Silence and Absence in Literature and Music

Word and Music Studies

VOLUME 15

The book series WORD AND MUSIC STUDIES (WMS) is the central organ of the International Association for Word and Music Studies (WMA), an association founded in 1997 to promote transdisciplinary scholarly inquiry devoted to the relations between literature/verbal texts/language and music. WMA aims to provide an international forum for musicologists and literary scholars with an interest in intermediality studies and in crossing cultural as well as disciplinary boundaries.

WORD AND MUSIC STUDIES publishes, generally on an annual basis, theme-oriented volumes, documenting and critically assessing the scope, theory, methodology, and the disciplinary and institutional dimensions and prospects of the field on an international scale: conference proceedings, collections of scholarly essays, and, occasionally, monographs on pertinent individual topics.

The titles published in this series are listed at *brill.com/wms*

Silence and Absence in Literature and Music

Edited by

Werner Wolf
Walter Bernhart

BRILL
RODOPI

LEIDEN | BOSTON

Library of Congress Cataloging-in-Publication Data

Names: Wolf, Werner, 1955- | Bernhart, Walter.
Title: Silence and absence in literature and music / edited by Werner Wolf, Walter Bernhart.
Description: Leiden ; Boston : Brill, [2016] | Series: Word and music studies ; volume 15 | Includes bibliographical references.
Identifiers: LCCN 2016000638 (print) | LCCN 2016007333 (ebook) | ISBN 9789004314856 (hardback : alk. paper) | ISBN 9789004314863 (E-book)
Subjects: LCSH: Music and literature. | Silence in music. | Silence in literature. | Absence in music. | Absence in literature.
Classification: LCC ML3849 .S5 2016 (print) | LCC ML3849 (ebook) | DDC 780/.08--dc23
LC record available at http://lccn.loc.gov/2016000638

Typeface for the Latin, Greek, and Cyrillic scripts: "Brill". See and download: brill.com/brill-typeface.

ISSN 1566-0958
ISBN 978-90-04-31485-6 (hardback)
ISBN 978-90-04-31486-3 (e-book)

This book is printed on acid-free paper and produced in a sustainable manner.

Printed by Printforce, the Netherlands

Contents

Preface

As in previous cases of the book series Word and Music Studies (WMS) the present, fifteenth volume in the series presents a selection of revised papers originally given at one of the biannual conferences of the International Association for Word and Music Studies (WMA). The event in question was the ninth conference held at the University of London in August 2013. In accordance with a long-standing tradition this conference was again dedicated to a topic of general interest for the study of both literature and music, namely 'silence and absence'.

The topic 'silence and absence' has a particularly wide relevance since we encounter these 'negative' phenomena not only in literature and music but – almost naturally – in a variety of fields in everyday experience, culture and the media. In fact, both silence and absence can be felt in real life as effects of actually or seemingly 'raw' reality, for instance in the quiet of vast forests or the absolute lack of light in deep caves, but also as the felt loss of beloved ones. Both phenomena can also be part of more openly culturally mediated facets of everyday life, be it the silence of meditation in churches or private prayer, a minute of silence dedicated to a deceased person, or the surprising impression of absence when expected events do not occur. In addition, contemporary life is being shaped by the interplay of absence and presence to a hitherto unknown degree through the digital revolution, which technically stems from the electronic exploitation of precisely this basic binary opposition in 'bits' (binary digits). Moreover, over the past century there has been a fascination with silence and absence in a specific cultural discourse, namely philosophy: from Wittgenstein's attempted quieting of metaphysical speculation in his well-known dictum from his *Tractatus logico-philosophicus* ("[...] wovon man nicht sprechen kann, darüber muß man schweigen"; 1921/1984: 85; cf. also 9) to Derrida absence looms large in recent thought. With regard to Derrida, one may, for instance, point out his critique of the "history of metaphysics" in which "Being" has been – allegedly in an erroneous way – always been equated with "presence in all senses of this word" (1966/1978: 279), an observation which has prompted Derrida and fellow-deconstructivists to emphasize the "absence of a centre" and moreover the absence "of a subject and [...] of an author" (ibid.: 287), in short, the absence of stable meaning both in individual texts and culture at large.

However, while these wider horizons are occasionally touched upon, the present volume is more modestly geared towards the exploration of silence and absence in literature and music (and its various combinations) as (*pace* deconstructivism) meaningful signifying practices. In fact, except for accidental cases of silence and absence, whenever we encounter or assume the presence of a frame 'communication', these seemingly 'negative' phenomena can assume a positive communicative and meaning-transmitting function and in this follow Watzlawick's observation according to which "One cannot *not* communicate" (Watzlawick/Beavin/Jackson 1967: 49). This is already true in everyday communication and also applies to the arts such as literature and music. Here, too, absence and silence can become as meaningful as visual and aural presence.

There are infinite forms of presence in both arts. In contrast to this, one may be tempted to think that this does not apply to the opposite of presence: in music, is this opposite not simply silence, while in literature it is merely absence of text or performance? Yet this assumption is false, as the contributions to this volume convincingly show. Indeed, there is a remarkably rich variety of forms of absence and silence, which, in semiotic terms, can operate on the level of the signifieds (and, where applicable, the referents) or on the level of the signifiers, or on both levels.

Absence operating exclusively or predominantly on the level of the signifieds can, for instance, occur in the form of a yearning for silence, the reverse of noisy modernity, as discussed by Axel Englund with reference to the poetry and the aesthetics of Rilke ("Silence and the Sawmill: Rainer Maria Rilke on the Nuisance of Sounding Music"). Absence can also take on the form of something conspicuously missing in the signification of a given work of literature or musical composition. This is what Laura Wahlfors presents in a case study of Schumann's *Kreisleriana,* where, as she argues, Romantic longing for the Absolute (an absent referent) can be heard in fragmentary musical quotations of Beethoven. This forms a considerable challenge to the pianist, which she addresses in detail ("How to Play the Music of Absence? The Romantic Aesthetics of Longing in Schumann's *Kreisleriana*, Part 4"). Another variety of absence in the signification structure of artefacts are cases of intermedial transposition or 'adaptation' in which the target work, the adaptation, lacks elements of the source work, a lack which nevertheless can cast a shadow of ghostly presence. Examples of this can be found in the contributions by Michael Halliwell, focussing on adaptations from Shakespeare ("The Sound of Silence: A Tale of Two Operatic *Tempests*"), and Naomi Matsumoto ("'Ghost Writing': An Exploration of Presence and Absence in *Lucia di Lammermoor*"). Yet another facet is addressed by Blake Stevens with reference to French baroque opera, namely the absence of important aspects of the performative representation of space and action which is shifted to a mere supplementation by means of verbal discourse ("The Spectacular Imagination and the Rhetoric of Absence in *Armide*"), while Beate Schirrmacher highlights a particularly unusual form of supplemented absence, namely the novelistic rendering of a Beethoven sonata (the *Appassionata*) not by means of descriptive acoustic evocation in the form of what Steven Paul Scher termed 'verbal music' (see 1968; 1970), but by a shift to the pianist's bodily performance, resulting in a "performative 'mute' ekphrasis" ("Mute Performances: Ekphrasis of Music, and Performative Aesthetics in Eyvind Johnson's *Romantisk berättelse*"; quotation see abstract below). Finally, Peter Dayan, while still locating his discussion in the field of absent signifieds, shifts his emphasis from literary or musical works to the aesthetic framing and comments on the remarkable absence of music in the reflections of early twentieth-century Dadaists ("The Inaudible Music of Dada").

Of particular interest are forms of absence and silence which do not principally occur on the level of the signifieds but more or less exclusively affect chains of signifiers. The most extreme case in this respect which, of course, comes to mind is the classic 'anti-composition' by John Cage, *4'33"*, which Karl Katschthaler explores in his contribution under the auspices of 'potentiality' ("Absence, Presence and Potentiality: John Cage's *4'33"* Revisited"). While Cage's 'work' appears to stage a totality of absence (there is no music in the conventional sense in the entire 'composition'), it nevertheless permits the experience of some forms of presence: on the one hand these are the accidental extra-musical sounds which may occur in the respective performance situations and aurally supplement the absent music, and on the other hand the body of the pianist and his or her gestures also form visual supplements to the performative absence of organized musical sound. The interplay between presence and absence may regularly be expected in plurimedial forms such as music theatre, in which silence and absence can operate on the level of one or two partial media (music, image, text) while other partial media are made to operate in the mode of presence. Various forms of such absence, together with their (metareferential) functions, are being discussed by Bernhard Kuhn with reference to Luigi Nono ("The Silence of an Elephant: Luigi Nono's *Al Gran Sole Carico d'Amore* (1975)"). Absence may assume yet different forms if one concentrates on one medium only – be it music (where the general rest comes foremost into mind) or be it literature, where blanks or a white page can become meaningful. Absence of this kind is explored by Mary Breatnach in her reading of Mallarmé's *Un coup de dés*, a work in which, as Breatnach shows, (silent) music also plays a role on the level of the implied aesthetics ("Silence and Music in Mallarmé's *Un coup de dés*").

As already said, absence can also affect the transition between different media involved in a performance: in a musical score the music is absent (or present as a potentiality only), while in the musical performance the shape of the score may be absent. Lawrence Kramer addresses this relationship for special cases in which the shape of the score, which he likens to 'hieroglyphs', can assume notably iconic meaning and produce an added value which may also influence the performance – or the reception – of the music in question ("Rosetta Tones: The Score as Hieroglyph").

In all of the forms of silence and absence discussed in the present volume it is assumed that this kind of negativity can, and in fact does, yield positive effects of meaning. In principle, this may be regarded as an unwarranted assumption begging the question under what conditions we are allowed to assume such a meaningfulness of what is actually not 'full' but empty. My own contribution is an attempt at answering this general question ("How Does Absence Become Significant in Literature and Music?").

The book series Word and Music Studies, since its inception in 1999, has repeatedly not only offered to its readers essays systematically focused on one leading topic per volume but has also presented, under the heading 'Surveying the Field', a forum for the discussion of individual issues of interest for both arts. In this volume, two essays can be signalled in this context: Emily Petermann addresses a hitherto largely neglected form of the interplay between word, music and image, namely "The Film Musical as a Subject for Word and Music Studies", while Jeppe Klitgaard Stricker contributes a facet to the larger issue of formal analogies to music in literature in his essay "Musical Form in the Novel: Beyond the Sonata Principle".

This volume is the result of the cooperation of various persons all of whom I would like to thank for their efforts. First and foremost there is the co-editor Walter Bernhart, who was kind enough to take on the brunt of the editorial matters. Then there are, of course, the contributors, without whose willing cooperation the present volume would not have come into being. The same applies to the organizers of the London conference, Robert Samuels and Delia da Sousa Correa from the Open University, who, as it were, laid the foundation to this book. I would also like to thank Masja Horn for her support in smoothing the transition from Rodopi to Brill | Rodopi as the new publishing house of Word and Music Studies. We all hope that the book series will continue to thrive under the auspices of the new publisher.

Werner Wolf
Graz, summer 2015

References

Derrida, Jacques (1966/1978). "Structure, Sign and Play in the Discourse of the Human Sciences". Jacques Derrida. *Writing and Difference*. Transl. with an introduction and additional notes by Alan Bass. London: Routledge & Kegan. 278–293; 339.

Scher, Steven Paul (1968). *Verbal Music in German Literature.* Yale Germanic Studies 2. New Haven, CT/London: Yale UP.

——— (1970). "Notes Toward a Theory of Verbal Music". *Comparative Literature* 22: 147–156 (Reprint: Walter Bernhart, Werner Wolf, eds. (2004). *Essays on Literature and Music (1967–2004) by Steven Paul Scher.* Word and Music Studies 5. Amsterdam/ New York, NY: Rodopi. 23–35).

Watzlawick, Paul, Janet H. Beavin, Don D. Jackson (1967). *Pragmatics of Human Communication: A Study of Interactional Patterns, Pathologies, and Paradoxes.* New York, NY: Norton.

Wittgenstein, Ludwig (1921/1984). *Tractatus logico-philosophicus.* Ludwig Wittgenstein. *Tractatus logico-philosophicus, Tagebücher 1914–1916. Philosophische Untersuchungen.* Werkausgabe vol. 1. Frankfurt a. M.: Suhrkamp. 7–85.

Silence and Absence in Literature and Music

∵

Theoretical Aspects

∴

How Does Absence Become Significant in Literature and Music?

Werner Wolf

The present contribution deals with a question which is fundamental for any enquiry into forms and functions of absence in literature and music, namely: how is it that absences can become significant parts of works or performances of literature and music in the first place? The answer to this question is the following hypothesis: recipients will tend to decode absences as meaningful or function-carrying parts of a work or performance if certain 'significance triggers' apply. In a first step the kind of absence that will be under discussion is specified: it is non-accidental gaps in or surrounding chains of verbal or musical signifiers (rather than chains of signifieds) as part of a communicative situation. The essay then discusses the most important of the aforementioned significance triggers which contribute to perceiving absences as non-accidental and potentially meaningful. Apart from the explicit marking of absence as such, there are various implicit forms: the marking of the cognitive frame 'art' is here most important, but individual conventions relating to absences in both literature and music and the deviation from certain conventions in these media (as a means of 'foregrounding' absence) may also play a role. These various possibilities are illustrated with musical and literary examples, and due attention is given to the functions of absence as well as to medial differences and similarities.

•••

1 Introduction

When reading texts and watching or listening to performances, how is it that in some cases we become aware of the absence of something in these texts and performances and endow such absence with significance while in other cases we do not? This is not a banal question in the context of a volume dedicated to *Silence and Absence in Literature and Music*, for it addresses two fundamental problems. The first one is: *how can one become aware of something that is not there*? It may indeed happen that one just does not notice an absence in the first place, since humans are cognitively hard-wired to perceive what is there, what sticks out as a 'figure' from a 'ground'. Only under certain circumstances and conditions do we become aware of 'conspicuous' absences. Lewis Carroll, in his novel *Through the Looking-Glass*, humorously

 | DOI 10.1163/9789004314863_002

addresses this problem, when the White King asks Alice to look for his Messengers "along the road" and Alice answers: "I see nobody on the road," which leads to the remarkable comment on the part of the King: "I only wish *I* had such eyes [...] to be able to see Nobody! And at that distance, too!" (1872/1970: 279) Like the holes of a Swiss cheese, absence can basically only be perceived in relation to a real or expected presence. In the case of the scene from *Through the Looking-Glass* just mentioned it is the expectation of some messengers who then do not come, and, on a more fundamental, metalingual level, the negative concept of absence is here shown to depend on the existence of a positive lexeme such as 'somebody', which is a prerequisite for negatives such as 'nobody'. For the purpose of the present contribution, the 'Swiss cheese' under consideration consists of various works of verbal and musical art, relevant conventions and performance conditions and corresponding recipient expectations.

The second problem is the question: *under what circumstances are we inclined to regard an absence* in the context of literature or music *as significant*, that is, as contributive to the meaning or functions of given texts, compositions or performances? Clearly, there are cases in which absences are *not* meaningfully to be perceived as significant in the above sense. After all, it is possible that in a theatrical performance the lights go out owing to a power cut; and one cannot exclude physical mishaps in performing artists, which may lead to the unfortunate situation that a pianist, who has sat down at his piano, is suddenly overcome by vertigo and is unable to play. As opposed to these cases, a completely different situation appears to apply in, for instance, the blackout at the end of the first act of Harold Pinter's play *The Birthday Party*, and the (relative) silence during the performance of John Cage's famous 'non-composition' 4′33″ – works of art in which we would be inclined to consider absence (be it of visibility or musical sound) to be somehow meaningful. Yet again, how is it that we tend to perceive the last two and similar cases as significant, while we would not do so in the first two examples – unless under a misconception?

2 What Kind of Absence? Significant, Intentional, Textual or Performative Absences in Chains of Signifiers in Peripheral or Internal Position as Part of a Literary or Musical Communication

Before we can address this question, some preliminary reflections are required. The first refers to a general precondition of becoming aware of absences in the first place. Paul Watzlawick et al. have famously claimed that "one cannot *not* communicate. Activity or inactivity, words or silence all have message value" (Watzlawick/Beavin/Jackson 1967: 49; cf. Meise 1996: 47). Indeed, man is a meaning-seeking animal, and we can in fact be tempted to read messages into almost everything. Yet, in our context, which is concerned with the meaning of individual works of art, it would hardly make sense, for instance, to discuss the absence of concert performances or poetry readings in a given location as a consequence of cuts in funding on the part of supporting institutions or as the result of a lack of interest on the part of the audience. For these absences would not be part of a communicative situation in which the works under consideration are involved, and such absences would therefore not be part of their meaning. As we can see here, and as Katrin Meise put it, for absence to become a meaningful, "constitutive element" of a work of art, "it is at least necessary to presuppose a *communicative situation*" (ibid.). In fact it is the presence of such a communicative situation which creates the necessary framework in which absence can be perceived in the first place and be regarded as a meaningful part of a 'message'.

When talking of a 'message', a further reflection is necessary. In true communication, genuine, and not merely metaphorical, 'messages' are not only *de*coded by recipients but are previously and intentionally *en*coded by senders. This leads to an important reformulation of the distinction 'significant vs. non-significant absences' underlying the present discussion: in communicative situations, we do not tend to ascribe significance to *accidental* occurrences, but rather to *intentional* ones. Significant absences of the kind that are in focus here can therefore be conceived of as encoded by the composer or the author on purpose so that they are loaded with intentional meaning or with at least one intended function. Consequently, such absences will not be perceived as mere chance occurrences, which have no 'message' (save one that a given recipient may construct for him- or herself).

Yet another distinction must be made, which refers to the *kind of absence* under discussion in terms of semiotics. In both literature and music one may distinguish between absence relating to *chains of signifieds* and absence in *chains of signifiers*. The former case would, for instance, include in literature, 'ellipsis' as a rhetorical figure but also what Wolfgang Iser called "*Leerstellen*" (1970/1975: 235) – gaps of meaning in the signification of a text. A case in point illustrating such gaps may be the absence of information on the identity of the murderer during the major part of a work of detective fiction. In music which follows traditional Western harmonics, an equivalent (if one considers harmonic position and function as 'signifieds') would perhaps be the juxtaposition of a C major and an F sharp minor chord without duly modulating chords in between. Interesting as such gaps in chains of *signifieds* may be in themselves, they will nevertheless be excluded in the following, since they would detract from what – in contrast at least to literary ellipsis and *Leerstellen* – so far has hardly found attention in scholarship dealing with more than one medium, namely absences in chains of *signifiers*, that is, discernible lacunae on the medial surface of given works of music or literature. This type of absence will be in focus in the ensuing transmedial discussion.

Another preliminary reflection concerns the *position* of such absences. For absences cannot only occur *within* a communication proper but also, so to speak, *at its margins*. We may therefore distinguish between *peripheral* and *internal* absences, and both variants will be of interest in the following.

A last distinction must be made with reference to the *type of musical and literary communications* under scrutiny: in both literature and music one may be concerned with *texts* (or scores) only or with *performances*. Consequently, visual *blanks* and aural *silences* are both relevant in our context, even though different ways of decoding absences apply in both cases. For brevity's sake both manifestations of a significant lack in medial signifiers will be subsumed under the umbrella term of 'absence'.

After these preliminary reflections we may now come back to our principal concern: the question of how absences become significant parts of works or performances of literature and music. A preliminary answer to this is: recipients will tend to decode absences as meaningful or function-carrying parts of a work or performance as a consequence of what I would like to call '*significance triggers*'. In the following, I will discuss such triggers individually, although in practice they may also operate in conjunction with one another.

3 The Framing of an Aesthetic Communicative Situation/the Marking of the Frame 'Art' as a Basic Significance Trigger for Rendering Absences Potentially Meaningful

According to what has been said, the most basic significance trigger must be of a kind to fulfil at least one function, namely to make the recipients aware of the existence of a communicative situation, or more precisely of a specific, *aesthetic* communicative situation. In non-aesthetic cases, for instance a prolonged silence occurring before the beginning of a lecture, the absence of words may be ambiguous as to its meaningfulness, for the cognitive frame 'lecture' is just about to be established by means of certain 'framings'[1] or markers.

1 For the frame-theoretical distinction of 'cognitive frame' vs. 'framing' as a marker of such a frame see Wolf 2006.

On the one hand, the physical framings of the lecture room, the presence of an audience and a speaker standing behind a lectern may be read as such markers. On the other hand, a lecture conventionally begins with an opening formula of address, and everything that precedes it would not normally be seen as part of the lecture proper. Yet even if we disregard the position of the absence outside the frame defined by the beginning markers, the absence of the frame 'art' in a lecture may also induce parts of the audience to not consider an initial silence as meaningful (they may, for example, attribute it to the speaker trying to concentrate or fiddling with his papers). It is indeed the frame 'art' which most readily induces us to regard almost everything happening in a corresponding communicative situation derived from a text or a performance – and perhaps also in its immediate context – as meaningful. For, as opposed to what applies to non-aesthetic communication, artistic communication is understood to be intentional and meaningful *in all its parts* (this is what may be called the 'premiss of artistic meaningfulness'). We have learnt to apply this premiss to art by default, with the consequence that it makes us anticipate significance even where none is apparent at first sight, and that applies also to cases where this non-appearance is due to the fact that no signs can be perceived.

The importance of the frame 'art' is best to be seen with reference to 'peripheral absences', and this most notably includes absences at the beginning of aesthetic communication. The problem here is: where or when does the communicative situation begin? In texts, if one disregards the fact that, as a rule, they are taken from some already framing contexts, the communication starts with our interaction with the physical materiality of the 'text' at hand and its paratexts. In performances, the performative situation and pertinent conventions must be taken into account. John Cage's *4'33"* is an extreme case, for here silence cannot be divided into peripheral and internal position since this 'composition' blurs the distinction between music as 'figure' and background noise or silence as 'ground'. Yet for all those familiar with Western conventions of musical performances there are nevertheless framings of 'art' and consequently significance triggers establishing an aesthetic communication that work even in Cage's case: an audience assembles in a room with an instrument (preferably a piano), an instrumentalist sits down in front of it and sets a score in front of him- or herself (as can, e.g. be viewed on *YouTube*[2] in a performance by William Marx). All of this raises expectations and renders the abovementioned possibility that the ensuing non-performance may be due to accidental reasons highly unlikely. Rather, the constitutive (relative) silence which forms Cage's work – for anyone prepared to go to such extremes – may be considered

2 See http://www.youtube.com/watch?v=JTEFKFiXSx4 [04/02/2014].

a liminal case of music as organized sound. It is indeed a case in which the absence of such organized sound makes the audience aware both of the essence of the medium (this would be a metamusical function) and of the existence of random sound, which may still be heard instead of the expected sound of an instrument (this would be a perceptual or sensitizing function of the composition under discussion).

John Cage's *4'33"* is only one among an amazing plurality of avant-garde 'silent musical compositions'. For all of them the significance trigger 'art' may be assumed to be a first and major incentive to make sense of the partial or complete absence of music. The entry "list of musical compositions which consist mostly or entirely of silence" is even a key-word in *Wikipedia*, where some 43 compositions are adduced.[3] The *Wikipedia* list is not even complete – for it does not, for instance, include Heinz Holliger's musical meditations on Hölderlin's 'Scardanelli' poems. Interestingly, one of Holliger's compositions dedicated to Hölderlin is entitled *(T)AIR(E)* – a portmanteau-expression combining the French words *air* with *taire* ('to be silent') – and starts with a curious instruction "dal niente," which, after only five bars, finds its counterpart in "al niente". Within the 14-minute composition for solo flute this trajectory 'from nothing to nothing' forms an initial experiment with eliciting sound from a flute coming in fact 'out of nothing', that is, out of silence.[4] Here, too, the framing indicating a musical performance operates as a significance trigger and makes the audience aware of the fact that the performance has already begun, while nothing is heard as yet.

More traditional cases of the phenomenon that peripheral absences can become meaningful owing to the frame 'art' would include the 'pregnant' silence in orchestral performances before the first note is played and while the conductor is raising his baton (a silence full of suspense, expectation and, perhaps, anticipation). It could also include – after the beginning of the music – the pianissimo openings of some musical compositions, such as the hardly perceptible D-minor chord at the beginning of Bruckner's ninth symphony or Wagner's prelude to *Rheingold*, where the initial 'Ur-Es' (the 'primeval E flat') is barely audible at the beginning, before it swells to *fortissimo* dimensions. In these cases music, as it were, emerges out of silence as in the case of Holliger's *(T)AIR(E)* and thus includes absence (as a starting point) into the composition. The interval between the conductor raising his or her baton and the beginning of the first instrumental sound thus gets extra meaning.

3 See http://en.wikipedia.org/wiki/List_of_silent_musical_compositions [11/07/2012].

4 I am grateful to Carolin Abeln (Basel-Freiburg) for having drawn my attention to this composition and having sent me extracts from the musical score.

The aforementioned question as to where an aesthetic communication may be assumed to begin has its counterpart at the end of a text or performance. Here, a previously established frame 'art' can also have an effect for the time or space immediately outside the actual textual or compositional limits (that is, after the last full stop or last written bar, or after the last heard word or chord). Conductors may, for instance, produce a terminal silence after particularly sublime endings by 'freezing', thus permitting the music, as it were, to be carried over into the framing world, before gesturally releasing the applause; one may in this context also think of the terminal silence that traditionally concludes performances such as J.S. Bach's *Passion according to St Matthew*, where the conspicuous absence of applause becomes meaningful as a marker and an acknowledgement of the religious content and solemnity of the composition which just has come to an end.

Another example to the point, this time taken not from music but from literature, and not from a performance but from a text of fiction, is the ending of James Joyce's short story "The Dead". There is something about this conclusion which arguably only becomes remarkable owing to the existence of the frame 'verbal art': in a negative epiphany, which shattered his entire married life, the story's hero, Gabriel Conroy, has just learnt that his beloved wife Gretta had a lover, Michael Furey, before she was married to Gabriel, and that she apparently still loves this Michael in spite of his being dead. In the last paragraph of the story, which also concludes the story cycle *Dubliners*, the reader gets access to the following stream of consciousness in Gabriel's mind:

> A few light taps upon the pane made him turn to the window. It had begun to snow again. He watched sleepily the flakes, silver and dark, falling obliquely against the lamp-light. The time had come for him to set out on his journey westward. Yes, the newspapers were right: snow was falling all over Ireland. It was falling on every part of the dark central plain, on the treeless hills, falling softly upon the Bog of Allen and, farther westward, softly falling into the dark mutinous Shannon waves. It was falling, too, upon every part of the lonely churchyard on the hill where Michael Furey lay buried. It lay thickly drifted on the crooked crosses and headstones, on the spears of the little gate, on the barren thorns. His soul swooned slowly as he heard the snow falling faintly through the universe and faintly falling, like the descent of their last end, upon all the living and the dead. (Joyce 1914/1993: 203f.)

This being the ending of the story – and at the same time the conclusion of the fictional text of the entire book – the last words, "the dead", are followed by the white space of the (in most editions) not fully printed last page. In a non-aesthetic context, the absence of words on this white space would hardly be noticeable, yet this being literature, it may elicit an awareness of a meaningful absence, and this has indeed been the case: in a comparison between Joyce's text and John Huston's film version, the critic Eric Paul Meljac observes:

> Joyce's text forces the reader to stop. A period followed by nothing, by wordlessness, forces the reader to cease reading, to complete the mental and visual exercise, and be faced with very real silence, a silence of sound, of vision, of mental processes, and of the heart. (2009: 295)[5]

The correspondence (if it is perceived) between the white snow thematized in the text, the atmosphere of 'paralysis' typical of *Dubliners* and, indeed, emotional as well as physical death on the one hand and, on the other hand, the textual materiality of nothingness on a white page are here an instance of what I have termed 'iconicity of absence' (see Wolf 2005). It is a frequent means of giving meaning to blanks in works of art. Yet in this liminal position it is a questionable one; for one could argue that *all* texts must end somewhere and are consequently followed by white space without print. It is only owing to the aforementioned premiss of a potential ubiquity of meaning which frames our reception of artworks, including their immediate context or periphery, that a reading such as Meljac's makes sense.

4 Absence-Related Conventions as Triggers for Rendering Silence or Blanks in Literature and Music Meaningful

Once the frame 'art' or literary or musical communication has been established, specific conventions and expectations start to apply – including conventions that work as significance triggers when it comes to evaluating absences. In print literature, a basic example of such a convention operating as a significance trigger would be the large empty space traditionally surrounding short versified texts on a page (as opposed to the narrower margins in prose, which, in addition, are both left and right justified). This conventional absence of text in the page layout bespeaks poetry and thus operates as a generic marker.

Another example would be blank pages between the individual parts or 'books' of a long novel, a convention which our cultural knowledge allows us to

5 I am grateful to my student Maximilian Feldner for having drawn my attention to this reading by Meljac.

read as segmentation markers. Sometimes, in the case of the cliff-hanging chapter endings so frequently used by Charles Dickens in his originally serialized novels, the sudden absences of (explanatory or concluding) text at a crucial moment also serves the affective function of creating suspense in addition to a pragmatic one (namely inciting readers to buy the next instalment of the periodical in which the novel in question is published).

With respect to the function of indicating intracompositional segments, the extended rests between the movements of a symphony in musical performances are analogons to the blank pages separating novel chapters.[6] In baroque preludes and fugues, for instance, absence-related conventions do not only render the silence following the last chord of a baroque prelude meaningful but also the absence of at first three, then two, and then one voice at the outset of the fugue (if it has four parts). Since these partial silences – together with the imitative structure of the composition – are so typical of the beginning of fugues they serve as conventionalized generic markers of this compositional form.

5 The Deviation from Literary and Musical Conventions and Expectations ('Foregrounding') as a Means of Rendering Absence Significant

When it comes to the potential of significance triggers for absences, however, *deviations from conventions* are more powerful and, as a rule, even more pregnant with meaning than absence-related conventions. Like conventions themselves, this type of significance trigger, which takes habitual expectations as a basis for meaningful non-fulfilment (often leading to the foregrounding of the respective convention itself), is of a very general nature and is not limited to the reception of art. For instance, it operated in London on April 17, 2013, when Big Ben was silent during the funeral of ex-prime minister Margaret Thatcher. In music, the ending of Joseph Haydn's symphony No. 45 in F sharp minor, entitled 'Farewell', is a case in point. The dwindling number of instrumentalists playing (and, in the original performance, actually present on stage), and the *adagio* tempo of the concluding section of the fourth movement with its diminishing volume of the music, iconically approaching the condition of a concluding silence, thus adding peripheral to internal absence; these are all

6 The fact that the 'reading' of such rests requires some cultural knowledge and a certain familiarity with performed compositions in particular can be seen in the 'misreadings' of compositional units by inexpert concert audiences applauding in between the movements of, for instance, a symphony.

clear deviations from the conventional ending of the last movement of a classical symphony in *fortissimo* and with full orchestra rather than with the first violins playing *pianissimo* and *con sordini*, almost fading into silence. Tradition has it that this was meant to remind Haydn's aristocratic patron Nikolaus I Esterházy of a holiday the orchestra musicians had wanted to obtain for some time. Besides this contextual reference, arguably another function of this curious playing with absence may be seen to operate here, namely a metamusical function, more precisely the foregrounding of traditional compositional practice. Be that as it may, both functions are heavily dependent on the remarkable departure from convention which this symphony ending implies.

Absence-related functions other than metamusical ones can repeatedly be encountered in Johann Sebastian Bach's oeuvre, where one may also find several examples of rests that particularly become meaningful owing to their forming noticeable deviations from conventions. In his motet for choir and basso continuo, *Jesu, meine Freude* (*Jesu, Joy of Man's Desiring*), BWV 227, there is, for instance, the surprising general rest after the word "nichts" ('nothing') in No. 2, "Es ist nun nichts Verdammliches an denen, die in Christo Jesu sind" ('There is nothing damnable in those that dwell in Jesus Christ'), a clear case of musical iconicity of absence. In his cantata BWV 105, *Herr, gehe nicht ins Gericht* (*Lord, Do Not Pass Judgment*), the 3rd movement, an aria on the text "Wie zittern und wanken / Der Sünder Gedanken" ('How tremble and waver / The sinners' thoughts') sports a sustained absence of the conventional *basso continuo*, which iconically expresses the groundlessness of the sinner who has no anchorage in God.

A particularly intriguing example containing several general rests which also conspicuously depart from conventions can be found in the last few bars of Bach's *Prelude and Fugue in C major for Organ*, BWV 547 (see Example 1).

Here, a tremendous build-up of tension is created in the last section of the five-part fugue, in which the pedal – after pages of silence – finally and majestically enters with the fugue theme in augmented form. This is followed after some bars by diatonic and then chromatic falling notes in the bass (in Bach frequently announcing the imminent conclusion of a composition); after this, the theme appears again conspicuously in the pedal, this time in mirrored form, first in G major and then – adding to the tension – in C minor. Instead of the expected G major chord which should follow this theme entry, possibly previous to a conclusion of the whole composition in C major, we are now entering a whole series of deviations from the conventions regulating the conclusion of regular fugues. At first we hear a surprising diminished seventh chord, followed by a spectacular general rest. In this and the next bar three more diminished chords follow, separated each time by general rests, before we finally come to the concluding organ point, a sustained C in the pedal. Here again a powerful tension is created, with all four other voices sounding the

EXAMPLE 1 *J.S. Bach,* Prelude and Fugue in C major for Organ, *BWV 547*

theme or its inversion at times simultaneously (*stretto*). After so much tension and absence-related breakings of conventions[7] we are confronted with a last

7 Arguably, it would be misleading to describe the effect of the absence of notes in these cases as actual 'silence', owing to the reverberation of the full organ sound in most performative situations.

surprise: the final C major chord is not, as in most other compositions, prolonged, usually at least a minim with a fermata, but rather a semiquaver without a fermata. Unfortunately, in most performances and recordings, organists tend to lengthen this note unduly, but it ought to be a mere suggestion of a final chord with the emphasis thus being placed on the general rest *after* it, with the reverberations of this adumbrated chord gradually fading into silence – arguably an absence of ephemeral *musica instrumentalis* merging into the imagined presence of the eternity of *musica mundana*, in which the purest chord, the C major chord, can sound on.[8]

General rests of the kind found in music also exist in literature – more precisely, in performed metrical literature with metre functioning as the convention from which significant departures are possible. A classic example of a significant metrical deviation within the most frequent metre in Elizabethan drama, blank verse, is to be found in *Macbeth*. It is the eponymous character's nihilistic monologue of despair, "Life's but a walking shadow," in act five, after he has received notice of his wife's suicide. This monologue ends with a catalectic verse containing only three 'feet' followed by, as it were, a through-composed general rest, which iconically illustrates the last verbal phrase, "Signifying nothing," by an emphatic silence.

> Life's but a walking shadow, a poor player
> That struts and frets his hour upon the stage,
> And then is heard no more. It is a tale
> Told by an idiot, full of sound and fury,
> *Signifying nothing.* /x/x
>
> Shakespeare, *Macbeth V.* v. 23–27; 1605/1997: 2613; my emphasis[9]

In print literature, expectedly, the same principle of deviating from conventions is frequently used to give absences significance. A crude humorous

8 A further, particularly well-known example of an unconventional rest would be the general rest before the concluding cadence of the "Halleluja" in G.F. Händel's oratorio, *The Messiah*; see also Wolf 2005.

9 In the *Norton Shakespeare* (see 1605/1997), verse 26 may be said to be catalectic only in appearance, since Macbeth's following utterance, "Thou com'st to use/Thy tongue: thy story quickly." seems to complete the blank verse. However, after "nothing," the stage direction reads "*Enter a* Messenger," and in a performance this would certainly require a pause in Macbeth's speech, so that the coherence of the verse would in practice be lost to the audience regardless of its print appearance. It is therefore no coincidence that in the First Folio, the line "Signifying nothing" is also printed as a stand-alone verse (1623/1998: 758). For a discussion of the iconicity of such foreshortened verses (as well of unusually long ones) see Nänny 2001.

example outside verbal art is a book by "Professor Sheridan Simove MSc DPhil", advertised on the front cover as "The worldwide best-seller", promising "Amazing Truth Inside!" and entitled: *What every MAN thinks about apart from SEX*. This hoax, published in 2012, consists of 196 empty pages, arguable the most radical departure from the convention of communication in written form. More inventive and at least as radical in metafictionally playing with our convention-induced expectations is Laurence Sterne's *Tristram Shandy*, which is a mine of examples of meaningful absences, mostly having humorous and metafictional functions. In this novel a plethora of absences and deviations from conventions can not only be found on the level of the signifieds but also on the level of the signifiers of print fiction: there are several pages where print is replaced by typographical gimmicks such as charts illustrating the narrative (non-)progress made so far;[10] moreover, besides black, marbled or white pages,[11] at one point (in volume IV) ten pages are indicated as 'missing', also in the pagination,[12] and at another point (volume IX) entire chapters have been omitted (to be inserted later on).[13] Literature, in particular modernist and post-modernist fiction, is full of various metareferential games based on conspicuous deviations from conventions, and many of them sport absences. The significance trigger always being the same, some few examples may suffice. There is, in the field of text segmentation, Flann O'Brien's novel *At Swim-Two-Birds*, which starts with Chapter 1 (cf. 1939/1967: 9) never to come to Chapter 2; or there is Samuel Beckett's *Molloy*, which omits paragraph segmentations after the first page. In B.S. Johnson's experimental novel *Albert Angelo*, absence is achieved by virtually affecting textual materiality in cutting out a 'future-seeing hole' in one of the pages (cf. 1964/1987: 149). Beckett's œuvre would require a whole treatise on its own dealing with his absurdist variations on the theme of absence and reduction, with his play *Breath* looming large as the shortest drama in world literature (35 seconds!), displaying absences not only on the level of setting, in the form of a bare stage except for "miscellaneous rubbish" (1970/1971), but also on the level of characters (no character appears on stage, only a recorded voice is heard), language (no words, only a cry and an inspiration followed by an expiration and another cry are heard) and action

---

10 E.g. in IV.40 (cf. Sterne 1759–1767/1967: 453f.).

11 Black page (referring to Yorrick's death) I.12 (cf. ibid.: 61f.); marbled pages III.37 (cf. ibid.: 233f.), a "motley emblem of my work," as the narrator says (ibid.: 232); white page (as a projection space for the reader to subjectively picture the beauty of Widow Wadman for himself) VI.38 (cf. ibid.: 451f.).

12 Cf. ibid.: 300–311 (with pages 301–310 missing).

13 This concerns Chapters 18 and 19 of volume VI, which are re-inserted into Chapter 25 of the same book (cf. ibid.: 592f.; 602–605).

(nothing happens except for an increase in luminosity followed by a decrease and the aural happenings just mentioned). Clearly, Beckett's variations on absence are readable as iconic correlatives of the absence of meaning in an absurdist universe.[14]

6 The Explicit Marking of Absence as a Significance Trigger

All of the devices and triggers of significance mentioned so far operate more or less implicitly. While absence in many of Beckett's texts is a conspicuous feature, there are other cases where this is not the case and where it consequently may create problems of awareness. Implicit triggers are therefore frequently used in combination with *explicit* ones, in particular where the implicit variant is felt not to be clear enough or where absences are in danger of being overlooked or misinterpreted. Yet explicit significance triggers may also be used independently of such cases of potential doubt and are an important category of triggers of their own, operating both on the para- as well as on the intratextual and metatextual levels.

As far as musical 'paratexts' are concerned, 'peritextual' examples of such explicit marking would be titles, such as Schubert's *Unvollendete* (*The Unfinished*, announcing the lack of a third and a fourth movement), or designations such as one can find on the aforementioned *Wikipedia* entry, "List of silent musical compositions"[15], for instance *A Lot of Nothing*, *Two Minutes Silence*, or *Pregnant Pause... Intermission*. Paratexts in a wider 'epitextual' sense also include comments on absences in the *con*text of respective works – to the extent that the recipient is aware of them. Such contextual paratexts may be an author's or composer's self-interpretation or aesthetics (e.g. John Cage's 1959 "Lecture on Nothing"; see 1959/1961) but also art-historical interpretations dealing with the significance of what is not to be seen or heard in aesthetic communication.

On the intracompositional level of musical scores, performance instructions as in the case of Holliger's *(T)AIR(E)*, "dal niente", "al niente" may serve

14 For 'nothing' and 'absence' in Beckett see Caselli, ed. 2010. (I am grateful to Catherine Laws for pointing out this book to me.)

15 Sometimes apocryphal titles serve to prepare the recipient for an unusual amount of absences, such as the title *Pausensymphonie* ('symphony of rests') applied to Bruckner's symphony no. 2 in C minor, but these cannot be counted as true 'compositional' (or intended) significance markers.

both for the production of silence or near-silence on the part of the musician and as explicit significance triggers for score-reading recipients. Performance instructions are often verbal, yet need not be. Words are, however, requisite as significance triggers of a particular kind of blank in chains of signifiers, namely iconicity of absence in literature and vocal music. This kind of absence is in fact only discernible if in the immediate context, for instance, of a general rest or the white space after the last full stop of a story, there are words that denote or connote nothingness and absence such as death, loss etc. The aforementioned ending of Joyce's story "The Dead" is a case in point. The last word "dead" of the concluding phrase about the snow falling on "the living and the dead" may indeed be viewed as a hint that the ensuing absence of text is arguably more than a necessary white space or silence following a text, even if one may object that the connection between the respective verbal marker and the absence must be made by the recipient.

In other, non-iconic, cases, the connection between explicit verbal significance triggers and the respective absence is even clearer: Henry Mackenzie, for instance, does not merely start his seemingly fragmentary sentimental novel *The Man of Feeling* with Chapter 11 but also explains the fragmentary nature of the text. The reason for the ten missing opening chapters, and indeed for many other similar absences, becomes clear in a framing "Introduction", in which the origin and fate of the allegedly reprinted manuscript is narrated (it was used by a curate with apparently little literary sensitivity as "excellent wadding"; Mackenzie 1771/1970: 5). As if this were not enough, a footnote attached to the first chapter number also explicitly warns the readers that they will be confronted with "scattered chapters, and fragments of chapters" (ibid.: 7). Similar metatextual thematizations of absences can also be found in *Tristram Shandy*, for instance the one following the missing ten pages (the actual absence of the pages may easily be overlooked): "– No doubt, Sir, – there is a whole chapter wanting here – and a chasm of ten pages made in the book by it [...]" (Sterne 1759–1767/1967: 311).[16]

16 Sadly, the pagination continues uninterrupted in the otherwise authoritative Norton edition (cf. Sterne 1759–1767/1980: 219). The whole episode is yet another metafictional and tongue-in-cheek discussion of the merits and nature of the text we are reading, for we learn that Tristram himself tore out the respective pages, because the journey of his father, Uncle Toby and Obadiah which they contained (and of which we nevertheless get a summary!) was allegedly "so much above the stile and manner of anything else I have been able to paint in this book, that it could not have remained in it, without deprecating every other scene" (Sterne 1759–1767/1967: 313).

7 Conclusion

In the foregoing examples, besides explicit triggers which alert recipients to the potential meaningfulness of absences, several implicit types were discussed, namely, firstly, the establishment of the cognitive frame 'aesthetic communication', secondly, conventions, and, thirdly, deviations from conventions. The discussion might have given the impression that not only absences themselves but also the means of marking their significance are, as a rule, clear and distinct phenomena and, moreover, that they are similar in literature and music. This, however, must be relativized to some extent.

One must point out first that the extent of absences as well as their significance and the intensity of their marking vary in their degree. The wide margins surrounding a poem on a printed page have obviously less functional load than the missing feet at the end of Macbeth's above-quoted monologue of despair. The intensity of the marking can equally differ – from conventions that have become so automatized that we are hardly aware of them to exceptional and emphatic marking as in the case of combining an implicit foregrounding with an explicit metatextual thematization of absences. In addition, as in all questions of significance, an interplay between work, recipient and cultural context must be taken into account, an interplay which greatly influences the reading not only of signs present but also of those absent.

A further qualification concerns the influence the media literature and music have on the *nature* and *transmission* of absences and of relevant significance triggers. While in music – owing to its acoustic nature and the conventions of musical notation – aural absences predominate (with rests being conventionally marked in scores), in literature, both visual and aural absences can equally occur, depending on the genre and its performative or non-performative quality. And while implicit significance triggers are in fact equally applicable to both music and literature, inducing us to invest absences with more or less meaning, others, notably in the field of explicit triggers, are not. This applies, in particular, to intracompositional thematizations. Clearly, music, and above all performed instrumental music, cannot use this device, since it does not have a denotational language by means of which absence can be thematized.

The question which I have tried to answer here, namely how does absence become significant in literature and music, is obviously not restricted to these media. Rather, it is of relevance within a general 'aesthetics of absence'. One may, for instance, think of Kasimir Malevich's *Suprematist Composition: White on White* (1918) or of Robert Rauschenberg's white paintings (produced in 1951), which apparently influenced Cage's *4′33″*.[17] In spite of what essay titles such as

17 See *Wikipedia*, s.v. 4′33″.

Susan Sontag's "The Aesthetics of Silence" (see 1967/1969) appear to promise, such an aesthetics still needs to be written, in particular from a transmedial point of view. If in the present volume music and literature are singled out, this is interesting in itself, because it highlights to what extent not only presence but also absence and the interplay between both forms contribute to the richness of these media and the overall meaning of individual texts or compositions. Yet, like many other phenomena (such as framing, description, metareference or aesthetic illusion[18]) significant absences in chains of medial signifiers are neither confined to literature nor to music but are a transmedial phenomenon that ought to be investigated on a larger scale, for there is still a lot to be discovered in meaningful absences as the often forgotten reverse side of what is present in medial communication.

References

Beckett, Samuel (1970/1971). "Breath". Samuel Beckett. *Breath and Other Stories*. London: Faber and Faber. 11.

Cage, John (1959/1961). "Lecture on Nothing". John Cage. *Silence*. Middleton, CT: Wesleyan UP. 109–124.

Carroll, Lewis (1872/1970). "Through the Looking-Glass". Lewis Carroll. *The Annotated Alice:* Alice's Adventures in Wonderland *and* Through the Looking-Glass. Ed. Martin Gardner. Harmondsworth: Penguin. 165–354.

Caselli, Daniela, ed. (2010). *Beckett and Nothing: Trying to Understand Beckett.* Manchester: Manchester UP.

Iser, Wolfgang (1970/1975). "Die Appellstruktur der Texte: Unbestimmtheit als Wirkungsbedingung literarischer Prosa". Rainer Warning, ed. *Rezeptionsästhetik: Theorie und Praxis.* UTB 303. Munich: Fink. 228–252. (Orig.: *Die Appellstruktur der Texte: Unbestimmtheit als Wirkungsbedingung literarischer Prosa.* Konstanzer Universitätsreden 28. Constance: Universitätsverlag).

Johnson, Brian Stanley (1964/1987). *Albert Angelo.* New York, NY: New Directions.

Joyce, James (1914/1993). "The Dead". James Joyce. *Dubliners.* Eds. Hans Walter Gabler, Walter Hettche. New York, NY: Vintage. 159–204.

Mackenzie, Henry (1771/1970). *The Man of Feeling.* Ed. Brian Vickers. Oxford: OUP.

Meise, Katrin (1996). "On Talking about Silence in Conversation and Literature". Gudrun Grabher, Ulrike Jessner, eds. *The Semantics of Silences in Linguistics and Literature.* Heidelberg: Winter. 45–66.

18 See vols. 1, 2, 4, and 6 of the book series Studies in Intermediality (Wolf/Bernhart, eds. 2006; Wolf/Bernhart, eds. 2007; Wolf, ed. 2009; Wolf/Bernhart/Mahler, eds. 2013).

Meljac, Eric Paul (2009). "Dead Silence: James Joyce's 'The Dead' and John Huston's Adaptation as Aesthetic Rivals". *Literature/Film Quarterly* 37/4: 295–304.

Nänny, Max (2001). "Iconic Functions of Long and Short Lines". Olga Fischer, Max Nänny, eds. *The Motivated Sign*. Iconicity in Language and Literature 2. Amsterdam: Benjamins. 157–188.

O'Brien, Flann (1939/1967). *At Swim-Two-Birds*. Harmondsworth: Penguin.

Shakespeare, William (1605/1997). "Macbeth". Stephen Greenblatt, ed. *The Norton Shakespeare*. New York, NY: Norton. 2555–2618.

——— (1623/1998). "Macbeth". William Shakespeare. *Mr William Shakespeares Comedies, Histories & Tragedies: A Facsimile of the First Folio, 1623*. Ed. Doug Moston. London: Routledge. 739–759.

Simove, Sheridan (2012). *What Every Man Thinks About Apart from Sex*. Chichester: Summersdale.

Sontag, Susan (1967/1969). "The Aesthetics of Silence". Susan Sontag. *Styles of Radical Will*. New York, NY: Farrar, Strauss and Giroux. 3–34.

Sterne, Laurence (1759–1767/1967). *The Life and Opinions of Tristram Shandy, Gentleman*. Ed. Graham Petrie. Harmondsworth: Penguin.

——— (1759–1767/1980). *Tristram Shandy*. Ed. Howard Anderson. Norton Critical Edition. New York, NY: Norton.

Watzlawick, Paul, Janet H. Beavin, Don D. Jackson (1967). *Pragmatics of Human Communication: A Study of Interactional Patterns, Pathologies, and Paradoxes*. New York, NY: Norton.

Wolf, Werner (2005). "Non-supplemented Blanks in Works of Literature as Forms of 'Iconicity of Absence'". Costantino Maeder, Olga Fischer, William J. Herlovsky, eds. *Outside-In and Inside-Out*. Iconicity in Language and Literature 4. Amsterdam: Benjamins. 115–132.

——— (2006). "Introduction: Frames, Framings and Framing Borders in Literature and Other Media". Wolf/Bernhart, eds. 1–40.

———, eds. (2007). *Description in Literature and Other Media*. Studies in Intermediality 2. Amsterdam/New York, NY: Rodopi.

———, ed. (2009). in collaboration with Katharina Bantleon and Jeff Thoss. *Metareference across Media: Theory and Case Studies. Dedicated to Walter Bernhart on the Occasion of his Retirement*. Studies in Intermediality 4. Amsterdam/New York, NY: Rodopi.

Wolf, Werner, Walter Bernhart, eds. (2006). *Framing Borders in Literature and Other Media*. Studies in Intermediality 1. Amsterdam/New York, NY: Rodopi.

Wolf, Werner, Andreas Mahler, eds. (2013). *Immersion and Distance: Aesthetic Illusion in Literature and Other Media*. Studies in Intermediality 6. Amsterdam/New York, NY: Rodopi.

Rosetta Tones: The Score as Hieroglyph

Lawrence Kramer

The first half of the nineteenth century produced a significant handful of scores based on the same visual model understood to govern Egyptian hieroglyphics both before and after the deciphering of the Rosetta Stone in 1825. The sources of this practice include the abandonment of figured bass, the growing commerce in printed scores, and the rise of the 'work' as the musical object par excellence. Equally influential was the conjectural history linking the rise of civilization with the development of writing systems. This project involved an ideologically charged polarization of glyphic and alphabetical writing. Hieroglyphs were understood as a middle term between nature and spirit, the sensuous and the conceptual, the pictorial and the phonetic. The same understanding sometimes extended to scores, which, like hieroglyphs, could be deciphered only by closing the necessary gap between symbol and meaning. With music this deciphering necessarily took the form of a passage from silence to sound. Making this passage required the action not only of a thinking subject but of an embodied one, a subject who interprets the symbol by animating it acoustically – giving life, as Liszt remarked, to the "still, lifeless notes" on the page.

•••

Musical scores are fictitious pictographs. They look, that is, like arrays of marks – pictograms – that signify by resemblance, marks that picture what they mean. Scores look the way Egyptian hieroglyphics must have looked before the translation of the Rosetta stone. They look the way hieroglyphics still do look to most of us, we who can't read the inscriptions that the man who deciphered them, Jean-François Champollion, called "a complex system, a writing simultaneously *figurative*, *symbolic*, and *phonetic*, in the same text, the same phrase, I would almost say in the same word" (1828: I/375). Scores can look this way even to musicians, not just to those who don't read music. The small grace notes, the graceful slurs, the carefully angled beams – all suggest the pictorial representation of sound, and at the same time a representation of the sound's expressive value; the pictograph incorporates an ideograph. But of course scores are actually not like this at all, are they? Scores are code. If we continue the comparison to linguistic writing systems, we read scores phonetically, not symbolically. Don't we?

Well, yes. But also no.

 | DOI 10.1163/9789004314863_003

Pictograms are signs full of absence, pictures only to a minimal degree. They depend on a wide gap, an ellipsis, between the shape of the signifier and the content of the signified. Just think of the little figures that tell you what restroom to go to in any airport, and you'll get the point immediately. Pictograms are reduced symbols; pictographic representation is defective in principle. The opposite was generally supposed to be true of alphabetic writing until Saussure came along with the idea that there are no positive terms in language. Prior to that, phonetic signification by letters was understood to be complete, and in practice, Saussure or not, it is still treated as if that were so. Most linguists, moreover, still think that pictograms alone cannot make up a complete writing system. Writing must refer to language, not to what language signifies.

In this respect scores are indeed more like pictographic than like alphabetic writing. Of course scores obviously do refer to musical sounds. The sounds stand to scores as speech stands to writing. But scores are always defective in their representation of music. And precisely that defectiveness may encourage the use of pictographic supplements, as much as it does of verbal supplements such as *espressivo* or *appassionato* or *nicht schleppend!* As Schenker observed in his edition of Beethoven's piano sonatas, clues to both structure and performance may lie in the visual display of musical information (cf. 1923/1975: I/xif.). So it is worth looking into the possibilities that scores, at least some of them, have a genuine resemblance to pictographs – and, historically speaking, to those other fictitious pictographs that have had the strongest hold on the European imagination since the eighteenth century: Egyptian hieroglyphs.

The first half of the nineteenth century produced a significant handful of scores with a strong hieroglyphic element. Unlike Baroque eye-music, these hieroglyphic passages primarily depict the music they help to notate, not what music depicts. Or rather, as I suggested at the outset, such passages incorporate a depiction of the music's expressive value into a depiction of its sound. Unlike ordinary tone painting, which is a form of mimetic reference, musical pictographs refer not to scenes or objects but to the process of referring to such things. In other words, the pictographs or hieroglyphs are typically as much or more about the problem and process of mediation than they are about the things mediated. These musical hieroglyphs compose what Walter Benjamin called a "perfecting mimesis": their visual form is "an imitation whose most hidden core is an intimation"[1] of how things should sound (qtd. Hansen 2012: 190). Their inscription in a score expands the ever-present gap between symbol

1 "[...] ein Nachmachen, dessen verborgenstes Innere ein Vormachen ist"; translation modified.

and meaning and at the same time shows how the gap should be narrowed, if never closed.[2]

The sources of this phenomenon arose mainly in the eighteenth century and had fully crystallized by the turn of the nineteenth, though the phenomenon itself was relatively short-lived; musically, it was largely exhausted by 1840. (The mid-twentieth century avant-garde would revive the tradition in the form of graphic scores, but that is another story – and a different animal.) The determinants of the score as hieroglyph include the abandonment of figured bass, the growing commerce in full printed scores, and the rise of the 'work' as the musical object par excellence. Equally influential was the conjectural history linking the rise of civilization with the progressive development of writing systems. This project, extending from Condillac and Rousseau to Hegel and Grimm, involved an ideologically charged polarization of pictorial and alphabetic writing. Hieroglyphs, understood to be neither the one nor the other, occupied a transitional role in the resulting narratives. Both before and after Champollion deciphered the inscriptions on the Rosetta stone in 1825, Egyptian hieroglyphs provided a middle term between the pictorial and the phonetic. From that position the mediating capacity of hieroglyphic writing could extend to a series of other, more obviously fraught oppositions including nature and spirit, the sensuous and the conceptual, the primitive and the evolved.

Hieroglyphs in this guise had long been associated with religious mystery and the mysteries of nature. The association was both positive and negative. On one hand, hieroglyphics were traditionally understood as a secret priestly code meant to protect sacred knowledge from the uninitiated. On the other hand, this secret language transmitted esoteric knowledge more fully than any other. Giordano Bruno, writing at the end of the sixteenth century, surmised that hieroglyphic writing "was taken from the things of nature and their parts. By using such writings and voices, the Egyptians used to capture with marvelous skill the language of the gods" (Bruno c. 1590; Grafton/Most/Settis, eds. 2010: 300). For Sir Thomas Browne early in the seventeenth century, the ancient Egyptians, "using an alphabet of things and not of words, endeavored through the images and pictures thereof to speak their hidden contents in the letters and language of nature" (Browne 1646–1672; Grafton et al., 2010).

About a century later, William Warburton sought to weigh this conception against a rigorous history of writing systems. For Warburton, Egyptian writing bypassed the more common progression from pictures to letters; its original alphabet remained one of things, not of words. As Jan Assmann explains, Warburton thought that the transition from this pictorial pre-writing to real writing systems

2 For discussions of similar self-referential procedures, see Bernhart/Wolf, eds. 2010.

"developed only during a process of what Warburton calls 'abridgment', that is, the introduction of rules and frames [to] limit the inventory of signs [both pictorial and arbitrary] and turn it into a conventional system" (2009: 105).[3]

In the second volume of his *Divine Legation of Moses* (1741), Warburton corrected the traditional idea that all hieroglyphics belonged to secret priestly codes. Only what Warburton called symbolic hieroglyphics – those involving metaphor and metonymy – were enigmatic in form and esoteric in content. This focus on some inscriptions rather than all, together with the identification of the figurative basis of that 'some', anticipates the language of hieroglyphic scores. But Warburton's refinement of the mystery trope seems to have done little to impede its circulation. The association of Egyptian writing in general with secret wisdom not only remained in force – Mozart and Schikaneder's *The Magic Flute* helped popularize it, for instance, and vice versa – but it also set up a shadow heritage for the cultural and spiritual advance of the West. Fascination with the Egyptian mysteries forms an esoteric parallel to the idealization of Classical Greece that developed at the same time, especially in the German-speaking world. Although the era's histories of alphabetic writing openly depended on an assumption of European superiority that they were also meant to demonstrate, Egyptian hieroglyphs tended to escape the deprecation visited on the Chinese and Aztec scripts with which hieroglyphic writing was usually classed. And although, as Jacques Derrida has shown, the elevation of alphabetic writing made common cause with the logocentrism of Western metaphysics, the mystique of Egyptian writing flourished in part precisely because the hieroglyphs resisted any ideal of transparent signification even after being decoded. As Derrida put it with respect to Hegel, "the hieroglyph [would] furnish the example of that which resists the movement of dialectics, history, and logos" (1982: 83). This resistance took on a coloring of both awe and glamor that encouraged the formation of the double heritage and the sub rosa (or sub-Rosetta) career of the hieroglyph as a locus of hidden truth.

The need for this esoteric double to the bright light of Greek antiquity may lie in a persistent but understated sense that something is lacking, inevitably so, in the modern experience of the latter. This scruple would develop into full-fledged antagonism late in the nineteenth century with Nietzsche's exaltation of Dionysus, which in turn fed the brutal image of antiquity found in Hofmannsthal's and Strauss's *Elektra*. But Hegel detected the same dissatisfaction as early as *The Phenomenology of Spirit*: "[The fruits of antiquity] cannot give us the actual life in which they existed, nor the tree that bore them, not the earth and the elements which constituted their substance [...] [nor] the spring and summer of the ethical life in which they blossomed and ripened, but only

3 Assmann also cites the comment by Sir Thomas Browne quoted above (cf. 2009: 104).

the veiled recollection of that actual world" (1807/1977: 456). The veil recalls the image, well known to Hegel, of the veiled statue of Isis in the ancient Egyptian city of Sais, subject of a famous poem by Schiller, object of a memorable allusion by Kant, and source of an inscription that Beethoven kept on his desktop: "I am all that was, that is, and that will be; no mortal yet has lifted my veil." In Hegel's text the veil falls, displaced, over the organic community of ancient Greece, the same pristine origin that Heidegger would later celebrate as if unconcealed in his essay on the origin of the work of art (see 1950).

The musical extension of the hieroglyph as esoteric wisdom invites and tests the initiate. It sees in the typography of the score the potential for secreting inscriptions that resemble symbolic hieroglyphs, figures that will reveal their secrets only to the performer or score-reader who has the learning and who takes the trouble to interpret them. The production of these score-symbols overlaps with an increasing awareness of the role of symbolic expression in art and culture, although, as always, the symbol meant different things to different people. Coleridge, influenced by both Goethe and Schelling, regarded the symbol as the medium permitting "the translucence of the eternal through and in the temporal" (1816/1854: I/437). Hegel thought almost the opposite; he regarded symbolic expression as only the starting point for such translucence, and in some ways a stumbling block.

For Hegel, hieroglyphics are the equivalent in writing of what he calls symbols in art. Symbols in Hegel's sense are signs that give glimpses of a meaning in the dimension of free spirit but that also block the view with their material presence. Symbols are signs that get in their own way. Hieroglyphic script "is largely symbolic, since it *either* [...] sketches actual objects that display not themselves but a universal related to them, *or* [...] in its so-called phonetic element this script indicates the individual letters by illustrating an object whose initial letter has the same sound as the one to be expressed" (1835/1998: II/357). In other words, hieroglyphs either sketch metonyms or form rebuses. More broadly, any sign that works by offering a "rough sketch" of an actual object falls under the category of the hieroglyphic (ibid.: II/761).

In his critique of Hegel's semiology, Derrida showed that Hegel associates the self-realization of Spirit in history with the passage from hieroglyphic to alphabetic writing. But although Hegel regards Egyptian art and writing as only a first step in the direction of fully-realized spirit, the step is a real one; indeed, it is a breakthrough. "It is not splendor, amusement, pleasure or the like", he wrote, "that [Egyptian Spirit] seeks. The force which urges it is the impulse of self-comprehension; and [...] to teach itself what it is – to realize itself for itself – [it resorts to] this working out its thoughts in stone; and what it engraves in stone are its enigmas – these hieroglyphs" (Derrida 1982: 97n.). The effort to resolve the enigmas is exemplary, even if the effort itself produces an enigma that no reading, Champollion notwithstanding, can wholly undo. Thus Hegel finds in hieroglyphics the same split between mark and meaning, symbol and sense that Derrida finds in writing and language generally. The results are literally monumental, because for Hegel they include not only writing on stone but writing on landscape *with* stone, "those enormous masses of architecture and sculpture, with which Egypt is furnished" (ibid.).

The latter-day understanding of hieroglyphics is, unsurprisingly, more complex than Hegel's, and it is much less ideologically invested in the pictorial element of the script. But the basic conception persists: hieroglyphics consist of two types of sign, one of which is phonetic while the other (in different varieties) is pictographic. For example, in the symbol

the first inscription is a phonogram for the sound *nfr* and the second is an ideogram for just what it looks like, a jug. The meaning that results is metonymic: wine or beer.[4]

It is in its role as a middle term between image and code that the hieroglyphic inscription provides a model, or at least a parallel, to the musical score. Explicit musical hieroglyphs, of the sort we will examine shortly, embody the underlying principle of this model and intimate that the principle extends to scores in general. The score-hieroglyph is both code and image. It can be deciphered only by filling the pictographic gap, only by correcting the imperfect relation between the reduced symbol and its meaning. With music this requires the action not only of a thinking subject but also of an embodied one, a subject who interprets the symbol by animating it. From one perspective, developed by Hegel, the act of animation would actually be a reanimation. Musical experience arises from an act of restoration that turns the symbol, formerly a pyramid-like tomb of its meaning, into a house where the meaning dwells.[5] For

4 In addition to such ideograms, hieroglyphic writing also uses logograms, marks that represent words or morphemes. Both types of character are typically also pictograms, so that is the category under which I have grouped them here. As the example in the text illustrates, the pictograms may be metonymic (and sometimes metaphorical) rather than directly iconic. I should add that the relationship of pictograms and ideograms is a fraught subject beyond the scope of this essay. And, perhaps needless to say, the complexities of hieroglyphic writing go well beyond my own 'hieroglyphic' sketch of them.

5 As Derrida observes, Hegel treats the pyramid differently in different venues: "If the Egyptian pyramid, in the *Encyclopedia* [*of the Philosophical Sciences*] is the symbol or sign of the sign, in the *Aesthetics* it is studied for itself, that is, as a symbol right from the outset" (Derrida 1982: 85).

Hegel, such reanimation is impossible with pictographs; its possibility arises only with the musical score.

The task of the modern musician faced with a score is to act as the rising sun did on those Egyptian colossi said to emit a musical sound when struck by the sun's rays at dawn. Hegel deciphers the colossi as symbols of Spirit in its first self-realization. Their sound "bears proportion and beauty", but it lacks subjective inwardness: "Instead of being able to draw animation from within [...] [the colossi] require for it light from without which alone liberates the note of the soul from them" (1883/1998: I/358). The musician supplies the light from within, "the light of consciousness", that the colossi lacked, so that the musical symbol reveals more than it conceals and assumes "the clarity [that] makes its concrete content shine clearly through the shape belonging and appropriate to itself" (ibid.: I/361).

Hegel did not make this connection directly, but he came close. His chapter "The Execution of the Musical Work of Art", which closes the section on music in the *Aesthetics*, refers performance to the spirit of the composition rather than to the score from which the performer discerns that spirit. If the score is symbolic writing, it is symbolic writing that erases itself as it is read. But the erasure is never complete, and the score's unspoken presence as symbolic form is indelible. Regardless of whether the spirit of the composition requires self-effacement from the performer or invites creative intervention, the performer's task is to animate the music, to infuse it with the force of a living soul rather than with the impetus of a rote mechanism. The task can be accomplished only if the performer is also an interpreter, one who has to overcome the recalcitrance of the musical symbol much as virtuoso performers, as Hegel understands them, overcome the materiality of their instruments.

What Hegel left implicit Liszt later made explicit, writing that the task of the performing musician – he had virtuosos like himself in mind – was precisely to "infuse life" into the "still lifeless form" of the score (Samson 2003: 81). The performer brings music (back) to life through an act of deciphering. Or rather decrypting: in performance the music entombed in silence departs from its Hegelian pyramid and rings out with a sound bearing "subjective inwardness" – feeling revived as sound loosed from its source.

The process of animation projects the score as a form of writing that, like the Egyptian hieroglyph, possesses an esoteric appeal that the triumph of alphabetic writing can never quell. This trend only gained strength from Champollion's achievement. The realization that hieroglyphic writing is phonetic as well as pictorial had the effect of turning scores and hieroglyphics into potential mirror images of each other. Both counted as symbolic inscriptions of sound. Although there is no simple cause-and-effect relationship that connects the hieroglyph as inscribed wisdom with the score as hieroglyph, the concurrence of the two belongs to a historically specific practice of cultural self-understanding.

Probably the best known of musical hieroglyphs is the "Dreimalige Accord" (the Triple Chord) that divides the two acts of *The Magic Flute* and also bisects the opera's Overture (see Example 1). This score image – three repetitions of a threefold chord, with the top voice of each threefold ascending through the tones of the triad – not only mimics an esoteric inscription but actually is one. The caption that names it, 9a, is both supernumerary and the only caption in the score that does not refer to a musical genre or ensemble. The score prints the six isolated measures of the passage as a complete number in a pattern of 3 times 2, with a fermata at the end of each of the three couplets. And the ceremonial sound of the Triple Chord's performance smoothly conjoins the opera's Masonic and Egyptian elements.[6]

EXAMPLE 1 *W.A. Mozart,* Die Zauberflöte, *9a: "Der dreimalige Accord"*

6 There is more. The chord involved is B-flat, which in the Overture is the dominant (of a key, E-flat, with three flats in the signature), but which in the body of the opera, between the

EXAMPLE 2 *Robert Schumann,* Carnaval: *"Sphinxes"*

But the majority of hieroglyphic scores involve the piano, whether as solo instrument, accompaniment to the voice, or member of a chamber ensemble. The best known pianistic instance is also the most explicit: the "Sphinxes" of Schumann's *Carnaval* – a score consisting of three detached sets of double whole notes forming cryptographs of the motivic cells that underpin this cycle of short piano pieces (see Example 2). The model is just about perfect. The double whole notes are both conventional and exotic, and they are also both arbitrary code and pictographic symbols of an enigmatic creature – or of several: the sphinx moth, symbol of twilight thought for Schumann's favorite Romantic author, Jean Paul, and the dark double of the "Papillons" that follow "Sphinxes" in the cycle; the Theban sphinx whose fatal riddle only Oedipus could solve; and the inscrutable Sphinx of the Egyptian desert.[7] When "Papillons", as both sound and notation, metamorphoses from the "Sphinxes", the music comes to life with a flourish of "subjective inwardness", much as Hegel had imagined.

Another exemplary aspect of Schumann's inscription is its sketch- or rebus-like character.[8] The images identified as sphinxes are not quasi-iconic but quasi-pictographic, so their effect depends on visual allusion, not pictorial resemblance. The shape of the double whole notes may equally allude to wings (the moth, the Theban sphinx) or hands (the Egyptian sphinx) without genuinely looking like either one. The view suggested is frontal, the position from which a riddle or enigma would be posed to a spectator.

Nearly as iconic as "Sphinxes" is the incipit to Schubert's song "Ihr Bild". The score inscribes an isolated pair of dotted half notes under the treble staff to form a hieroglyph of both eyes and gaze – those of the lover in the poem, who

---

March of the Priests and the subsequent Aria with Chorus ("O Isis und Osiris"), is, so to speak, a counter-dominant, deferring plagal movement from F to C by inserting itself as the subdominant of F. In every respect, written and sounded, the Triple Chord is both transparent and esoteric.

7 On the complex chain of associations centered on the sphinx moth, see Jensen 1998: 135–137.

8 John Daverio suggests that the "Sphinxes" derive in part from rebuses familiar in nineteenth-century German children's literature (cf. 2007: 74f.).

EXAMPLE 3 *Franz Schubert, "Ihr Bild", mm. 1f.*

is staring at his beloved's picture, and those of whoever is reading the score (see Example 3). This doubling is present visually twice over: in the pairing of the 'eyes' over two measures, and in the doubling of the 'eye' notes at the lower octave in the bass. The score reader or pianist looks at these hieroglyphic eyes as if into a mirror, but the mirror is musical, not visual. The notes may look eye-like, but what they depict is the way music rivets the gaze. Just that, the gaze, and not its equivalent in the ear for which we have no name. This is a gaze that sees only with the mind's eye, a gaze that paralyzes vision, just as the sight of the beloved's painted eyes in the text by Heine causes the observer's vision to cloud: "Ich stand in dunkeln Träumen / Und starrt' ihr Bildnis an / [...] Und wie von Wehmutstränen / Erglänzte ihr Augenpaar. // Auch meine Tränen flossen [...]."[9] (Stanford *Schwanengesang*) The lover's tears reflect the beloved's in a clouded mirror as the partially obscured 'eyes' in the bass reflect the exposed 'eyes' in the treble.

But Heine's poem is almost irrelevant in its tearful sensibility. Its romantic plot becomes significant mainly as an illustration of the contest between sight and sound for primacy as an intellectual sense. The blind gaze 'sees' as sound. Like the double whole note 'sphinxes', the dotted half-note 'eyes' are both pictographic and encoded, both image and writing. At one level the eyes and sphinxes are enigmas while at another they form the ground of a meaning or,

9 'In darks dreams I stood / And stared at her image / [...] /And as from tears of woe / Her paired eyes glistened. // My tears flowed too [...].' (My translation).

if you will, a grammar. These instances are important as anchors for what is in the end a necessarily speculative account of musical hieroglyphics because they show the distinct possibility of thinking of music in hieroglyphic terms during this period, at least where the piano is involved.

The causes of the focus on the piano may include the instrument's iconic status in the era's musical training and musical culture, together with the peculiarity that the two staves of keyboard notation already offer a potential image of musical totality including both individual lines and their vertical integration. Other pianistic hieroglyphs can be found in the Adagio of Beethoven's "Moonlight" Sonata, the Largo of his "Ghost" Trio, and numerous passages in the last four piano sonatas; Schubert's Impromptu in G-flat, segments of the slow movement of his *Wanderer Fantasy*, and several songs in addition to "Ihr Bild" including "Die Stadt", "Der Doppelgänger", and "Meeres Stille"; Chopin's C-major, D-flat major, and E-flat minor *Preludes*, plus the Funeral March and Finale from his "Funeral March" Sonata; and Schumann's "Der Dichter spricht" from *Kinderszenen*, "Fabel" from *Fantasiestücke* and, from the same cycle, the end – aptly enough – of "Ende vom Lied".

As this list indicates, it is rare for the whole score to be hieroglyphic, which is in most cases a practical impossibility. The inclusion of hieroglyphic segments, even if only one or two bars long, suffices to activate the fiction of the score as hieroglyph despite the score's function as code. The hieroglyphic passage initially acts as a visual metaphor for what and how the score writes; it forms what W.J.T. Mitchell calls a metapicture (cf. 1995: 35–38). But as soon as it does so the score as a whole assumes hieroglyphic status on terms not confined to metaphor. The score acts like an ideographic extension of the hieroglyphic particle, the pictographic nucleus, that it incorporates.

A portion of this ideographic value extends to scores with no hieroglyphic elements. As Mitchell has suggested, there are no texts without an imagistic element, no images without a textual dimension. More broadly, as Lydia Liu has sought to show, writing as such, a technology independent of particular languages or even of language in general, is ideographic at its root (2011: 15–37). It has become customary of late to question the authority of scores because they fail, and must fail, and *should* fail, to determine in full the sounds they write down. The questioning is fair enough, given a historical tendency to overvalue scores, even to fetishize them. But a plausible alternative emerges when we treat scores not as venerable texts but as extended ideographs. The authority of scores so treated is not dogmatic but conjectural. The hieroglyphic scores of the earlier nineteenth century candidly say so, and ask us to hear as much.

Of course, the line between the hieroglyph and purely accidental forms of iconic symbolism is hard to draw; we need specific reasons to single a score out. But we should be wary of automatically assuming that iconic scores are conceived acoustically first and visually second. It may actually be the other way around. Better yet, the question of priority may not make any sense; the priority may be impossible either to set or determine.

The Schubert G-flat Impromptu is a good test case. Its unusual time signature, double cut time, allows for a distinctly pictorial display of white and black notes – white in the treble and bass, festoons of black in the middle (see Example 4). The score looks like an allegorical emblem. More exactly, it looks like an allegorical emblem for how it sounds, which is devotional, as if Schubert were following J.G. Herder in regarding reverent contemplation – *Andacht* – as the spiritual peak of expression in instrumental music.[10] The scoring of this sound looks like an image of such spiritual elevation, the sublimation of motion into contemplative stillness. But in relation to its sound this score also inscribes the imperfection that goes with its identity as a hieroglyph. Like its image, the music's sound is layered; its devotional rhetoric comes wrapped in lush harmonies that implicate the music, together with its archaic-looking score, in an early-nineteenth-century dialectic between traditional worship and ad hoc pantheism. It is not clear, and cannot become clear, whether the music is reviving a lost spirituality, expressing nostalgia at the loss, finding a modern surrogate, or secularizing the religious in the form and sensory medium of the aesthetic.

The score thus requires the pianist to act simultaneously as executant, listener, and reader. These roles may divide and reunite, but whoever assumes any of them becomes, in doing so, a figure who must master an enigma, a musical Champollion tasked with decoding the score as Rosetta stone. The iconic score thus – to recall Benjamin's terms – makes its most hidden core an intimation: it comments on the music via a performance guided by the hieroglyph, through which the music becomes an allegorical embodiment of the cosmic harmony that the hieroglyph qua mystic writing symbolizes. As with 'real' hieroglyphs, the music is encoded, but some of the code's signifiers are neither 'arbitrary' nor 'unmotivated', as in alphabetic writing, but iconic or evocative.

---

10 Herder's comment is from his *Kalligone* (cf. 1800/1880: 186), a riposte to Kant's aesthetics: 'What was that something that set [music] apart from everything foreign [*fremd*], from spectacle, dance, gesture, even from the accompanying voice? Devotion [*Andacht*]. Devotion it is that elevates individuals and gatherings above words and gestures so that nothing remains of the feelings but – sounds.' (My translation).

EXAMPLE 4 *Franz Schubert,* Impromptu in G-flat, *mm. 1–6*

Another strong example from Schubert is "Meeres Stille". The text, by Goethe, describes a becalmed ship in terms that redouble the state of paralysis: 'Deep stillness rules the water, / Without motion rests the sea.'[11] The piano part of the song mirrors this dead calm visually as well acoustically – perhaps even more so. Each measure contains a static column of whole notes marked as arpeggios; the score fits onto a single page (see Example 5[12]). There is no absolute reason to sustain this arrangement except that it gives a visual impression of absolute

11 My translation. ("Tiefe Stille herrscht im Wasser / Ohne Regung ruht das Meer").

12 The metronome marking of quarter=27 is obviously too slow. Most recorded performances range from about quarter=40 to quarter=58.

EXAMPLE 5 *Franz Schubert, "Meeres Stille"*

lack of change or motion. Anything else would mar the image. Schubert could have made the acoustic stillness even deeper by tying measures together at a crucial point or points, or he could have exacerbated the stillness by allowing slight stirrings of motion, aligned with the voice, to emerge and come to nothing. We can't know that he declined those options because they would have lessened the visual effect, but we can know the effects of the option he chose. The frozen stacks of whole notes frame the piano part of the score as an image of the lack that the score embodies. The arpeggio marks may even be taken as depictions of unachieved wave motion. And the music is performed in a state of arrested motion; no one turns a page.

In this frame of reference, a performance of the song is less a realization of the score than a description of it. The words assume an ambiguity that detaches them from their meanings and frames them as empty, or rather as emptied, signifiers. What the words say refers to the fictitious ocean voyage, to be sure, in both its figurative and literal dimensions, but the same words, at the same time, also refer to the music that 'sets' them. The words become acoustic inscriptions whose material presence matches the visual inscription that frames them. The dead calm of the sea becomes a metaphor for the even deeper stasis of the score as both seen and heard – and felt, since for the pianist in "Meeres Stille" the repetitive hand motion is as much a hieroglyph for unrelieved stasis as the notation that elicits it and the sound that it elicits.

Schubert's autograph score (see Schubert Autographs) differs in some details from the printed text, but as a visual sketch it is an equally arresting hieroglyph of sheer stasis.[13] (There will be more to say about autographs later.) One point of interest is that after a fermata on the last syllable of the fraught phrase "Todestille fürchterlich!" ('fearsome dead calm!'), a marking that appears in both scores, Schubert's autograph adds two measures of vocal silence. The published score omits these measures, as if their presence broke the stillness in the very act of being appalled by it. Despite its psychological depth, the vocal silence had to yield to the image, both acoustic and visual, of a voice in thrall to the dead calm and thus unable to keep from giving it utterance. The result is a contradiction that rules the song as the stillness does the water: the music moves in time but not in space. Such motion as there is only amplifies stillness.[14]

One obvious but crucial feature of the hieroglyphic score is that it must be seen to be appreciated. As our Schubert examples suggest, 'the listener' is not an operative category here, except insofar as the listener is also a performer. Historically speaking, the score would not have been addressed to a listener who follows the inscription without performing it. The hieroglyphic segments of a score were genuinely esoteric; for a merely listening audience, their mysteries would be doubly veiled. Such music cannot be understood fully unless it is seen as well as heard, or, better, unless the score is seen as part of an endless loop: the sounds that the score requests interpret the score; the score interprets the sounds made at its request. Neither comes first. As noted earlier, the

13 The score is a full but incomplete draft on a single page of brown paper.

14 For more on the immobility of this song, see my "The Schubert Lied: Romantic Form and Romantic Consciousness" in Frisch, ed. 1996: 210–215.

score as hieroglyph does not designate something the music expresses or represents; it designates the music that does the expressing or representing.

Another way to say this is that the hieroglyphic score constitutes (in whole or in part) a constructive description of the music it projects. Like the diverse 'imagetexts' – loose collections of textual and pictorial antecedents – that always go along with music,[15] the hieroglyph forms a primary source of the music's expressive identity. For instance, the score of Schubert's G-flat Impromptu plays on the assumption that note values carry an informal time feeling. Schubert's double cut time again turns out to be as much or more symbolic as it is practical. This score sounds faster than it looks. The melody proceeds almost exclusively in long white notes – whole notes, dotted halves, and half-notes – that float serenely over an inner voice in eighth-note triplets; the triplets move much more quickly than their note-value and their spacing on the page would seem to suggest – something they must do precisely in order to give the melody its serene breadth. There is thus a contradiction between the visual velocity of the triplets and their acoustic identity as a steady murmur between treble and bass. To perform the triplets is to abolish them, to etherealize them, as if they were imaginary sixteenths or thirty-seconds, and this effort is part of what the music means, part of its image of transcendent contemplation or prayer. One can even feel this in the fluttering or weaving motion of the fingers between the warp and the woof of the treble and the bass. The score multiplies these effects visually by the spacing that allows for only two measures per system and that widely separates the notes of the melody. The way the score looks – looks, not reads – reinforces the *sostenuto* impression made by the way it plays.

This bond between looking and playing also depends on the specific medium of the printed score, and not just because the score set in music type is what the performer would be looking at. There is an important subtext to this relationship involving the process of transforming the composer's autograph score into a published document. Autographs are often messy, even if not as notoriously so as Beethoven's, and they are often typographically wrong or idiosyncratic. Stemming and beaming are often haphazard; pitches sometimes need to be surmised more than read. Fair copies are by definition neater and more correct, but they too are often idiosyncratic and they often assume

15 Mitchell's *Picture Theory* coins the term 'imagetext' to refer to "composite, synthetic works (or concepts) that combine image and text" (1995: 89). But since, as Mitchell observes, all texts have an imagistic dimension and all images a textual one, the term may also refer to the general system of representation in Western cultures, which is defined by the polarity of text and image, the verbal and the visual. This system excludes music; for a critique, see Kramer 2002: 145–172. On constructive description, see Kramer 2010: 52–66.

the expressive force of calligraphy. Beethoven, for example, made a fair copy of the second and third movements of his "Les Adieux" Sonata – more properly *Das Lebewohl* – for presentation to its dedicatee, the Archduke Rudolph.[16] The first page is careless about stem placement but it gives great visual weight to slurs and beams. Especially notable is the beaming of the doleful inner voice in the bass in mm. 1, 2, 5, and 6, where the beams rise dramatically from under the first note, stem down, to over the remaining three notes, stems up.

None of this survives in the printed scores. The process of publication is thus also a process of normalization. The resulting gain in legibility and transmissibility is its own justification, but it is also possible to register a corresponding loss. The printed score removes the intimacy of writing; it erases the trace, the weight, the material mark of the composer's hand. To some extent, the composition of hieroglyphic passages acts as a way of reclaiming such tokens of real presence. Just insofar as the visual array goes beyond its neutral function as pure code and assumes hieroglyphic force, the composer's hand as it were merges with the knowing performer's and smudges the print.

To some extent, too, this audiovisual handprint is a fantasy, although that does not mean it is 'false' or merely fictitious. The phrase the "intimacy of writing" comes from Derrida, who acknowledges the force of that intimacy, for himself as well as for others, while also observing that the act of writing by hand is bound to both the reproducibility of the written signs and the technological means of reproducing them (2005: 27).[17] The mark of the composer's handiwork must, so to speak, cross out, or scribble across, those features. The musical hieroglyph arises in and through this act of overwriting. That is exactly what happens in the fair copy of Beethoven's "Les Adieux" or "Lebewohl" Sonata, which depicts the sound it prescribes with ad hoc marks that neither would nor could be reproduced mechanically at the time of their inscription.

Another cardinal instance of hieroglyphic scoring is the whole note counterpoint in the coda of the first movement of this piano sonata, call it what

16 The autograph can be viewed on the digital archives of Beethoven-Haus, Bonn (see online).

17 The exact phrase is "presumed intimacy of writing", which does little to counteract the force of the presumption: "I began writing with a pen [...]. For the texts that mattered to me, the ones I had a slightly religious feeling of 'writing', I even banished the ordinary pen. I dipped into the ink a long pen holder whose point was gently curved with a special drawing quill [...]. My idea must have been that my artisanal writing really would break its way through [...] as near as possible to that hand of thought or word evoked by the passage in Heidegger I later tried to interpret in 'Heidegger's Hand' [...]. But I never concealed from myself the fact that, as in any ceremonial, there had to be repetition going on, and already a sort of mechanization" (Derrida 2005: 20).

you will. To review quickly the pertinent facts about the piece, all of them famous: Beethoven entitled the three movements "Lebewohl", "Abwesenheit", and "Wiedersehen" – Farewell, Absence, and Reunion – and inscribed the syllables "Le-be-wohl" over the falling three-chord motive that begins the slow introduction to the first movement. This farewell inscription finds an echo in the rising three-note motive that begins the movement's main theme. The whole notes come much later to replace alphabetic writing by hieroglyphic inscription.

Unlike the white notes in Schubert's Impromptu, the whole notes in Beethoven's Sonata involve compression rather than expansion. The notes strip the "Lebewohl" chords down to their essence to bid both the traveler and the movement a final farewell. Or rather a reluctant series of final farewells, whose whole-note phrases entwine with and echo each other. These phrases trace out a fourfold contrapuntal rotation that isolates each whole note in a single measure (see Example 6). The visual result is a depiction of the notes' utter solitude and hence of the equally stark solitude following the farewell that the movement has narrated. The subsequent slow movement produces a similar impression by writing its melody in very slow dotted-sixteenth and eighth notes, as if to depict a traumatic slowing down of time or thought in the void of absence – the very absence opened by the empty circles of the previous movement's isolated whole notes.

Where do those notes come from? From the beginning; for the sonata begins by anticipating the absence that arrives as the first movement departs. The slow introduction writes the opening "Lebewohl" motive in quarter notes. But when the coda shifts over to whole notes, the difference in tempo means that the motive is played at roughly the same pace in both places. The expressive difference lies initially in the resulting accentuation. The movement is in 2/4 time. In the introduction, the first and third notes of the motive fall on downbeats and the second note is unaccented, whereas in the coda each note falls on a downbeat, so that the second note is also accented. As the fourfold rotation proceeds – in two voices, one in the treble, one in the bass – the first

EXAMPLE 6 *Ludwig van Beethoven,* Piano Sonata in E-flat, *Op. 81a, first movement, mm. 181–191*

note in one voice coincides with the third note in the other. Each time this happens, the third note disappears; it shrinks to a quarter note over or under the other voice's first whole note. The phrases intertwine only to slip away from each other. The process is as much visual as it is acoustic. In both media, it forms an emblem of the separation of partners in an act of farewell. The burden of the resulting isolation falls on the newly accented second note, which sounds naked, without counterpoint or counterpart except silence.

It is up to the performer to make the expressive difference felt by the controlled effort of finger, wrist, and shoulder, and to make the terrible isolation of that second note heard without making it obtrusive. The isolation must in fact be barely perceptible, the mark of dwelling on a threshold. The difference lies ultimately in the symbolic value of this isolated whole note on the page, something obvious to the original audience, who would be players, not listeners. The singleness of the note symbolizes the importance of the singular, the condition of solitariness, the absence of the one from the other, the condition of remaining when contact has been broken, the incommensurable condition of becoming a remainder.

Shortly before the end of the movement there is a strange visual echo of this inscription paired with an acutely painful sound (see Example 7). Only one measure is involved. In the bass are two whole notes fused into one form, the edges soldered into a common border: a low E♭ and the D a semitone below it. In the treble there is – nothing. The two hieroglyphic notes become one in the anguish of separation; the mark of separation hovers above them in the notation of the silence (faintly crisscrossed by clashing overtones) that hovers over the dissonant bass. It remains unclear whether what I am describing here is an

EXAMPLE 7 *Ludwig van Beethoven,* Piano Sonata in E-flat, *Op. 81a, first movement, mm. 242–244*

effect of sight translated into sound or vice versa. What is clear is that the performer, once again, must realize this redoubling of solitariness in the act of playing the double note, shading its pianissimo dynamic so that the ugliness of the sound is neither exaggerated nor mollified.

How often have these hieroglyphics of farewell been noticed, or at least intuited? Impossible to say, perhaps, but the difference between noticing and intuiting may be significant. To anyone who has studied the piano repertoire, these passages from the score of the misnamed "Les Adieux" are perfectly familiar; there might seem to be no reason to think twice about them. To some extent, this is true of all the passages we have – literally – looked at. But the particular familiarity of the Beethoven offers a good opportunity for reflection. I suggest that we customarily see these passages from the "Lebewohl" Sonata, and others like them, without fully recognizing what is there to be seen. Even without words, music has never been a matter of sound alone – a principle, of course, that is by no means limited to the matter of hieroglyphics. But on that matter, we can hear such music better by seeing it – again, literally seeing it – as a fragment in phonoglyphics, as sound not merely encoded, but inscribed for the eye to hear.

References

Assmann, Jan (2009). *Moses the Egyptian: The Memory of Egypt in Western Monotheism.* Cambridge, MA: Harvard UP.

Beethoven, Ludwig van (1923/1975). *Complete Piano Sonatas*. Ed. Heinrich Schenker. 2 vols. New York, NY: Dover Books.

Beethoven-Haus, Bonn (online). http://www.beethoven-haus-bonn.de/sixcms/detail.php?id=&template=dokseite_digitales_archiv_en&_dokid=ha:wm966&_seite=1–2 [04/10/2014].

Bernhart, Walter, Werner Wolf, eds. (2010). *Self-Reference in Literature and Music.* Word and Music Studies 11. Amsterdam/New York, NY: Rodopi.

Browne, Sir Thomas (1646–1672). *Pseudodoxia Epidemica* (online). http://penelope.uchicago.edu/pseudodoxia/pseudo19.html [4/10/2014].

Bruno, Giordano (c. 1590). *De Magia* (online). http://www.esotericarchives.com/bruno/magia.htm [4/10/2014].

Champollion, Jean-François (1828). *Précis du système hiéroglyphique des anciens égyptiens* (online). 2nd ed. 2 vols. Paris: Treutel & Würtz. Google Books [4/10/2014].

Coleridge, Samuel Taylor (1816/1854). *The Statesman's Manual* (online). Ed. William G.T. Shedd. The Complete Works of Samuel Taylor Coleridge. 7 vols. New York, NY: Harper. Google Books [08/12/2013].

Daverio, John (2007). “Piano Works, I: A World of Images”. Beate Perrey, ed. *The Cambridge Companion to Schumann*. Cambridge: CUP. 65–85.

Derrida, Jacques (1982). “The Pit and the Pyramid: Introduction to Hegel’s Semiotics”. Jacques Derrida. *Margins: Of Philosophy*. Trans. Alan Bass. Chicago, IL: University of Chicago Press. 69–108.

——— (2005). *Paper Machine*. Trans. Rachel Bowlby. Stanford, CA: Stanford UP.

Frisch, Walter, ed. (1996). *Schubert: Critical and Analytical Studies*. Lincoln, NE: University of Nebraska Press.

Grafton, Anthony, Glenn W. Most, Salvatore Settis, eds. (2010). *The Classical Tradition*. Cambridge, MA: Harvard UP.

Hansen, Miriam Bratu (2012). *Cinema and Experience: Siegfried Kracauer, Walter Benjamin, and Theodor W. Adorno*. Berkeley, CA: University of California Press.

Hegel, G.W.F. (1807/1977). *Phenomenology of Spirit*. Trans. Arnold V. Miller. Oxford: Clarendon.

——— (1835/1998). *Aesthetics: Lectures on Fine Art*. Trans. T.M. Knox. 2 vols. Oxford: Clarendon Press.

Heidegger, Martin (1950). *Der Ursprung des Kunstwerkes*. Stuttgart: Reclam.

Herder, J.G. (1800/1880). *Kalligone*. Ed. Bernhard Suphan. Herders Sämmtliche Werke. Berlin: Weidmannsche Buchhandlung.

Jensen, Eric (1998). “Explicating Jean Paul: Robert Schumann’s Program for ‘Papillons’, Op. 2”. *19th Century Music* 22: 127–143.

Kramer, Lawrence (2002). *Musical Meaning: Toward a Critical History*. Berkeley, CA: University of California Press.

——— (2010). *Interpreting Music*. Berkeley, CA: University of California Press.

Liu, Lydia (2011). *The Freudian Robot: Digital Media and the Future of the Unconscious*. Chicago, IL: University of Chicago Press.

Mitchell, J.W.T. (1995). *Picture Theory: Essays on Verbal and Visual Representation*. Chicago, IL: University of Chicago Press.

Samson, Jim (2003). *Virtuosity and the Musical Work: The Transcendental Studies of Liszt*. Cambridge: CUP.

Schubert Autographs (online). http://www.schubert-online.at/index_einzelansicht_en.php?werke_id = 499 [4/10/2014].

Stanford *Schwanengesang* (online). http://opera.stanford.edu/iu/libretti/schwan.html [4/10/2014].

Warburton, William (1741). *The Divine Legation of Moses* (online). http://archive.org/stream/divinelegation01warbuoft/divinelegation01warbuoft_djvu.txt [4/10/2014].

Historical Studies

∵

The Spectacular Imagination and the Rhetoric of Absence in *Armide*

Blake Stevens

The *tragédies en musique* of Jean-Baptiste Lully and Philippe Quinault range widely across spatial and temporal boundaries, rejecting the unity of place as postulated by classical poetics in favor of frequent set changes and transformations through stage machinery. Criticism of the *tragédie en musique* has only recently begun to engage with the reverse side of spectacular display: the strategic concealment of actions that are manifested onstage through discursive reference. This reading of *Armide* demonstrates that techniques of absence and disclosure, located in the spatial awareness of characters, lend spatial and temporal complexity to the fictional worlds represented in the *tragédie en musique*.

•••

The *tragédies en musique* of Jean-Baptiste Lully and Philippe Quinault produced between 1673 and 1686 manifest a perpetual fascination with place. Palaces, temples, gardens, forests, caverns, deserts, and other sharply differentiated sites not only stage actions and expressive utterances but at times transform them. In *Atys* (1676) and *Amadis* (1684), for instance, woods and forests are thematized as spaces of solitary reflection. The opening scenes of *Atys* reveal that Atys has been overheard by his confidant delivering an amorous lament in a moment of unguarded – and, he believes, unobserved – expression, having sought refuge 'in a solitary and dark wood' ("dans un bois solitaire et sombre") beyond the frame of the stage (Quinault 1999a: 180; this and all subsequent translations are by the author). By contrast, Amadis appears within a forest in his monologue air, "Bois épais, redouble ton ombre". Whereas the site of Atys's lament is only disclosed through narrative description and reenactment by his confidant, the wooded scene of Amadis's monologue is depicted onstage: he addresses the 'dense woods' ("bois épais") and casts his song rhetorically as an attempt to persuade them to hide his 'unfortunate love' ("malheureux amour") in their deep shade (Quinault 1999b: 167).

Armide, the final collaboration of Lully and Quinault (1686), presents a particularly compelling instance of the interaction of character and stage space in Renaud's monologue "Plus j'observe ces lieux et plus je les admire". Having left his companion Artémidore behind as he wanders through a verdant countryside, the crusading knight Renaud sets his weapons down and rests at the edge

 | DOI 10.1163/9789004314863_004

of a river. His awareness is gradually absorbed by the space enveloping him, as he perceives the motion of water depicted in the sinuous, muted strings of the orchestra and fuses his voice with the sonorous landscape. The monologue is set throughout in the present tense and avoids the vivid play of apostrophe, exclamation, and interrogation typical of monologic discourse. Renaud instead describes the animated and resonant *tableau* of flowing water, flowers, wind, harmonious sonorities, thick foliage, and shade, all features of what is likely an enchanted space under the control of the sorceress Armide:

Plus j'observe ces lieux et plus je les admire.
  Ce fleuve coule lentement
Et s'éloigne à regret d'un séjour si charmant.
Les plus aimables fleurs et le plus doux Zéphyr
  Parfument l'air qu'on y respire.
Non, je ne puis quitter des rivages si beaux.
Un son harmonieux se mêle au bruit des eaux.
Les oiseaux enchantés se taisent pour l'entendre.
Des charmes du sommeil j'ai peine à me défendre.
  Ce gazon, cet ombrage frais,
Tout m'invite au repos sous ce feuillage épais.[1]

The site is well suited to the presentation of a *sommeil*, given the topical associations between the *locus amœnus* of pastoral poetry and states of repose and reverie (cf. Curtius 1953: 195–198). Renaud's monologue is materialized through the setting itself: the *locus amœnus* appears not only as a site for lyrical utterance but also as a force that actualizes the verbal description of place through instrumental music. As he sings, Renaud's interior state merges with an encroaching spatial presence, and he in turn brings the stage world into a mediated and psychologically transfigured presence for the audience.

The portrayal of spatial awareness, in which characters engage with immediately present and sonorous or resonant sites, demonstrates the impact of stage spectacle on the dramatic text and performance of the *tragédie en*

1 Quinault 1999b: 265. ('The more I observe this place, the more I admire it. This river flows slowly and leaves behind so charming a space with regret. The loveliest flowers and the calmest wind perfume the air one breathes. No, I cannot leave shores so beautiful. A harmonious sound mixes with the noise of the waters. The enchanted birds silence themselves to listen to it. I can hardly defend myself against the charms of sleep. This grassy bank, this fresh shade, everything invites me to rest beneath this dense foliage').

musique. This fictional absorption or astonishment is doubled in early critical reception of the form. Critics writing in the 1670s and 1680s, such as Charles Perrault, Jean de La Bruyère, and Claude-François Ménestrier, noted opera's singular dependence on spectacle. For these critics, the frequent set changes and transformations realized through stage machinery (the *merveilleux*) constituted one of opera's most basic deviations from theatricality as defined by the tragedies of Pierre Corneille, Jean Racine, and their contemporaries. Ménestrier articulated this important thread in reception by locating opera's distinguishing feature in its fusion of epic subject matter with immediate enactment. Integrity of dramatic construction was the hallmark of spoken tragedy, with its 'well-managed intrigues and the linking of scenes'; by contrast, opera was marked by striking, even extravagant display: 'Here, subjects of pure invention or those drawn from fables are most appropriate, because they allow more for extraordinary machines, decorations, open skies, hells, seas, shipwrecks, clouds, gods who fly from the sky to the earth or who carry mortals up to the heavens, monsters, extraordinary animals, enchanted palaces that descend from the sky or that rise into it, etc.'[2] This appeal to the *merveilleux* was calculated to meet the distinctive objectives of opera, conceived 'more for pleasure and divertissement than for instruction', and 'where one searches more for the *merveilleux* than the *vraisemblable*'.[3] The consequences for dramatic representation included subject matter drawn from classical mythology and chivalric epic as well as the diverse sets, machinery, costumes, and dances that enacted these subjects.

It is in counterpoint with this foregrounding of spectacle that the crucial role of absence in the *tragédie en musique* emerges. The striking and seemingly essential effects of spectacle may be suspended at will, as characters deflect the immediacy of embodied presence to invoke absent figures and spaces. The robust critical tradition initiated by Ménestrier and La Bruyère that has placed the techniques of opera within the horizon of classical poetics has only recently begun to register the complex construction of space in the *tragédie en musique*.

2 "[…] des intrigues bien conduites, & un enchaînement de Scenes qui se lient les unes aux autres. Icy les sujets de pure invention, ou ceux qui sont tirez des fables sont les plus propres, parce qu'il y entre plus de machines extraordinaires, & de decorations, des Cieux ouverts, des Enfers, des Mers, des Naufrages, des nuées, des Dieux qui volent du Ciel en terre, ou qui enlevent des mortels dans le Ciel, des Monstres, des animaux extraordinaires, des Palais enchantez qui descendent du Ciel, ou que y montent, &c." (Ménestrier 1972: 239).

3 "Comme les pieces de Theatre composées en Musique, sont plus faites pour le plaisir & le divertissement que pour l'instruction, on y cherche plus le merveilleux que le vrai semblable [sic]" (ibid.: 170).

This shift in perspective has brought attention to the discursive and musical representation of imaginary and unseen events rather than treating opera as a kind of 'saturated' spectacle fundamentally at odds with the representational techniques of classical tragedy.[4] An important insight of this new perspective is that a shared attraction to offstage space generates a striking difference between the forms: because opera admits not only stage transformations and spectacular manifestations but also strategies of intimation associated with tragedy, it operates according to a wholly distinctive representational syntax split between the possibility of display and the concealment of space. Whereas the use of offstage space is a common feature of diverse theatrical forms, the denial or retraction of spectacle acquires a marked theatrical force in the *tragédie en musique* precisely through its normative violation of spatial unity and appeal to visual display (cf. Thomas 2002: 100–107; 116–118).

This 'spatial turn' in studies of the *tragédie en musique* has opened a broad field of investigation into its strategies of representation. In this essay I explore the discursive means by which offstage space is constructed in *Armide* as well as the impact of these techniques on the experience of illusion and imagination so critical to seventeenth-century models of spectatorship. I examine selected dramaturgical writings of Jean Chapelain and the abbé d'Aubignac to locate two such techniques: expository dialogues and entrance and exit discourses that 'place' unseen events in entr'actes. In *Armide*, I will argue, the awareness of offstage space exhibited by characters articulates important structural points in the plot; these key moments link the 'internal' unfolding of the fictional action to the 'external' interplay of presence and absence directed to the spectator's capacity for imaginative response.

A Poetics of Concealment

In contrast to the *tragédie en musique*, French classical tragedy has long been defined according to its investment in concealed action. Ménestrier's catalogue of visual effects and settings in opera stands in stark contrast to d'Aubignac's observation that 'very few actions' appeared in spoken tragedy of his time, and furthermore, that 'nearly all of them, at least the most important,

4 Important analyses along these lines include Burgess 1998: 190–195 and 313–337, Thomas 2002: 100–128, and Naudeix 2004: 170–193 and 448–474. The contrary tendency of identifying the *tragédie en musique* with absolute subjection to spectacle, firmly rooted in operatic criticism of the seventeenth and eighteenth centuries, is exemplified by the work of Catherine Kintzler (cf. 2006: 147–243; 275–278).

were almost always imagined to be outside of the stage'.[5] The strong articulation of onstage and offstage space in classical tragedy was rooted in the concept of spatial unity. Part of a set of practices that included the rules of unified action and time, the unity of place emerged in the 1630s and 1640s in opposition to the simultaneous 'multiple décor' of preclassical or irregular French theater, which had divided the stage into several distinct sites and allowed characters to move freely from one place to another. As John D. Lyons has observed, this conception of a "porous, loosely structured stage setting" was eventually supplanted by the "rigorous dualism" of a single décor that firmly established offstage space as constitutive of representation (1991: 71).

The results of spatial unity were ideally productive rather than constraining. Integrated with the unities of action and time, the *décor unique* reinforced effects of compression and psychological analysis. Jean Chapelain's analysis of these effects in his "Lettre sur la règle des vingt-quatre heures" focused on the techniques of narrative and the entr'acte. Because the unity of time required that the action as distilled by the poet be initiated as closely as possible to the catastrophe, Greek tragedy introduced the narrations of messengers to clear the stage of accessory incidents that would detract from this compression (cf. 2007: 227f.). For Chapelain, the unities of time and place were interdependent, as the spectator could not plausibly imagine events unfolding across a long duration yet confined to a single location. Represented fictional time and action, therefore, are by necessity incomplete: not only must prior actions be introduced through narrative, but fictional time and objective time are virtually never fully synchronized, however much a perfect equivalence between the two might be aesthetically or dramaturgically attractive. The difference was balanced out by the entr'acte, which as Chapelain described was a means of temporal expansion that compensated for the discrepancy between the two or three hours of unfolding theatrical time and the broader expanse of implied fictional time. In the performance of French classical tragedy, the curtain was only raised at the beginning of performances; between acts, while the stage remained exposed, stagehands altered the physical properties of the set as needed and musicians filled the time and diverted the audience's attention with instrumental airs (cf. Rosow 1993: 232f.). Beyond the objective clock-time of the entr'acte and the vacant stage, cleared of dramatic agents, fictional time stretched to include an imaginary passage of time and unseen events.

---

5 "Voire même est-il certain, qu'il fait paraître fort peu d'Actions sur son Théâtre; elles sont presque toutes supposées, du moins les plus importantes, hors le lieu de la Scène" (d'Aubignac 2011: 408).

Chapelain did not directly couple the entr'acte, which suspends speech and stage action, with narrative as a discursive mode. D'Aubignac's *La Pratique du théâtre* supplies this link in terms of entrance and exit speeches that define notional actions transpiring offstage.[6] For d'Aubignac, the entire problematic of theatrical representation was centered on the internal justification, or *couleurs*, of onstage enactment. The disposition of onstage and offstage events was accordingly a pivotal determination made by the poet in the earliest stages of composition (cf. 2011: 78–82; 166).[7] This determination responded to widely shared assumptions about the *bienséances* (decorum) and *vraisemblance* (dramatic plausibility), elements of the external disposition of the work that fulfill the requirements of 'representation' ("Représentation") for an audience; at the same time, judgments concerning onstage enactment responded to the autonomous level of the dramatic action, the internal disposition that corresponds to the 'true action' ("Action véritable") (ibid.: 78–81). This economy of representation is not founded simply on the avoidance of displays of violence or other unrepresentable actions. Instead, d'Aubignac stressed the active nature of extended narrative speech in staging the passions of the narrator. The *récit* is at once a compensation for lost onstage action and a potentially powerful discursive action in itself that appealed to the passions and imagination of the spectator (cf. ibid.: 343f.; Hawcroft 1992: 218–221).

The offstage actions that compel these discourses, which may range from brief allusions to large-scale narrative speeches, were understood to occur principally before the inception of the represented action and during the entr'actes. The advantage of the entr'acte over dramatic scenes for the placement

---

6 D'Aubignac used a wide range of expressions to describe offstage space: "des lieux éloignés de la Scène" (2011: 253), "hors le Théâtre" (ibid.: 307) and "hors de la Scène" (ibid.: 317), "un autre lieu que celui de la Scène" (ibid.: 313), "derrière la Tapisserie" (ibid.: 352), and more generally, "hors de la vue des Spectateurs" (ibid.: 164) or simply "ailleurs" (ibid.: 349).

7 The principle was foundational for Pierre Corneille as well in his *Discours des trois unités, d'action, de jour, et de lieu*: 'The poet is not bound to expose to the sight all of the individual actions that lead to the principal action. He must choose those that are most advantageous to him to present [*faire voir*], whether by the beauty of the spectacle, the brilliance and vehemence of the passions that they produce, or by some other attraction associated with them, and hide the others behind the stage [*scène*] and to make them known to the spectator either through a narration or by some other artful means.' ("Le poète n'est pas tenu d'exposer à la vue toutes les actions particulières qui amènent à la principale. Il doit choisir celles qui lui sont les plus avantageuses à faire voir, soit par la beauté du spectacle, soit par l'éclat et la véhémence des passions qu'elle produisent, soit par quelque autre agrément, qui leur soit attaché, et cacher les autres derrière la scène, pour les faire connaître au spectateur, ou par une narration, ou par quelque autre adresse de l'art." 1987: 176.)

of offstage events lay in its shift in mode. The entr'acte allowed the rational faculty of sight to be supplanted by the imagination. The withdrawal of actors and the displacement of discourse with instrumental music conspired to 'trick' ("tromper") the spectator that a rapid passage of fictional time had occurred: 'during this absence of all sorts of characters, the imagination, which shortens time as it pleases, makes moments pass for years, all the more easily in that the eyes do not contradict it'.[8] Although offstage action may also transpire within acts, the entr'acte was privileged in this regard because dramatic scenes may establish too precise a sense of temporality to facilitate the expansion of conjectural time offstage (cf. d'Aubignac 2011: 351).

The importance of offstage action in the spectator's experience of dramatic illusion is illustrated by d'Aubignac's claim that the dramatist must fashion dialogue to reveal the objectives of exits, to guard against charges that the actors are 'lazy' and that they 'cease playing their characters when they are lost to sight'.[9] The principle applies to all scenes but is critical at the ends of acts, where proleptic or forecasting language establishes an extra-scenic continuance of character and action. This speculative activity in the audience is subject to the poet's control: the spectator's supposition that characters circulate through an unseen space is shaped and constrained by discourses that mark exits and entrances, as well as allusions to offstage events made in the course of dialogue (see Barnwell 1986).

This strategic elision of visible action and its fabrication in discourse shifts the scene of selected actions into the spectator's mind. As Timothy Murray has argued, d'Aubignac's theory of "non-representation" advances the receptive mind as a "*figural place* of the representation of theater's rhetoric of desire", positing the imagination as an interior faculty that represents sensuous appearance in the absence or loss of objects (1982: 72; cf. d'Aubignac, 2011: 408; Lyons, 2005: 105). The spectator is mobilized in the unfolding of a tragic action through the dynamics of identification, through imaginative experience that is associated above all with states of agitation and disorder. We should recall that the terms used by d'Aubignac to characterize offstage actions include 'impossible', 'unpleasant', and 'obstructing'.[10] The imagination is accordingly their only available stage, and vivid language their most effective vehicle.

8 "Durant cette absence de toutes sortes de personnages, l'imagination, qui raccourcit les temps, comme il lui plaît, faisait passer les moments pour des années, d'autant plus aisément que les yeux n'y contredisaient point" (d'Aubignac 2011: 318).

9 "[…] afin que l'on sache qu'ils ne seront pas oisifs, et qu'ils ne laisseront pas de jouer leurs personnages encore qu'on les perde de vue" (ibid.: 146).

10 "Impossible", "désagréable", "embarrassantes" (ibid.: 352f.).

The Spaces of *Armide*

The central characters in *Armide* are keenly aware of the space that surrounds them. Pivotal moments in which they turn to invoke absent beings or sites demonstrate the importance of spatial reference and placement for characterization, plot, and the appeal to the spectator's imagination. Three such passages in Acts 1, 3, and 5 mark important junctures in the action: the liminal scenes of opening and closing, and the medial rupture of Act 3 effected by a radical spatiotemporal transformation in which Armide and Renaud fly from Damascus to a remote desert.

The spatial articulations of Act 1 define both topography and character. Armide and her confidantes, Phénice and Sidonie, appear in dialogue before a 'grand place ornamented with a triumphal arch' ("une grande place ornée d'un Arc de Triomphe"; Lully 1686: 255) in the environs of Damascus. The expository path of the dialogue is directed by the confidantes, who take the lead in a series of gentle rebukes at Armide's conspicuous sadness. Their verbal exchange moves freely through offstage sites and unseen agents, creating a picture of the *fabula* that from the very beginning eclipses stage space and sketches in features of the geographical space and the broader context of the action.[11] Among these references are allusions to the ravages of war, the banks of the Jordan that separate the 'tranquil shores' ("tranquilles rivages") of Damascus from the site of warfare, hell, the camp of Godefroi's crusading knights, and finally Renaud, who stands apart from the knights in his resistance to Armide (ibid.).

After Armide invokes Renaud, her confidantes once again attempt to lead her away from somber reflection. In response, Armide discloses an ominous dream about the knight in an extended *récit*. This narration is thus integrated into the dialogue as a reply to her confidantes and as a continuation of this syntax of revelation: as the offstage space and its agents have been sufficiently established, now the matter at hand shifts to interior space. The exposition is motivated not by an appeal to the spectator but by the affective state of Armide. What d'Aubignac would term the *couleur* that motivates discourse in this opening scene is Armide's pensive state of mind.[12] The dialogue establishes the

11 I adapt the term 'geographical space' from David Maskell's study of performance and theatricality in Racine. Maskell introduces the terms "scenic place" and "geographical place" to express the distinction between onstage and offstage space: the "scenic place" is the onstage site of enactment that presents the imitation of action directly before the eyes of the spectator; the offstage space, or "geographical place", is realized through the discursive allusion of an onstage speaker and encompasses the entire notional world metonymically displayed in the scenic place (1991: 17f.).

12 The expository dialogues in the first acts of Racine's *Iphigénie* and *Phèdre* illustrate similar strategies in the practice of spoken tragedy. In *Iphigénie*, Agamemnon's restlessness at

deeper spatiotemporal field of the plot as well as the thematic opposition between exteriority and interiority that Downing Thomas has emphasized in his reading of the opera (cf. 2002: 116–118). Thomas suggests that Armide's dream narrative redirects our attention to an inner drama, the realm of affect and fantasy that cannot be represented visually. The presentation of the dream within the expository dialogue is not however a turn from spectacle to interiority but rather a mutation in the economy of narrative reference, from the notional positing of an invisible offstage space to the assertion of an onstage presence of startling immediacy. This mutation is effected through the irruption of orchestral accompaniment for the first time in the scene and is announced by an agitated bass line with which Armide pivots from dialogue into the extended *récit*. The dotted rhythms and rapid strokes of the "Prélude" to the *récit* evoke an entrance or change of scene, here conceived figurally as a discursive and psychological shift (see Examples 1a & b).

The orchestral accompaniment charges the dream with the premonitory force of an oracle that exceeds the informative function of a retroversion in a narrative sequence. Compared to the previous invocations of offstage sites and figures, the musical setting of the dream renders Renaud strikingly 'present', and he will retain his hold over onstage events and awareness throughout the remainder of the act. His presence is felt in the celebrated 'parenthesis' in her discourse in which Armide reveals a complex mixture of fear and admiration of Renaud's strength (cf. Quinault 1999b: 258; Norman 2001: 331–333). His proximity is manifested most dramatically when Aronte interrupts the *divertissement* of Act 1 to report that Renaud has freed the captive knights and injured Aronte in the process. This concise messenger scene draws the 'real' physical threat of Renaud onto the stage by grounding the phantasmagorical projection of him through Armide's dream in greater proximity and 'reality'. The exact nature of Armide's first physical encounter with Renaud is never clarified by her; likewise, in Act 2 Renaud indicates an awareness of Armide without detailing the circumstances of this encounter, although he offers Artémidore a brief narrative account of his exile from Godefroi's camp after killing Gernand

---

dawn initiates an extended dialogue with his servant, Arcas, outside his tent in the Greek camp at Aulide. While centered on Agamemnon's inner conflict concerning Iphigénie's sacrifice, the dialogue also defines the wider space Agamemnon and his fellow Greeks inhabit. Arcas's celebrated line invoking the sleeping army, winds, and the sea or Neptune ("Mais tout dort, et l'Armée, et les Vents, et Neptune") intimates the broader geographical space surrounding this tense moment and limited stage perspective (Racine 1999: 703; cf. Maskell 1991: 30). In *Phèdre*, Hippolyte's desire to leave Trézène initiates an extended dialogue with Théramène that introduces the principal agents of the tragedy at the same time that Théramène's description of his travels in search of Thésée allows him to introduce a wider topographical perspective to the scenic space (cf. Racine 1999: 821–825).

(cf. Tasso 2000: 97f.). The spectator's first contact with Renaud in Act 1 occurs through multiple displacements: he is cast in the offstage space as one of many physical agents among Godefroi and the other knights, he is 'internalized' and transformed through dream imagery, and he is invoked as a powerful force by Armide and a messenger whose wound manifests this force onstage. Whereas Renaud's subsequent appearance in the opening of Act 2 fulfills the convention in classical dramaturgy according to which any remaining major characters must appear onstage, his physical absence from Act 1 as it shapes the action and awareness of characters has already established his agency in the plot.

When Sidonie dismisses the content of Armide's dream as an 'insubstantial image' ("image légère") and a 'vain illusion' ("vaine chimère"), she introduces a narrative enigma of truth and falsity that the remainder of the opera will be tasked with resolving (Lully 1686: 257). Recalling d'Aubignac and Corneille's observations about the poet's determination of representational modes, it remains to be seen which components in the register of images and allusions in this opening dialogue will be manifested onstage and how their implications will be realized. The exposition frames the stage space as a site in which

EXAMPLE 1A *Jean-Baptiste Lully,* Armide, *act 1, scene 1, mm. 146–162*

EXAMPLE 1B *Jean-Baptiste Lully,* Armide, *act 1, scene 1, mm. 146–162*

an initially notional, even phantasmagorical world will either be realized, contradicted, or permanently suspended.

Act 3, which opens with Armide alone in a desert, lies at the furthest remove from the site of exposition. Armide delivers a monologue air of regret and despondency framed as an apostrophe to an absent Renaud, once more presenting him in figural or imaginary form rather than immediately.[13] In the prior act, Armide had failed to carry out her planned murder of Renaud as he lay in an enchanted sleep in the *locus amœnus*. Suspending her action in confusion and self-doubt, she commanded the demons under her power to transform into zephyrs and carry them away to the 'most remote deserts (…) at the end of the universe' ("les plus reculés deserts […] au bout de l'Univers"; ibid.: 267). During the entr'acte separating Acts 2 and 3, Armide has not only arrived with Renaud in the desert; sufficient time has elapsed for the two to consummate their desire and for Armide's love to develop in complexity and self-consciousness. Her monologue reveals the regretful awareness of the disparity between Renaud's enchanted love and her own passion. She has also been joined in this retreat by her confidantes. In a scene that parallels the expository dialogue of Act 1, Armide is led to describe these unseen events occurring during the entr'acte. In terms of the spectator's contact with the fictional world, these are not so much 'events' placed in the entr'acte as dispositions and psychological states that unfold in real time, as they appear in an ever deepening analysis of the situation through dialogue.

In this way, Acts 2 and 3 engage in a structural play of concealment and disclosure. Armide's exit discourse at the end of Act 2 projects a refusal of mimesis by removing the spectacle of her pity from Hidraot and the people of Damascus; the gradual picture that emerges in Act 3, sketched by Armide's monologue and the confidential disclosures that follow in dialogue with Phénice and Sidonie, is one of recovery and allusiveness to past time. By eliding visual incidents not amenable to direct representation through the entr'acte, Quinault observed the *bienséances* by necessarily avoiding the display of lovemaking. Yet he and Lully also exploited the entr'acte as a means of temporal expansion. The revised entr'acte music was drawn from the Prologue rather than from the preceding act, as had been Lully's custom in previous operas. Lois Rosow has argued that he chose the *entrée grave* to allow additional time for the machine to carry away Armide and Renaud and to establish a more serious affect (cf. 1993: 236f.). The longer entr'acte music has the additional advantage of suggesting a broader passage of fictional time. In their exchange in Act 3, Armide and her confidantes avoid precise indications of

13 D'Aubignac singled out apostrophe among the figures of rhetoric for its 'theatrical' ("Théâtral") effect in evoking an 'object of the imagination'; the figure, prompted by the passionate 'impulse' of the speaker, in turn 'carries away the imagination of those who listen to him'. ("Comme c'est un effet de l'emportement de l'esprit de l'Acteur, elle emporte avec elle l'imagination de ceux qui l'écoutent"; 2011: 476.)

time; by contrast, the first nominal indication in Act 1, scene 1 is "jour", a temporal gesture that points to the importance of the 'day' that will witness the arrival of Hidraot and the celebration of Armide's (illusory) triumph in the Act 1 *divertissement*. This avoidance of spatiotemporal indicators in the Act 3 dialogue aids in sustaining the dramatic illusion of extensive passage of time.[14]

The final actions of the opera assert once more the evocative power of offstage space. After a prolonged absence from stage space, during which Renaud has been diverted by the dances of fortunate lovers and allegorical Pleasures, Armide returns to find a now disenchanted Renaud being led away by Ubalde and the Chevalier Danois. Armide vainly calls upon the demons to stop him and then implores him to remain or take her captive, ultimately fainting before him and thus realizing her vulnerability as intimated by her dream. Ubalde and the Chevalier Danois prevail over Renaud's pity – and not, as the dream had predicted, murderous cruelty – and forcibly remove him from this spectacle into the offstage space. Quinault exploits the technique of teichoscopy (literally, "seeing through the wall"; Pavis 1998: 381) when Armide regains consciousness and responds to Renaud's departure with rage, torment, and incredulity. She calls out to the absent Renaud, but whether or not he hears her, and how he might be reacting, is concealed from the spectator. Observing that 'he is already close to the shore' ("Il est déjà près du rivage") and that her efforts at stopping him are useless, she pivots from direct address in a series of ellipses and fragmentary utterances to a confused projection of violence and a loss of awareness, requiring her to re-orient herself in discourse ('What am I saying?') and space ('Where am I?'):

> Traître, attends...je le tiens...je tiens son cœur perfide...
> Ah! je l'immole à ma fureur...
> Que dis-je? où suis-je? hélas! Infortunée Armide!
> Où t'emporte une aveugle erreur?[15]

This moment of inarticulation acquires urgency as a disruption of Armide's commanding power of voice and enunciation. It recalls the silences and hesitations in her Act 2 monologue, "Enfin il est en ma puissance", in which an equally unresponsive Renaud had provoked passionate excess (cf. Lully 1686:

14 For the abbé Gabriel Bonnot de Mably, however, writing in a later period (1741), this extreme traversal of space destroyed the experience of dramatic illusion (cf. Rosow 1993: 238).

15 Lully 1686: 287. ('Traitor, wait...I hold him...I hold his treacherous heart...Ah! I sacrifice him to my rage...What am I saying? Where am I? Alas! Unfortunate Armide! Where does blind error carry you?')

266f.). As with the Act 2 monologue, too, her passion finds release in magical invocation, here commanding the demons under her control to destroy the enchanted palace.

The final scene encapsulates the dual enunciatory power of Armide, as she summons and directs the actions of magical beings as well as projects her awareness of unseen space. This terminal *récit* fulfills an informative function in describing Renaud's departure as it unfolds beyond the stage, yet the emphasis is placed firmly on Armide's passionate response. The action of the opera is thus rooted in spatial awareness by shaping the emergence and disappearance of Renaud not through immediate representation but through discursive allusion. The boundary of scenic space represents a threshold leading from the real to the visionary and imaginary as projected by the mediating consciousness of Armide.

Staging Absence

Armide has provoked a wide range of critical responses from the early eighteenth century to the present. These responses have often centered on Armide's monologue of Act 2, "Enfin il est en ma puissance", as a demonstration of the expressive possibilities (or limitations) of *récitatif* and the compelling immediacy of performers who incarnated the role, in particular Marie Le Rochois. In addition to commenting on this scene and Le Rochois's interpretation, Le Cerf de la Viéville noted the distinctive effect of the opera's conclusion: he reported that it left spectators 'full of passion' and that they 'returned home' in a state of 'reverie, saddened at the despondency of Armide'.[16] Le Cerf did not further specify why spectators remained absorbed in thought after performances of *Armide*. Thomas has suggested that the spectator in Le Cerf's account is "haunted by the figure of Armide" and her loss of Renaud (2002: 121). The incompletion of the action and loss extend to Renaud as an agent as well, whose heroic victory and resolute commitment to *gloire* are compromised onstage. He expresses profound pity when roles are reversed and he faces an unconscious but powerful enemy. Crucially, he does not choose to abandon Armide but is compelled to do so by his fellow knights. The drama of Renaud's conflict between sensuality and martial glory is therefore suspended rather than resolved, and it is projected offstage, like Renaud himself. The spectator is left to ruminate over an absent yet implied continuation of the action, no

16 "L'Auditeur plein de sa passion [...] s'en retourne chez lui pénetré malgré qu'il en ait, rêveur, chagrin du mécontentement d'Armide" (Le Cerf 1972: 60).

longer placed in the entr'acte but in the site of the imagination beyond the theater. Not only Armide's vivid teichoscopy, through which we glimpse Renaud for the last time, but Renaud's own exit discourse suspends resolution and solicits memory and imagination for continuance or closure.

This projection of action into the spectator is only one of many instances in which *Armide* illustrates the technique of 'non-representation' as defined by d'Aubignac. The opera is permeated with effects of absence and evocation. As in spoken tragedy, these effects extend from fleeting inflections of discourse to large-scale dramatic events like the *récit*. Unlike spoken tragedy, however, opera places these references in structural play with onstage spectacle that also impinges upon characters' spatial awareness, as in Renaud's absorptive monologue in the *locus amœnus* of Act 2 or Armide's solitary reflections in the desert of Act 3. Throughout the opera Quinault and Lully exploit the "discourse of the invisible", as Lyons has characterized dramatic narrative, to fashion characters whose accounts of their world are marked by anxiety and the projection of fantasy (Lyons 1991: 74). The ruins of the enchanted palace are a compelling figure of the 'spectacular imagination' of *Armide*, so frequently divided between absence and presence, concealment and disclosure: the palace collapses as the onstage site of representation after the action itself has already moved beyond the threshold of the 'real' to occupy the spectator's pensive imagination.

References

Barnwell, H.T. (1986). "'They Have Their Exits and Their Entrances': Stage and Speech in Corneille's Drama". *The Modern Language Review* 81: 51–63.

Burgess, Geoffrey (1998). "Ritual in the *Tragédie en musique* from Lully's *Cadmus et Hermione* (1673) to Rameau's *Zoroastre* (1749)". PhD dissertation, Cornell University.

Chapelain, Jean (2007). "Lettre sur la règle des vingt-quatre heures" [1631]. Alfred C. Hunter, Anne Duprat, eds. *Opuscules critiques*. Geneva: Droz. 222–233.

Corneille, Pierre (1987). *Discours des trois unités, d'action, de jour, et de lieu* [1660]. Ed. Georges Couton. *Œuvres complètes*. Vol. 3. Paris: Gallimard. 174–190.

Curtius, Ernst Robert (1953). *European Literature and the Latin Middle Ages*. Willard Trask, trans. Princeton, NJ: Princeton UP.

d'Aubignac [François Hédelin], abbé (2011). *La Pratique du théâtre* [1657]. Ed. Hélène Baby. Paris: Honoré Champion.

Hawcroft, Michael (1992). *Word as Action: Racine, Rhetoric, and Theatrical Language*. Oxford: Clarendon.

Kintzler, Catherine (2006). *Poétique de l'opéra français de Corneille à Rousseau*. 2nd ed. Paris: Minerve.

Le Cerf de la Viéville de Freneuse, Jean-Laurent (1972). *Comparaison de la musique italienne et de la musique françoise* [1705–1706]. 2nd ed. 3 vols. Facsimile ed. Geneva: Minkoff.

Lully, Jean-Baptiste (1686). *Armide: Tragédie mise en musique*. Paris: Christophe Ballard.

Lyons, John D. (1991). "Unseen Space and Theatrical Narrative: The 'Récit de Cinna'". *Yale French Studies* 80: 70–90.

——— (2005). *Before Imagination: Embodied Thought from Montaigne to Rousseau*. Stanford, CA: Stanford UP.

Maskell, David (1991). *Racine: A Theatrical Reading*. Oxford: Clarendon.

Ménestrier, Claude-François (1972). *Des Représentations en musique anciennes et modernes* [1681]. Facsimile ed. Geneva: Minkoff.

Murray, Timothy (1982). "Non-Representation in *La Pratique du théâtre*". *Papers on French Seventeenth-Century Literature* 9: 57–74.

Naudeix, Laura (2004). *Dramaturgie de la tragédie en musique (1673–1764)*. Paris: Honoré Champion.

Norman, Buford (2001). *Touched by the Graces: The Libretti of Philippe Quinault in the Context of French Classicism*. Birmingham, AL: Summa Publications.

Pavis, Patrice (1998). *Dictionary of the Theatre: Terms, Concepts, and Analysis*. Christine Shantz, trans. Toronto/Buffalo, NY: University of Toronto Press.

Quinault, Philippe (1999a). *Livrets d'opéra*. Vol 1. Ed. Buford Norman. Toulouse: Société de Littératures Classiques.

——— (1999b). *Livrets d'opéra*. Vol 2. Ed. Buford Norman. Toulouse: Société de Littératures Classiques.

Racine, Jean (1999). *Œuvres complètes*. Vol.1: *Théâtre – Poésie*. Ed. Georges Forestier. Paris: Gallimard.

Rosow, Lois (1993). "Making Connections: Thoughts on Lully's Entr'actes". *Early Music* 21: 231–238.

Tasso, Torquato (2000). *Jerusalem Delivered: Gerusalemme liberata*. Ed. and trans. Anthony M. Esolen. Baltimore, MD/London: The Johns Hopkins UP.

Thomas, Downing A. (2002). *Aesthetics of Opera in the Ancien Régime, 1647–1785*. Cambridge: CUP.

'Ghost Writing': An Exploration of Presence and Absence in *Lucia di Lammermoor*

Naomi Matsumoto

When Salvadore Cammarano was adapting Walter Scott's *The Bride of Lammermoor* (1819) for Donizetti's new opera, *Lucia di Lammermoor* (1835), the librettist removed several characters. The most striking deletion was that of Lucy's mother, Lady Ashton, who in the novel seems to be the prime mover in the narrative, alongside the character of Lucy herself.

This paper first discusses Lady Ashton's absence in relation to general theories of 'opera-as-adaptation', and contrasts Donizetti's opera with earlier stage works based on the same novel. Central to the dramaturgical analysis here is the notion of 'presence-through-absence': Lady Ashton's influence is present in spite of her bodily absence; Lucy's 'angelic' personality masks darker aspects not directly acknowledged; and the silent presence of the ghostly girl killed by an ancestor of Lucy's lover Ravenswood turns Lucia into what we might call (borrowing from Derrida) a 'corporeal ghost'. Indeed the metaphysics of presence/absence, conceived in Derridean terms, has a great deal to do with this opera, and offers a hermeneutic window into its effects and layers of activity.

•••

Introduction

When Salvatore Cammarano was adapting Walter Scott's *The Bride of Lammermoor* (1819) for Donizetti's new opera *Lucia di Lammermoor* in 1835, the librettist altered the novel in a number of ways.[1] For example, minor protagonists such as Caleb Balderstone (Edgar Ravenswood's faithful servant), Ailsie Gourlay (a witch all but in name) and Cragengelt (the Jacobite who challenges Edgar) were removed. Also, events and motivations associated with the heroine's parents (Lord and Lady Ashton) and brothers (Sholto and Henry) were compressed into those of a single character, 'Enrico Ashton'.

* My thanks to Dr David Francis Urrows and Prof Dr Walter Bernhart for their insightful comments upon an earlier version of this article.

1 The libretto was first published as Cammarano 1835.

 | DOI 10.1163/9789004314863_005

However, the most striking alteration was the deletion of the villainess, Lady Ashton, who throughout the original novel seems to be the prime mover in Lucy's fatal story.

At one level, those subtractions may seem simply to fall within the usual realm of the adapter's "surgical art" (Abbott 2002: 108), a supposedly inevitable process in media changes such as those from novel to opera which involve compression of the plot. However, the 'absence' of Lady Ashton on the stage in *Lucia di Lammermoor* is much more significant than that. For one thing, accounting for her absence invites us to explore more deeply the phenomenon of 'opera-as-adaptation', and the processes involved. After all, 'adaptation studies' (as opposed to the related issues of 'intertextuality') are relatively underdeveloped in musicology,[2] and although this is not the place to adumbrate a full theory of adaptation in opera, a few observations may help to place the observations in this article into some kind of wider context.

At first glance Donizetti's opera may seem simply to be a case of what we might call 'scale adaptation' – précis of the novel that involves a selective shortening of the action without significant changes of motivation and consequence. However, when scale changes (by reduction or expansion) are accompanied by genre or medium changes the adaptive process becomes more complex. This is because different media favour certain types of vivid presentation and eschew others, and although various subplots are erased in Donizetti's opera when compared with the novel, other events come into their own. In Walter Scott's version, for example, Lucy's famous mad scene is passed over in two or three pages (cf. Scott 1819/1991: 337–339) and takes up a couple of minutes of the reader's time, whereas in the opera it can last twenty minutes or more (as it does in recordings by Joan Sutherland and Maria Callas, for example) – and this in spite of the fact that it takes much longer to read the 350-page novel than it does to listen to the opera.

Again, different media offer different kinds of access to elements of essentially the same story, and a performance art such as opera provides the chance for musical sounds, action and staging to make many kinds of reference simultaneously. Moreover, performance, through the use of a human agent (the performer), also provides a very concrete route by which to empathise with a character and participate in his or her emotions – not just to acquaint ourselves with them by description as it were. This means that the kinds of scenes that take on a symbolic or iconic status within the plot will differ according to the medium, irrespective of the process of compression or expansion that

2 Recent general work in the field includes Halliwell 2005; Sanders 2005; Hutcheon 2006/2012; MacArthur/Wilkinson/Zaiontz, eds. 2009; and Bruhn/Gjelsvik/Hanssen, eds. 2013.

takes place in the transfer from one genre to another, or their functions within the overall needs of the plot. Therefore changes or conflations of characters, and alterations in the foregrounding of events (or even in the events themselves) do not mean that there is *ipso facto* a fundamental 'hermeneutic adaptation' or change of purpose (as there might be in the case of parody, for example) between the two media. We should beware of thinking of the opera as perpetrating a completely different set of aims and consequences from the novel.[3]

Even so, the absence of Lady Ashton in the opera did not go unnoticed – at least by some British critics. For example, Henry Chorley wrote:

> "Lucia" would generally be named as Donizetti's best opera. I am not able to share in the admiration it has excited. Never, assuredly, was a story so full of suggestion for music as Scott's "Bride of Lammermoor", tamed into such insipid nothingness, even by an Italian librettist, as this. The supernatural tone of the legend entirely taken way; – the dance on the bridal night, with its ghastly interruption, replaced by a sickly scene of madness, such as occur by scores in every southern serious opera; – the funeral, with its one superfluous mourner and unbidden guest, abolished, to make room for the long final scene so cherished by tenors; – the character of *Lady Ashton,* affording such admirable material for contrast, obliterated – here are so many injuries to one of the most moving tragic tales existing in any literature. – It would be a good deed to arrange Scott's novel anew – and anew to set it. (1862: I/157f.)

This criticism of Donizetti's opera at first seems right: Lady Ashton does not appear on stage in the opera, and indeed she is dead before it begins. However, in some studies of the opera, her removal by the librettist Cammarano has been justified as a positive act, one that lends a sharp focus to the action and thus allowing it "to concentrate on the love story between Edgar and Lucy" (Mitchell 1977: 144f.). Also, by providing that focus, some believe that that allowed

3 Linda Hutcheon's *A Theory of Adaptation* (2006/2012) based upon her exhaustive survey of examples from different media, divides adaptation into the following three types: (1) forms seemingly faithful to the original but which prove to be either a "theoretical ideal" or a "practical impossibility" (e.g. translations/transcriptions in music); (2) condensations and bowdlerisations; and (3) continuum adaptation (retelling and revisions) (171). My (tentatively suggested) adaptation categories – scale, medium, genre, and hermeneutic adaptations – operate rather differently, and allow (I hope) for complex interactions and varied consequences.

Donizetti to bring about changes in "the dramatic and musical language of Italian opera" (Gossett 1985a: [vii]). Those recent remarks seem to suggest that that we should view the opera as a drastic 'hermeneutic adaptation', one that changed the motivations and purposes of the novel and made the relationship between Lucy and her lover a new focus as though it had never been the central crucible of narrative interaction in the novel (even though it had).

In fact, these two opposing views – one deploring the absence of Lady Ashton, the other welcoming it – may arise from a different kind of misunderstanding, the mistake of drawing too brutal a distinction between presence and absence in an opera that is, after all, pervaded by dark family histories (the plot has much in common with Shakespeare's *Romeo and Juliet*), haunting melodies and mysterious ghosts. This paper will discuss three aspects of presence and absence in relation to Donizetti's opera: first, how they are negotiated in relation to Lady Ashton; second, how the ambiguity between them is vital for the portrayal of the ghosts in the plot; and third, how the operation of Lucy's character relies on a complex mix of apparently absent but obliquely present attributes. It will soon become clear that presence and absence do not form a mutually exclusive dichotomy; rather there is inescapable interplay between the two. The operation of presence-through-absence offers a valuable hermeneutic window on causes and motivations in such literary, musical and dramatic works – and especially on those in Donizetti's opera. In the end, this discussion will open up the possibility that the opera is not in fact a hermeneutic transformation of Scott's novel. However, we should begin by trying to understand a little more clearly what Chorley was complaining about, and we shall begin with Lady Ashton's role in the novel.

The Presence and Absence of Lady Ashton in Scott's Novel

In the novel, Lady Ashton is an imperious character with "strong powers and violent passions" (Scott 1819/1991: 29f.), but without much love or affection for her daughter Lucy. Her family belongs to the powerful, land-owning Douglas clan that, in the past, had actually intermarried with the Ravenswood family. This initially makes her opposition to Lucy's marriage to Edgar Ravenswood puzzling, but it emerges that there are three reasons for it. First, in recent times there has been much enmity between the families and the Ashtons managed to dispossess the Ravenswoods of their land and castle. Second, the Ashtons, nonetheless, are short of money, and Lucy needs to make a 'good match' in financial terms, and Edgar cannot provide this because his family is now poor. And third, there is a rival suitor, Bucklaw, who is rich and owns lands in which there is a vacant seat for Parliament, and Lady Ashton wishes her favourite son Sholto to be able to take up that seat. These factors explain Lady Ashton's implacable opposition to the Lucy–Edgar marriage. She resorts to tampering with the correspondence between them, and when Edgar appears unannounced just after Lucy signs her marital contract with Bucklaw, it is Lady Ashton who tears the golden love-token from her daughter's neck, given to her by Edgar (cf. Scott 1819/1991: 328f.). The scene is vividly depicted in a well-known painting by W.P. Frith (see Figure 1; cf. Altick 1985: xviii).[4]

In the novel it is Lady Ashton who is portrayed as the prime mover in all the disasters that befall the families. Indeed, at the end of the book we are told: "Lady Ashton lived to the verge of extreme old age, the only survivor of the group of unhappy persons whose misfortunes were owing to her implacability." (Scott 1819/1991: 348f.) How could such a motivating female force be omitted from operatic and dramatic works based on Scott's novel? The answer, of course, is that it could not be entirely, and in fact several theatrical and operatic adaptations of Scott's novel do indeed retain Lady Ashton as a living character on the stage.

Lady Ashton on the Stage

One example of this 'physical presence' approach can be seen in John Calcraft's stage-play adaptation, *The Bride of Lammermoor: a Drama* (1823), which starred the famous Scottish actress Harriet Siddons as Lucy. Lady Ashton accompanies her daughter in the action, though the balance of power between them is softened slightly compared with the novel – Lucy is strong enough to challenge her mother occasionally and in her mad frenzy even manages to make her mother feel remorse (cf. Calcraft 1823: esp. 61f.; White 1927: 76–79).[5] Some slightly later Continental dramatisations seem to have found the cruelty of Lady Ashton towards her own daughter rather difficult to accept, and Victor Ducange's French version, *La fiancée de Lammermoor* (1828), for example, made the Lady Ashton character the stepmother of Lucy, a move which tends to align the drama with the sentimentality and cruelty of a fairy story.[6]

4 For an anecdote concerning the forgery of this painting, see Frith 1887/2006: 158f.

5 For a history of dramatic adaptations of *The Bride of Lammermoor*, see Bolton 1992: 267–334.

6 The drama was premiered at the Théâtre de la Porte Saint-Martin, Paris on 25 May 1828.

FIGURE 1 *W.P. Frith,* The Love Token
BY COURTESY OF MUSEUMS SHEFFIELD

By the time Donizetti and Cammarano were working on their *Lucia*, Scott's novel was well known to the Italians through a translation by Gaetana Barbieri (1824). They were also familiar with the plot through a stage play written by Ferdinando Livini (1828), although this was largely a translation from Ducange's French dramatization, portraying Lady Ashton as Lucy's 'matrigna' (evil stepmother).[7] Moreover, there were a number of musico-dramatic adaptations which pre-dated Donizetti's attempt.[8] Amongst them, I will focus upon *Le nozze di Lammermoor*, Michele Carafa's opera on a libretto by Luigi Balocchi (1829). This is not only because Carafa's music for *Le nozze* survives in full but also because this work retains Lady Ashton as a living character within the plot, in keeping with the original novel.

Balocchi's libretto is perhaps one of the most faithful to Scott's original story. The major deviation occurs in the final scene where Lucia takes poison before proceeding to the forced marriage, rather than stabbing her bridegroom and going insane (Act II, Scene 17; cf. Balocchi 1829: 54). Lady Ashton's formidable presence is clearly portrayed and the composer Carafa gives this contralto several important numbers. These include: (1) a grandiose entrance aria accompanied with the chorus, "Fu dei prodi all' alta gloria" (Act I, Scene 15); (2) a duet with Lord Ashton comparable in length and importance to that between Lucia and Edgardo, "Tu vuoi che di mia vita" (I, 17); and (3) another duet with Lucia, "D'aspro destin fremente" (II, 12). Of particular interest is the duet with Lucia where each character pours out not only her public frustrations but also her private reflections. Lucia reveals her inner determination to remain faithful to Edgardo while pretending to succumb to her mother's manipulations, and Lady Ashton celebrates her victory, offering at the same time caring words of support to Lucia. Interestingly, in this opera by Carafa, Lady Ashton is not particularly 'evil'[9] – in fact she is quite maternal. She simply believes that her plan is best for her "amata figlia" ('beloved daughter'), and in the duet with Lucia just mentioned repeatedly sings to Lucia, 'in the end you will be grateful for my tender zeal' ("Grata / al mio tenero zelo / sarai"; Balocchi 1829: 46). Her music conforms to, and reinforces, this characterisation. In that duet, for example, her florid passages interfere obsessively with her daughter's lyrical melodic contours but remain harmonious, and at times completely united with them (see Example 1).

---

7 Italy's reception of *The Bride of Lammermoor* does not seem to have been fully explored so far. It is rather regretful that Murray Pittock's anthology (see 2006) does not contain a chapter dedicated to the subject. Other translations into Italian prior to Donizetti's adaptation include C[ampiglio] 1828 and Sormani 1829.

8 Those include Adolphe Adam's *Le Caleb* (on a libretto by A. d'Artois premiered in 1827); Michele Carafa's *Le nozze di Lammermoor* (libretto by L. Balocchi, in 1829); Luigi Rieschi's *La fidanzata di Lammermoor* (libretto by C. Bassi, in 1831); I. F. Brendal's *Bruden fra Lammermoor* (libretto by H. C. Anderson, in 1832); Giuseppe Bornacini's *Ida* (libretto by Bassi, in 1833); and Alberto Mazzucato's *La fidanzata di Lammermoor* (libretto by P. Beltrame, in 1834).

9 For the musical portrayal of evil characters see Bernhart 2009.

EXAMPLE 1 *Michele Cafara,* Le nozze di Lammermoor (*Act II, Scene 12*)

In the premiere of the opera, the mother and the daughter were played by the contralto Benedetta Rosmunda Pisaroni (1793–1872) and the soprano Henriette Sontag (1806–1854), respectively. Pisaroni was noted not only for her magnificent vocal techniques but also for her relatively unattractive physical appearance[10] – and it is certain that her portrayal of Lady Ashton left a lasting

10 See for a 19th-century comment upon her appearance Rosselli 1995: 68f.

impression, particularly since she was placed alongside Sontag, a known beauty. That strong visual contrast seems to have proved a type of dramaturgical counterweight to the harmonious emotions between them.

Other solutions to retaining Lady Ashton's role as a motivating protagonist were of course possible. For example, her governing wishes could be made known and conveyed by others, or her views could be attributed to other characters, or her responsibility for the downfall of Lucy and Edgar could be diluted by a range of other causes and reasons. What is interesting is that all of these various examples of presence-through-absence were already embedded in the novel since Lady Ashton spends a good deal of the time away from the action on business in London and Edinburgh (cf. Scott 1819/1991: Chapters xv–xxi). The remarks of Chorley and others in fact make the mistake of assuming that, in contrast to the Donizetti opera, the presence of Lady Ashton in Walter Scott's novel, and her role as the prime mover of events, is unambiguous and exclusive. An obvious demonstration that this is not true is that, during her long absences similar views to hers are asserted or conveyed by Lord Ashton, by the witch-like character Alice, by the Reverend Bide-the-bent, a Presbyterian clergyman (who becomes Raimondo in Donizetti's opera), and by Lucy's brothers. Not surprisingly, therefore, her presence is still felt in the Donizetti opera even though she is dead before its story begins, as we shall now discover.

Lady Ashton off the Stage: The Donizetti–Cammarano Opera

From his correspondence dated 29 May 1835, it seems that Donizetti himself chose the Lucia story for his new work.[11] However, it is not recorded how the composer and the librettist decided to eliminate the overt presence of Lady Ashton. It has been previously argued that the deletion of the "machiavellistische Lady Macbeth-Figur" of Lady Ashton may have arisen from difficulties Donizetti had encountered with two *prime donne* in *Anna Bolena* in 1830 (Bernhart 2008: 12f.). It is true that Donizetti presented in *Anna Bolena* two important female characters – Anna Bolena (Anne Boleyn, created by the soprano Giuditta Pasta) and Giovanna Seymour (Jane Seymour sung by the mezzo-soprano Elisa Orlandi) – yet no surviving evidence directly demonstrates that there was an actual conflict between the two singers in this particular opera

11 Cf. Donizetti's letter to Antonio Santocelli qtd. in Zavadini 1948: 373f.

12 Gossett's detailed study of *Anna Bolena* tells us that "documentary sources concerning the preparation of *Anna Bolena* fail us", following a letter dated 5 October 1830 from Bologna which Donizetti wrote to inform his father of his forthcoming visit to Bergamo (1985b: 3f.).

nor that therefore Donizetti became unwilling to score for that combination again.[12] Although it is also true that two surviving autograph drafts corroborate the composer's compositional struggle to finalise the duet "Sul suo capo aggravi un Dio" between Anna and Giovanna in *Anna Bolema* (cf. Gossett 1985b: 108f.,[13] in the end he created a superb psychological confrontation between them.

On the other hand, the year preceding *Lucia*, Donizetti does seem to have witnessed a cat-fight between two sopranos (Giuseppina Ronzi de Begnis and Anna del Sere singing respectively the roles of Mary Stuart and Elizabeth I) in a rehearsal of *Maria Stuarda* (cf. Ashbrook 1982/2004: 85f.). But it is again difficult to link this event necessarily to any supposed reluctance on his part to write for two female protagonists again.

Even after *Lucia*, Donizetti continued to write operas with two important female roles, including Antonia and Irene in *Belisario* (1836) and Elisabetta and Sara in *Roberto Devereux* (1837). Those roles are not for two sopranos, but for a soprano and a mezzo-soprano, which implies a certain vocal and social hierarchy within the terms of the drama. This would have been the most obvious type of casting for Donizetti to use had he wished to present Lady Ashton in conjunction with Lucia on the stage. Indeed, prior to *Lucia*, the composer made a notable success in *Rosmonda d'Inghilterra* (1834) by composing parts for Rosmonda (the young mistress of the king, soprano) and Eleonora (the king's jealous wife, mezzo-soprano), and it was Fanny Tacchinardi-Persiani (who created Lucia at the premiere) that sang Rosmonda. Considering this, it is significant that in early productions, Lucia's entrance cavatina was replaced by an aria from *Rosmonda d'Inghilterra*, the replacement eventually being sanctioned by Donizetti.[14]

After all, it is unlikely that Donizetti and Cammarano eliminated the role of Lady Ashton in a 'make-shift' manner to pacify the *prima donna*'s ego. Donizetti made it clear in his letter of 29 May 1835 (mentioned earlier) that he had already had a very clear idea about the potential cast (including Fanny Tacchinardi-Persiani as Lucia),[15] even before the management of Naples' Royal Theatres approved his proposed plan.

---

13 The two drafts are US-NYpm, Cary 238 114433 and Cary 239 114434.

14 At least by 1837 Tacchinardi-Persiani replaced "Regnava nel silenzio" with "Perchè non ho del vento" from *Rosmonda d'Inghilterra*. When the composer revised *Lucia* for the Théâtre de la Renaissance in Paris in 1839, he officially sanctioned "Perchè…" with a French translation as the replacement of "Regnava…". The *Rosmonda* aria found its way into the publication of *Lucie de Lammermoor*. Cf. Poriss 2001: 2f.

15 The letter tells us that Donizetti submitted to the theatre authorities Cammarano's synopsis with a list of the cast. That document survives, specifying Tacchinardi-Persiani as Lucia. For an English translation of the synopsis, cf. Black 1984: 239–245.

Cammarano admits in the preface to the first published libretto that, although he is indebted to Walter Scott for the setting and general plot of *The Bride of Lammermoor*, he did not simply follow the novel but boldly changed the story by removing some important characters as well as altering the circumstances in which Edgar dies (cf. Cammarano 1835: 3f.). His argument is that he wanted to give the story its own "forma drammatica", but his motivations and literary decisions seem to have had more complex consequences than that singular agenda might suggest.

After all, Lady Ashton as a motivational force does survive in the opera not only in the sense that her dynastic views act as a prohibition on the behaviour of Lucy, but also because her recent death and her implied importance to Lucy are significantly invoked as reasons for her daughter's melancholic mood and erratic behaviour. This supposed quality of their relationship is suggested in many ways. In the opening scene, for example, Normanno – the captain of the guard for the Ashton family – explains that she had recently been walking along a 'lonely path in the park where her mother is buried' ("del parco / Nel solingo vial, dove la madre / Giace sepolta"; Part I, Act I, Scene 2; Cammarano 1835: 6f.).[16] Moreover, when Enrico attempts to justify to Arturo the unhappy

EXAMPLE 2 *Enrico's phrase "Madre estinta!" and the subsequent processional music from Gaetano Donizetti,* Lucia di Lammermoor *(Part II, Act I, Scene 4)*[17]

16 This paper follows the original scene divisions as found in Cammarano 1835. When setting the text to music, Donizetti altered some portion of Cammarano's text (for this, cf. Black 1984: 235–237), but the phrases I discuss in this paper found their way into the score.

17 For all the musical examples in this paper taken from Donizetti's *Lucia*, I have consulted Donizetti's autograph (I-Bgc, Cassa forte 6/12) and a mid-19th-century neat copy of the work (I-Nc, Segnatura 26.5.20-21). Donizetti's autograph contains some alterations in his own hand. The Naples manuscript seems to have been copied by various hands, probably during different periods. However, some features of the Naples MS seem to be related to the premiere of the opera (I am grateful for this information to Dr Tommasina Boccia and Francesco Melisi at the Biblioteca del Conservatorio S. Pietro a Majella, Naples). It should be noted that Donizetti originally composed two scenes for Lucia ("Regnava nel silenzio" and the mad scene) in higher keys than they are now customarily sung (semi-tone/a whole-tone higher, respectively). My musical examples are in the original, higher keys.

paleness of Lucia who is about to sign the marriage contract, he exclaims "la madre estinta" ('deceased mother') which initiates some sombre processional music that gives the cue for Lucia's entrance in despair (Part II, Act I, Scene 4; Cammarano 1835: 21f.; see Example 2). Furthermore the music pre-echoes that which introduces Lucia's mad scene later in the opera, and suggests that her relationship with her mother was (at least subliminally) a factor in her collapse into insanity. Donizetti made Enrico repeat the phrase "madre estinta" twice to emphasise its importance, even though the words occur only once in the libretto.

It is also significant that it is implied that Lady Ashton's standards and values are important to Lucy. When the priest Raimondo wants to persuade Lucia to yield to her brother's order to marry Arturo (who is equivalent to Bucklaw in the novel), he alludes to her mother in a way that he believes will have an effect on Lucia's self-respect and sense of duty. He says: 'otherwise because of you, your dead mother will tremble with horror in her grave' ("O la madre, nell' avello fremerà per te d'orror"; Part II, Act I, Scene 3; Cammarano 1835: 19f.; see Example 3). The music in this scene consists of a subtle but persistent staccato triplet-figure on the strings – a kind of palpitation as if to represent emotional disturbance and perhaps the evocation of some unsettled, ominous spirit.

It seems, then, that in so far as the barriers to the love between Lucia and Edgardo are financial, dynastic and worldly, they find a presence in the opera through the continual evocation of the mother and the force of her attitudes. There are, however, other ingredients in the story that resist the Lucy–Edgar union – supernatural and psychological ones – which raise their own issues of presence and absence. We shall turn next to supernatural elements and their treatment in the opera.

EXAMPLE 3 *Raimondo's reference to Lady Ashton (Donizetti,* Lucia, *II, I, 3)*

The Role of Ghosts

Donizetti's opera was not the first to feature ghosts since various kinds of apparition had appeared in works since at least Luigi Rossi's *Orfeo* of 1647.[18] However, although many of these earlier ghosts – including most famously the Commendatore in Mozart's *Don Giovanni* – had 'otherworldly qualities' (for example, they were pallid or white and walked awkwardly), they otherwise conversed and participated in the action like ordinary human beings. In other words, they were not gothic ghosts, and this new musical type presented Cammarano and Donizetti with some special problems. For example, how were they going to indicate their apparent presence and effect, while 'silencing' them completely? And how were they going to suggest their effect on the mind of a real character without the benefit of describing specific actions or events perpetrated by the ghosts?

Lucia herself, from the moment she appears first on the stage, is actively preoccupied not by her deceased mother (who never appears as a ghost) but by a more sinister figure: a female ghost whom she has encountered at a fountain in the castle garden of Lammermoor. As Lucia tells us in her first entrance aria, "Regnava nel silenzio" (Part 1, Act 1, Scene 4), the ghost is a girl who was murdered by an ancestor of Edgardo Ravenswood. This is a slight adaptation of the exact circumstance in the novel where the girl was not directly murdered by the ancestor, but rather, because she was an 'other-worldly' sprite, her detention after a certain hour by that ancestor led to her disappearance forever into the waters of the fountain, which then turned blood red. As Walter Scott then tells us, thereafter "that spot was fatal to the Ravenswood family" and "to drink of the waters of the well, or even approach its brink" was "ominous" (1819/1991: 57–59).

This well is the very place where Lucia was holding her secret meetings with Edgardo, and she tells the story of the dead girl at her first entrance with the aria just mentioned. Donizetti faces several dilemmas here. He must give some initial indication of Lucia's personality, but he must also outline the dark 'curse' on the place – and, by implication, the mysterious prohibition on the burgeoning relationship between Lucia and Edgardo. The result is somewhat odd, and has proved to be problematic in many performances.[19] Lucia is introduced by ethereal (or, perhaps, 'heavenly') music in the major key played on harp. This

---

18 Rossi's *Orfeo*, based upon a libretto by Francesco Buti, contains a scene where the ghost of Euridice haunts Aristeo (Act III, Scene 3). The opera was premiered in Paris.

19 Many sopranos introduced into this 'fountain scene' a variety of replacement arias. For the case of Tacchinardi-Persiani (the first Lucia), see above.

EXAMPLE 4 *(a) Lucia's entry music by the harp compared to (b) an incipit of her cabaletta "Quando rapito in estasi" (Donizetti,* Lucia *I, I, 4)*

opening melody is related to that of the cabaletta "Quando rapito in estasi" which Lucia will sing later in the scene when, excited, she is about to see Edgardo (see Example 4).

The overall impression of both passages is in keeping with Scott's description of Lucy as "an angel descended on earth" (1819/1991: 195f.), though we shall return to Lucia's ambivalent character shortly. The recitative that she sings at her first entry then explains that she trembles at the sight of the fountain because of the past events that happened there. The music of the recitative is mildly unsettled (there are a couple of diminished chords) but contains no great vocal flourishes. We then reach the *Larghetto* section based on four four-line stanzas of *settenari.* It is in these four-line stanzas that the story of the girl and her ghost is unfolded. But the style is somewhat in the manner of a strophic ballad – objective and slightly matter-of-fact. There is no special effect or pause when Lucia describes the girl's "gemito" ('groan') as she is dying; rather the whole has the air of an almost dream-like incantation as though dispassionately describing something comfortably familiar inside her head. There are two mini cadenzas, one as she describes the ghost at the "margine" ('edge') of the pool (marked *presto* and *forte*), and another for the phrase "di sangue rosseggiò" ('it became red with blood') (marked with a slight *crescendo* up from *piano*).

[Numbers in brackets indicates: poetic lines, boxed numbers stanzas, and boxed alphabet letters Musical structure.]

EXAMPLE 5 *Lucia's ghost-story aria with its flute part (Donizetti,* Lucia, *I, I, 4)*

Of course, many performers do their best to turn these fleeting increases in intensity into histrionic displays, but those passing 'extremes' should be seen in the context of the whole narrative, thirty bars of which are marked *piano* out of a total of thirty-six. In spite of the efforts of performers this narration is certainly not of the breathless, excitable, 'gothic horror' type (see Example 5).

On the other hand, Donizetti takes the trouble to underline the quiet presence of the ghost in two interesting ways. First, there is the ghostly, silenced

EXAMPLE 6 *Lucia and her ghostly Doppelgänger (flute) in the mad scene (Donizetti,* Lucia, *II, II, 5)*

'voice' in the melodic line of the flute which sketchily shadows that of Lucia and links her to it – a device he resurrects in the mad scene to much greater effect at the end of the opera, which culminates in the famous 'voice-and-flute cadenza'[20] (see Example 6).

Also in the final mad scene it is the flute which joins the singer in a fragmentary reminiscence of her last happy memory with Edgardo, which is symbolised musically by a quotation of their duet melody "Verranno a te" (Part I, Act I, Scene 5). It is this moment that is interrupted by Lucia's frantic cry 'ah!...that horrible ghost is rising up and driving us apart!' ("Ahimè!...sorge il tremendo/ Fantasma e ne separa!"; Part II, Act II, Scene 5; Cammarano 1835: 32), as she now openly admits to the presence of the ghost who attempts forcibly to separate them (see Example 7).

Alterations in the autograph score tell us that Donizetti originally wanted the glass harmonica to accompany Lucia's mad utterance. That instrument was strongly associated with phantasmagoria and popular entertainment in the 19th century (cf. Thomas 2012: 96f.), and its use would have underpinned for the audience Donizetti's attempts to indicate the ghostly presence of something absent.

Aside from these melodic devices Donizetti has another method to give presence to the ghost in the quiet, ballade-like narration of Act I – the use of

20 For the origins and an early development of Lucia's flute cadenza, see Matsumoto 2011.

EXAMPLE 7 *The "Verranno a te" Theme (Donizetti,* Lucia, *I, I, 5) and the appearance of the ghost (II, II, 5)*

dynamics (see Example 5 above). The cadenza that mentions the ghost at the edge of the pool *crescendo*s up to *forte* thus giving it the greatest 'sonic presence' in the narrative and a much louder effect than the later cadenza that mentions the blood-red pool. Moreover, after the 'ghost cadenza' Donizetti inserts the only stage direction in this whole section, and indeed in the whole opera independent of Cammarano:[21] Lucia "coprendosi colle mani il volto" ('hides her face in her hands'), and the clear implication is that she is covering her eyes so as not to catch the very real presence of the ghostly girl.

It is interesting to note that this ghostly female spirit haunting Lucia and striving to separate her from Edgardo shares significant attributes with Lady Ashton and seems to elide with her motivations as a driving force in the opera. Curiously, also, in the novel Lady Ashton is sometimes described in 'otherworldly' terms: she is a "predominating spirit" (Scott 1819/1991: 164f.) and, upon her unannounced return home, she is likened to an "apparition" and a "spectre"

21 Since Cammarano put no stage directions for this aria in the libretto (cf. 1835: 9f.), this indication (found in Donizetti's autograph on f.32[r]) might well have been Donizetti's own idea.

(ibid.: 231f.). Thus, the identity of the ghost who haunts Lucia until her death stands midway between representing the girl murdered by Edgardo's ancestor and those aspects of Lady Ashton that haunt and thwart her dreams and desires in everyday life. In Donizetti's opera, Lady Ashton is 'present' through 'absence', and her voice is silenced but at the same time eloquent. This contributes to the eerie depth of the supposed love story, whose prevailing 'Gothic' aura is strongly present in the original romance despite Walter Scott's rather critical attitude towards so-called 'Gothic' literature as such (see Scott, 1827).[22] What we should not do is to lay all the causes of misfortune in this story at the door of Lady Ashton or the ghostly murdered girl. The 'heavenly' and 'innocent' Lucy herself has a hinterland of suggested ambiguity and culpability, where her complex attributes come into play and then fade with disconcerting effects.[23] Now is the point at which to examine those present-yet-absent attributes.

Lucy's Character

Even in the novel there are hints that Lucy herself may have played a role in bringing about her own downfall, especially in view of her insistent contacts with Edgar. In Chapter XX of the novel, a raven (obviously a symbol for the Ravenswood family) is killed and Lucy is covered with its blood (cf. Scott 1819/1991: 209f.), suggesting that she will bring about Edgar's demise. Furthermore, although Lucy is frequently described as sweet and angel-like, there are hints in the novel that she has a more complex character. At one point she is teased for having sat with "handsome young gentlemen [...] twenty times" and had "a hundred sweethearts" (ibid.: 210f.). We also learn that "under a semblance of extreme indifference", Lucy "nourished the germ of those passions which sometimes spring up in one night [...] and astonish the observer by their unexpected ardour and intensity" (ibid.: 42f.).

This inner strength is not so very far from that of her mother (some aspects of Lucy's behaviour are what we might now refer to as 'passive aggressive'), and the mother–daughter resemblance is, on one famous occasion, accidentally exposed by Lord Ashton, who, in a rather Freudian manner, presents Lucy as "his wife, Lady Ashton" (ibid.: 235f.). In the end, Lucy is not simply docile and oppressed – not only her simple despair but her dark anger leads her to kill her

22 For a modern edition of Scott's essay, see Williams, ed. 1968/2010: 222–251.

23 Lucy's less than innocuous traits have been discussed previously in terms of the "ambivalence" of the characterisation in *The Bride of Lammermoor* (Shaw 1983: 214–226) and of "the female (particularly the 'mother'-type) as a source of persecution" (Hilliard 2010: 231–233).

newly-wed husband, and even her retreat into insanity may be seen as an act of defiance, a move to put herself beyond apology, remorse or sympathy.

Oddly enough this dangerous detachment is revealed in the one significant musical scene in the novel – a scene that, curiously, is omitted from the opera. In Chapter III, Lucy is heard playing on the lute, and the words she sings seem to reflect her inner removal from life:

> Look not thou on beauty's charming,
> Sit thou still while kings are arming,
> [...]
> Stop thine ear against the singer,
> From the red gold keep thy finger,
> Vacant heart, and hand, and eye,
> Easy live and quiet die.
> (Ibid.: 39f)

The sentiments here at a deeper level remain obscure and ominous. Is the "red gold" a portent of the marriage ring soiled by blood? Why is the "heart" "Vacant"? – is she unable to love? And is Lucy herself the singer, or is there some other presence that must not be listened to, that needs to be made 'silent'? It is as if, to adopt a term from Derrida's *Spectres of Marx*, Lucy herself is some kind of "corporeal ghost" (1993/1994: 191, n.13), perhaps a shade of that poor sprite who died by the pool generations ago, but lingers on in a real body, both present and absent at the same time. By omitting this significant musical scene Cammarano and Donizetti removed lines that are central to the complexity of Lucy's character, and were in any case destined to become well known by being cited in literature, set to music, and collected in anthologies of poetry.[24]

The Story and the Story-Teller

The analysis present in this paper has been based on a close reading of the texts of the novel and of the opera. But that approach has its weaknesses in

24 It is these words that were set to music by Henry Bishop as: *Look Not Thou on Beauty's Charming: Canzonet from the* Bride of Lammermoor ([c. 1820]), though the British Library Catalogue curiously gives the publication date "c. 1815", four years before Scott's novel was published. The poem reappears in E.M. Forster's novel *A Room with a View* (1908), Chapter 18, where it is sung by another Lucy, Lucy Honeychurch. It is also contained in Quiller-Couch, ed. (cf. 1900/1943: 638f.) amongst other collections of verse. It is to be hoped for the sake of Walter Scott that the title of this last refers to poetry in English rather than to the nationality of the poets.

relation to a tale such as this. First, to sense ghostly, silenced voices we cannot only take the route of searching for concrete evidence. As Derrida says, the valid existence of such a "ghostly voice" is not to be "proved" but to be "perceived" (1972/1981: 216f.). We must open ourselves to be a witness to it, since only our experience offers something 'irreplaceable' and can properly attest that some 'thing' has been presented to us (cf. Derrida 2000: 190). The writing down in words or music of the 'evidence-for-presence' is at best, in the Derridean sense, only a 'supplement' to the experience itself in that it both elaborates an explanation of the experience, and yet at the same time is a non-essential addendum to it, a non-substitution for it. Lucy's reticence shows that she herself understood this, that such experiences were a matter of sensibility rather than sense or description. Walter Scott tells us:

> Left to the impulse of her own taste and feelings, Lucy Ashton was peculiarly accessible to those of a romantic cast. Her secret delight was in the old legendary tales of ardent devotion and unalterable affection, chequered as they so often are with strange adventures and supernatural horrors. This was her favoured fairy realm, and there she erected her aerial palaces. But it was only in secret that she laboured at this delusive, though delightful architecture. (1819/1991: 40)

In other words, present within her there seems to be a wish to be at one with that absent ethereal realm, and the unification of that particular presence and absence leads to her bodily death and eternal silence.

The second weakness of a text-based approach to a ghostly tale is that we do not value such things for the story they tell so much as for the way in which the story is told. And the way in which the story is told is the responsibility not only of Cammarano and Donizetti but also of the performers of opera. They are 'supplements' and 'spectres' of a different kind who inhabit the plot in surprising and unpredictable ways. But that is another story.

References

Abbott, H. Porter (2002). *The Cambridge Introduction to Narrative*. Cambridge: CUP.

Altick, Richard Daniel (1985). *Paintings from Books: Art and Literature in Britain 1760–1900*. Columbus, OH: Ohio State UP.

Ashbrook, William (1982/2004). *Donizetti and His Operas*. Cambridge: CUP.

Balocchi, Luigi (1829). *Le nozze di Lammermoor*. Paris: Dreauche.

Barbieri, Gaetano (1824). *La promessa sposa di Lammermoor, a nuovi racconti dal mio ostiere* […]. Milan: V. Ferravio.

Bernhart, Walter (2008). "'Liebling der ganzen Welt': Sir Walter Scott als Inspiration für die romantische Oper und Donizettis *Lucia di Lammermoor*". *Programmheft Theater Graz*. Graz: Theater Graz. 6–18.

——— (2009). "'Pour Out…Forgiveness Like a Wine': Can Music 'Say an Existence is Wrong'?". Keith Chapin, Lawrence Kramer, eds. *Musical Meaning and Human Values*. New York, NY: Fordham UP. 170–184.

Bishop, Henry (c.1820). *Look Not Thou on Beauty's Charming: Canzonet from the* Bride of Lammermoor. London: Goulding D'Almaine and Potter.

Black, John (1984). *The Italian Romantic Libretto: A Study of Salvadore Cammarano*. Edinburgh: The University Press of Edinburgh.

Bolton, Philip (1992). *Scott Dramatized*. New York, NY: Mansell.

Bruhn, Jørgen, Anne Gjelsvik, Eirik Frisvold Hanssen, eds. (2013). *Adaptation Studies: New Challenges, New Directions*. London: Bloomsbury Academic.

C[ampiglio], G[iovanni] (1828). *La fidanzata di Lammermoor: romance storico di Walter Scott abbreviato nelle parti di minore importanze ed amenita*. Milan: Giovanni Campiglio.

Calcraft, John William (1823). *The Bride of Lammermoor: a Drama*. Edinburgh: John Anderson.

Cammarano, Salvatore (1835). *Lucia di Lammermoor, dramma tragico in due parti* […]. Naples: Flautina.

Chorley, Henry F. (1862). *Thirty Years' Musical Recollection*. 2 vols. London: Hurst and Blackett.

Derrida, Jacques (1972/1981). *Dissemination*. Trans. Barbara Johnson. London/New York, NY: Continuum.

——— (1993/1994). *Spectres of Marx: the State of Debt, the Work of Mourning and the New International*. Trans. Peggy Kamuf. New York, NY/London: Routledge.

——— (2000). "'A Self-Unsealing Poetic Text': Poetics and Politics of Witnessing". Trans. Rachel Bowlby. Michael P. Clark, ed. *Revenge of the Aesthetic: the Place of Literature in Theory Today*. Berkeley, CA/Los Angeles, CA: University of California Press. 180–207.

Ducange, Victor (1828). *La fiancée de Lammermoor*. Paris: Bouquin de la Souche.

Forster, E.M. (1908). *A Room with a View*. London: Edward Arnold.

Frith, William Powell (1887/2006). *My Biography and Reminiscences*. Whitefish, MT: Kessinger Publishing.

Gossett, Philippe (1985a). The Preface to Michele Carafa, *Le nozze di Lammermoor*, a facsimile edition of the printed piano-vocal score. *Italian opera 1810–1840: Printed Editions of Complete Operas and Excerpts by Contemporaries of Rossini and Donizetti*. New York, NY/London: Garland. Unpaginated [v–x].

——— (1985b). *Anna Bolena and the Artistic Maturity of Gaetano Donizetti*. Oxford: Clarendon Press.

Halliwell, Michael (2005). *Opera and the Novel: the Case of Henry James*. Word and Music Studies 6. Amsterdam/New York, NY: Rodopi.

Hilliard, Raymond F. (2010). *Ritual Violence and the Maternal in the British Novel 1740–1820*. Cranbury, NJ: Bucknell UP.

Hutcheon, Linda (2006/2012). *A Theory of Adaptation*. 2nd ed. London/New York, NY: Routledge.

Livini, Ferdinando (1828). *La promessa sposa di Lammermoor* [...] *traduzione dal francese*. Naples: Francesco Strada Pignatelli.

MacArthur, Michelle, Lydia Wilkinson, Keren Zaiontz, eds. (2009). *Performing Adaptations*. Newcastle upon Tyne: Cambridge Scholar Publishing.

Matsumoto, Naomi (2011). "Manacled Freedom: 19th-Century Vocal Improvisation and the Flute-Accompanied Cadenza in Gaetano Donizetti's *Lucia di Lammermoor*". Rudolf Rasch, ed. *Beyond Notes: Improvisation in Western Music of the Eighteenth and Nineteenth Centuries*. Turnhout: Brepols. 295–316.

Mitchell, Jerome (1977). *The Walter Scott Operas: an Analysis of Operas Based on the Works of Sir Walter Scott*. Tuscaloosa, AL: University of Alabama Press.

Pittock, Murray (2006). *The Reception of Sir Walter Scott in Europe*. London/New York, NY: Continuum.

Poriss, Hilary (2001). "A Madwoman's Choice: Aria Substitution in *Lucia di Lammermoor*". *Cambridge Opera Journal* 13/1: 1–28.

Quiller-Couch, Arthur, ed. (1900/1943). *The Oxford Anthology of English Verse 1250–1918*. Oxford: Clarendon

Rosselli, John (1995). *Singers of Italian Opera: the History of a Profession*. Cambridge: CUP.

Sanders, Julie (2005). *Adaptation and Appropriation*. London: Routledge.

Scott, Walter (1819/1991). *The Bride of Lammermoor*. Oxford World's Classics. Ed. with an Introduction and Notes by Fiona Robertson. Oxford: OUP.

——— (1827). "On the Supernatural in Fictitious Composition, and Particularly on the Work of Ernest Theodore William Hoffmann". *The Foreign Quarterly Review* 1/1: 60–98.

Shaw, Harry E. (1983). *The Forms of Historical Fiction: Sir Walter Scott and His Successors*. Ithaca, NY: Cornell UP.

Sormani, Giacomo (1829). *La fidanzata di Lammermoor: nuova traduzione*. Milan: Giuseppe Crespi.

Thomas, Sophie (2012). "Visual Culture". Joel Faflak, Julia M. Wright, eds. *A Handbook of Romantic Studies*. Oxford: Wiley-Blackwell. 87–104.

White, Henry Adelbert (1927). *Sir Walter Scott's Novels on the Stage*. New Haven, CT: Yale UP.

Williams, Ioan, ed. (1968/2010). *Sir Walter Scott: On Novelists and Fiction*. London: Routledge & Kegan Paul.

Zavadini, Guido (1948). *Donizetti: vita, musiche, epistolario*. Bergamo: Istituto Italiano d'arti grafiche.

How to Play the Music of Absence? The Romantic Aesthetics of Longing in Schumann's *Kreisleriana*, Part 4

Laura Wahlfors

The fourth piece of Robert Schumann's *Kreisleriana*, op. 16 (1838), the lyrical centre of the piano cycle, presents us with a Romantic discourse of absence, distance, and longing. Buried in the music is a fragment from Beethoven's piano sonata *Appassionata*, op. 57. In the context of E.T.A. Hoffmann's writings, with which Schumann's cycle has a well-known intermedial relationship, Beethoven's instrumental music represents the paradigm of 'romantic music' that reveals an unknown realm and thus approaches the Absolute, the forever-absent object of infinite longing. This Romantic aesthetics of longing can inspire the pianist in the performing of Schumann's fragmentary phrases and ambiguous harmonies, and in producing a Romantic sound. Playing this 'Tombeau de Beethoven', making the absent present at the piano, can constitute an uncanny experience for the pianist.

•••

Loss and Longing: Hermeneutic Windows

The fourth piece of Robert Schumann's *Kreisleriana*, op. 16, gives the impression of improvised music: processual, unsettled, not achieving closure. The same phrase is repeated over and over, as if searching and trying; from B flat major to E flat major, from there to C minor – and the modulations never find their way to a stable cadence. The music mainly consists of seventh sonorities, and the B flat major tonality of the piece is never explicitly stated, only projected in terms of its dominant. There is a sense of instability in the rhythm and metre too: the music starts with a syncope as if in the middle of a phrase, and the twelve-beat phrases do not quite find their home in the eight-beat measures.[1] The fragmentary music seems to hover around an absent centre.

1 The same kind of observations on the open, unstable, and improvisatory nature of the fourth piece of *Kreisleriana* have also been made elsewhere e.g. by Deahl 1996: 138; Loos 2005: 96; Münch 1992: 258; and Rosen 1995: 674f. The songlike middle section of this piece (structured ABA') differs from the syncopated unsettledness of the A sections. Apart from a passing remark, I leave the discussion of the middle Section (B) outside the scope of this paper.

 | DOI 10.1163/9789004314863_006

EXAMPLE 1 *Robert Schumann,* Kreisleriana, *op. 16, part 4, mm. 1f.*

EXAMPLE 2 *Robert Schumann, "Der Dichter spricht" (from* Kinderszenen, *op. 15), mm. 1–4*

The impetus for this paper arose from the practical question I asked myself as a pianist reflecting on this sense of absence: how to play this kind of music? It was not easy to bring a convincing improvisatory feel to music composed by someone else; the phrases seemed too heavy for my temperament, they did not fit my rhythm of breathing – and, they seemed to be pregnant with some meaning.[2]

Indeed, even the opening phrase contains several allusions (see Example 1). The motive decorated with the characteristic gruppetto figure is familiar from the last piece of Schumann's own piano cycle *Kinderszenen*, op. 15: "Der Dichter spricht" ("The Poet Speaks") (see Example 2). The same motive also appears in the epilogue of his piano piece *Arabeske*, op. 18, and in the piano epilogue of the last song of *Dichterliebe*, op. 48. This motive, which has been called Schumann's "most personal phrase" (Váznosyi 1972: 71), tends to appear in reflective epilogues and is associated with looking back, taking a certain distance in relation

2 As Weingarten notes, with this kind of Romantic music that aspires to individuality and originality, it is important for the performer to understand the spirit and atmosphere in which the composition was born, the influences, and the personality of the composer, while it is also essential for the romantic subjective expression that the performer engage her/his own personality and creativity (cf. 1972: 102–106). On the problem of bringing an improvised atmosphere to *Kreisleriana*'s fourth piece in the performance of this already-composed music, see Münch 1992: 258f. Münch argues that what works in improvisation does not necessarily work in a concert performance.

EXAMPLE 3 *Clara Wieck,* Andantino, *mm. 1–4*

to the composition and to the creative process. Not only is the motive reflective – it is also self-reflective: a recurring reference to Schumann himself as a composer, almost like his autograph (cf. Taylor 1990: 169–172; Perrey 2002: 217–219).

The opening phrase of *Kreisleriana*'s fourth piece also includes a citation of the famous 'Clara motive', a descending five-note scale from Clara Wieck's *Andantino* (see Example 3). Here it appears in major instead of the original minor. When composing *Kreisleriana*, Robert Schumann was ardently in love with Clara, from whom he had had to separate temporarily after Clara's father Ludwig Wieck refused to give his consent to their marriage (cf. Daverio 1997: 168). The motive appears in some form in all the pieces of *Kreisleriana* (cf. Arnsdorf 1976: 45f.).[3]

Through these allusions, Schumann, rethinking music as literature in the sense of the 'Literary Absolute', hence refers to *himself* as a *Dichter*, a poet, and also to his absent beloved Clara Wieck.[4] The thematisation of the subjectivity of the Romantic artist is here essentially intertwined with the artist's unfulfilled love as a source of inspiration.[5]

3 Schumann originally wanted to dedicate *Kreisleriana* to Clara but, presumably because of Ludwig Wieck's hostile reaction, he changed the dedication to Chopin. Robert wrote to Clara in a letter in April 1838: "You and one of your ideas are the principal subject, and I shall call them *Kreisleriana*, and dedicate them to you." (Qtd. Arnsdorf 1976: 27; Daverio 1997: 169).

4 The reference here is to the concept of "l'absolu littéraire" (Lacoue-Labarthe and Nancy, 1978). The Jena Romantics understood literature as an activity of production that aimed at offering a solution to the problem of the subject unrepresentable to itself. In this project, literature ('the Absolute of Literature') expanded to encompass all artworks in which the subject aspires to search and represent itself (cf. ibid.: 12–14, 20–22; Daverio 1997: 89; Perrey 2002: 7, 25). Schumann thought that the composer should be a poet; on the composer as *Dichter*, see e.g. Taylor 1990: 169f. On Schumann's rethinking music as literature, cf. Daverio 1997: 168f.; Deahl 1996: 132; Dill 1989: 175.

5 One more occurrence of the above-discussed gruppetto motive is in Schumann's song "Widmung" from *Myrthen*, op. 25, which was a wedding gift to Clara when they finally had

The composer qua poet who improvises, fantasizes and yearns in *Kreisleriana* is not simply Schumann himself, but – perhaps more importantly – the fictive character Johannes Kreisler, the melancholy Romantic artist from E.T.A. Hoffmann's collection of writings, after which Schumann's *Kreisleriana* is named (see Hoffmann 1989b). Kreisler also appears in Hoffmann's novel *Lebensansichten des Katers Murr nebst fragmentarischer Biographie des Kapellmeisters Johannes Kreisler in zufälligen Makulaturblättern* (see 1974).[6] This is a double novel consisting of alternating fragments of two narratives: an autobiography of Murr the cat, and a biography of the composer Kreisler. An analogous structure can be perceived in Schumann's *Kreisleriana*. *Kreisleriana* alternates between deeply reflective and musically complex Bb major parts – Kreisler's music – and more straightforward and structured but capricious, energetic, virtuosic G minor parts – music of Tomcat Murr.[7] This intermedial relationship to Hoffmann's writings is well known, and many scholars and pianists have associated the improvisatory character of *Kreisleriana*'s fourth piece with the improvised fantasies of Hoffmann's Kreisler (cf., e.g., Deahl 1996; Münch 1992: 260f.; Loos 2005: 96; Kautsky 2006: 47).

I have now just briefly opened some hermeneutic windows – to use the concept of Lawrence Kramer (cf. 1990: 9–14) – through which the process of interpretation could be set into motion. I will, however, focus more closely on another one, a quotation from Beethoven. Even though Schumann's technique of quotation has been studied quite extensively, this particular allusion has not (to my knowledge) received scholarly attention.[8] Furthermore, this allusion has been particularly meaningful to me as a hermeneutic window in practicing this music and in experiencing it as that of absence and longing.

---

each other. "Widmung" celebrates the idea that the beloved raises the artist above himself. On the appearance of the motive in this song, cf. Vaznosyi, 1972: 73.

6 The novel has been translated into English by Anthea Bell (see Hoffmann 1974).

7 For interpretations that associate the structure of Schumann's *Kreisleriana* with that of Hoffmann's novel in relation to the alternation of Kreisler and Murr parts, see, e.g., Deahl 1996; Kautsky 2006; Rosen 1995: 669–683. There are also interpretations that the whole piano cycle reflects the whims of Kreisler's eccentric personality (see, e.g., Münch 1992; Daverio 1997: 168f.).

8 Discussing the central role of quotations in Schumann's Romantic irony, Dill notes: "[T]here is hardly any composer who quotes – either from other composers' works or his own – as much as Schumann does." (1989: 185) On quotations in Schumann's music, also see, e.g., Todd 1994; Daverio 2007; Marston 2007.

EXAMPLE 4 *Robert Schumann,* Kreisleriana, *op. 16, part 4, mm. 5f.*

EXAMPLE 5 *Ludwig van Beethoven,* Piano Sonata op. 57 (Appassionata), *Finale, mm. 1–14*

Beethoven's Tomb?

The short phrase in the low register of bar 5 (see Example 4), starting from the diminished-seventh chord, can be interpreted as a citation from the beginning of the finale of Beethoven's Piano Sonata op. 57, known as the *Appassionata.* Beethoven has the exact same tones in the same rhythm but in a different register: they first appear three octaves higher (than Schumann's quotation) and are then repeated in lower octaves (see Example 5). In what follows, I will discuss this quotation as a Romantic fragment and as a reflection of absent music, a *tombeau.* How do I render in my performance the dialectic of presence and absence that the evocation of Beethoven creates in Schumann's music?

The *Appassionata* is charged with meaning both in the context of Kreisler's artist identity and that of Schumann's life and his relationship with Clara Wieck. Firstly, the citation of the *Appassionata* refers to Beethoven's instrumental music that had a mythical status in the German Romantic philosophy of music and in the aesthetic of autonomy, in the formation of which Hoffmann was a central figure (cf. Dahlhaus 1978/1989: 94f, 117–127; 1980/1989: 75–96; Goehr 1992/2007: 148–157, 205–234; Chantler 2006: 22–24, 54–66, 73–77). Moreover, the *Appassionata* belongs to those very works that according to Dahlhaus have a symbolic function in sustaining the so-called Beethoven myth, the Romantic image of Beethoven (cf. 1980/1989: 75f.).[9] In Hoffmann's *Kreisleriana*, Kreisler repeats the argument from Hoffmann's famous review of Beethoven's Fifth Symphony that Beethoven's instrumental music is "genuinely romantic, since its only subject-matter is infinity. [...] Music reveals to man an unknown realm, a world quite separate from the outer sensual world surrounding him, a world in which he leaves behind all precise feelings in order to embrace an inexpressible longing." (1989b: 96; 1989a: 236–238) This kind of infinite longing, or longing for infinity, was for Hoffmann and other Romantics "the essence of romanticism" (Hoffmann 1989b: 98; cf. Perrey 2002: 35). Schumann, too, idolised Beethoven, and Beethoven's music was a strong influence on his compositions.[10]

Secondly, the *Appassionata* had a specific significance in Schumann's life. This is because it belonged to Clara Wieck's core repertoire; it was by her celebrated performance of the *Appassionata* that she gained a considerable reputation as a pianist during the years 1837–1838 when Schumann composed *Kreisleriana* (cf. Reich 1985: 25; Worthen 2007: 277). The *Appassionata* thus refers to Schumann's absent beloved, which reinforces the connection between romantic love and the yearning for the Absolute associated with Beethoven. Perhaps also evoked here are the feminine musicians idealised by Kreisler as representatives of the 'other world' of music and as objects of his eternally thirsting and thus eternally inspiring artist's love.[11] The songlike

9 Dahlhaus clarifies, however, that these symbolic, mythical works are by no means 'representative' – they are not the 'major' works compared to all others, and they represent just a narrow selection from Beethoven's oeuvre (cf. 1980/1989: 76).

10 On the influence of Beethoven in Schumann's music, see, e.g., Jones 1988; Todd 1994: 96; Marston 2007: 52–55; Daverio 1997: 97–103. Perhaps the best known and most studied of Schumann's Beethoven citations is that from Beethoven's song cycle *An die ferne Geliebte* ('For a Distant Beloved') in *Fantasie*, op. 17 (cf. Rosen 1995: 110–112; Hoeckner 1997: 109–126).

11 Hoffmann was hopelessly in love with his student Julia Marc. This inspired him to create the character of Julia, the object of Kreisler's artist's love in *Kater Murr*, and other feminine musician figures (cf., e.g., Schoolfield 1966: 17f.; Charlton 1989a: 4, 38).

middle section – as a representation of music within music, as a music of imaginary plenitude – can be associated with the heavenly singing of a woman that lifts Kreisler out from his earthly misery in the part "Ombra adorata" of Hoffmann's *Kreisleriana* (1989b: 88–91).[12] The typical Romantic gesture is to elevate the longing as such; the longing becomes fetishized, when a material object – such as the beloved, or Beethoven's music here – is elevated to the status of an impossible love (cf. Žižek 1997/1999: 194, 196; Välimäki 2005: 238). As Novalis wrote in one of the influential texts of early Romanticism: "In the distance, everything [...] becomes romantic".[13]

The quotation of the *Appassionata* in *Kreisleriana*'s music slowly oozes forth, indeed like a distant memory. The sense of distance, of time having passed, is at least partly produced by the fact that the high-register opening of the *Appassionata*'s finale has, as it were, sunken down all the way to the bass register – as if the kinesthetic energy that could have evolved into the frenetic allegro of the sonata were exhausted long ago. Also, the citation is specifically marked to be played *piano*, which places it in the background in relation to the accented chord of the right hand. What we have here is a typical Romantic fragment, a "ruin whose wholeness has been lost" (Hoeckner 1997: 119). The longed-for Absolute of the Romantics cannot be represented; it is an infinity towards which one can only refer through fragments. This is why the fragment rather identifies with our dividedness, with the gap in our existence – with the fundamental lack that in Romantic melancholy is experienced as loss. (Cf. Perrey 2002: 27, 29–30; Hoeckner 1997: 55f., 119; Lacoue-Labarthe/Nancy 1978: 57–80, esp. 64; Žižek 1997/1999: 205) Sunken away to far distance and strangely distorted, the fragment of the *Appassionata* is like a lost object in an uncanny register. We might aptly call this a *tombeau*: a musical tomb. As Carolyn Abbate explains, a *tombeau* is a celebration for a dead composer, a remembrance and reflection of music through reproducing it in an altered form (cf. 1999: 470).

My first impression about this passage was that the role of the right hand would be to react to the recollection of the *Appassionata* with spontaneous, declamatory speech (the chord and the phrases in sixths). However, the accented chord of the right hand that appears together with the quotation is not simply a reaction in the present tense. It is the same F minor seventh-degree chord that – repeated in *fortissimo* – opens the finale of the *Appassionata*

12 This connection is also made by pianist Murray Perahia (see 1997, leaflet text).

13 "So wird alles in der Entfernung [...] romantisch [...]." (Novalis 1960–1988: 302; trans. and cited Hoeckner 1997: 55). This kind of dynamic in which love, melancholy, and sublimation are intertwined is thoroughly analysed by Julia Kristeva in her book *Black Sun* (*Soleil noir*) (see 1987/1989). Her theory of artistic creation draws on the Romantic tradition.

(just a different inversion). (See Examples 4 & 5) One might say that the chronological structure of the opening of the sonata's finale has been condensed into an image in which the components – the first chord and the sixteenth-note patterns – are superimposed. It can be interpreted as a Proustian kind of involuntary memory, as an experience of lost time recalled, of embodied time (cf. Kristeva 1994/1996: 15, 169–171, 193f.). The seventh chord continues its reverberation internally, as it were, and the present tense expands to comprise the past as well. This is how time expands into space, and the distance is bridged – a typical gesture of the Romantic aesthetics of distance and yearning, as described by Hoeckner (cf.1997: 56, 61).

This kind of musical representation of involuntary memory – of making the absent past present – is not uncommon for Schumann. As has been noted by Rosen (cf. 1995: 112, 103) and Žižek (cf. 1999: 205), it is typical of Schumann's technique of quotation that the fragment seems to be as if inevitably generated by the process of the music, as if Schumann's music could expand organically to produce a fragment of Beethoven. Indeed, the *Appassionata* fragment could also be interpreted as yet another ornamented variation of the descending scale of the opening phrase (cf. Arnsdorf 1976: 80).

How to play this passage, then? I have wanted to obtain a remote sound for the fragment of Beethoven, and a distance of longing between (Kreisler's) present tense and the *Appassionata* – a rendering where the recollection of Beethoven would sound through Schumann's Romantic music without assimilating too completely into its environment. When practicing this, it once occurred to me to experiment by playing the original Beethoven figure with my right hand and, at the same time, Schumann's quotation with the left, my hands three octaves away from each other (see Example 6). I wanted to feel the distance as a bodily experience. As I concentrated on this experiment, I felt and heard the two musics together, the different sounds of the different registers; the clearness and brightness of the *Appassionata* pattern could not be obtained in the bass register. The experience was uncanny – my hands became strangers to each other. Even if I played exactly similarly with both hands, the sound of the low chords faded away more slowly than that of the treble register

EXAMPLE 6 *Experiment*

played by the right hand – as if I had two voices, both of which could not possibly be my own. The circular connection between my hands and ears (which usually makes me feel whole as a pianist) was disrupted. The *Appassionata* in the bass register sounded as if from the depths of a tomb; I felt as if my left hand played in somebody else's voice, or – what was even more uncanny – that this foreign voice sounded through my hand, making it play.

As Abbate notes, there is something deeply disquieting about *tombeaux* because they have a symbiotic, even phagic relationship to dead thoughts and lost objects: the lost things become introjections, transpositions of otherness to self (cf. 1999: 470–473). A *tombeau* plays back a lifeless work, a voice from the past, but is also inspired *by* that work, "like a puppet in a theatre of reanimation, a lifeless object set in motion by some hand that moves from within" (ibid.: 470). Through my intense experiment with the *tombeau* of Beethoven in Schumann's *Kreisleriana* at the piano, I exposed myself to a classical Freudian experience of 'the Uncanny' ('das Unheimliche'), to an ambivalent confusion of familiar and unfamiliar, living and dead, active and passive (see Freud 1919/1981). I felt a loss of composure and control in the uncanny way reminiscent of the mechanicalness of unconscious symptoms.[14] Instead of one intimate voice, I had a vivid experience of my own intimacy as a tomb of other voices, and perhaps understood something about the decentredness of Romantic fragments; the fragment system's centre can never crystallise (cf. Perrey 2002: 32).

Yet, working at the piano, I reach for an ideal sound, for the crystal voice of my absent beloved comparable to Schumann's Clara, or to Kreisler's "Ombra adorata", the bell-like voice of a woman that "like a heavenly luminescence" carries Kreisler off to the realm of the mighty and the immeasurable (cf. Hoffmann 1989b: 89). To obtain a distant sound for the quotation of the *Appassionata*, I have used the soft pedal for the thirty-second notes. The sustaining pedal is definitely needed too – to produce the constant vibration essential to the romantic sound – but carefully, with rapid, quivering depressions and releases.[15] When practicing this, in a concentrated way, aspiring for the perfect sound, it occurred to me once that the sound I was searching for in the Beethoven fragment was a paradoxical sound: as dim as possible, almost smothered, but

14 Reminiscent of the repetition compulsion, these kind of experiences where somebody else (an unconscious mechanism) is driving one's mind are classical manifestations of the uncanny (cf. Freud 1919/1981: 227, 237f.; Kristeva 1988/1991: 183–185).

15 Schumann indicates that the fourth of *Kreisleriana* is to be played with pedal (see Example 1). As Rosen notes, in the piano writing of the Romantic generation of the 1830s, a fully pedalled sonority is the norm (cf.1995: 24; 2002: 30).

still radiant – perhaps something like the black sun ("an imagined sun, bright and black at the same time"), the metaphor that Kristeva borrows from Nerval for the impossible Thing of the melancholic (1987/1989: 13, 151f.). My work on the sound of this passage, the heavenly luminescence experienced in the shadow of the low register – triggered by conscious knowledge and research – drove me little by little towards the dark side of amatory idealisation, towards the point where all knowledge is forgotten. For the inner expansion towards the voice of the lost other borders on the loss of self: the shadow of the object, as Freud terms it, totally takes over the subject who identifies with the lost Thing (see Freud 1917/1981; cf. Välimäki 2005: 237; Kristeva 1987/1989: 16–21).

Eventually, however, I need to listen to the *Appassionata* fragment from the distance of longing. To be able to play this passage well, I need to distance myself somewhat from the experience of succumbing to the uncanniness of the *tombeau* and to the dazzlement of the black sun. Through repetition, I can teach my left hand to produce the fragment as if automatically, still making use of the experience of the uncanny I had – while shifting my focus to the spontaneous quality of the reaction of the right hand, differently every time. Abbate somewhat overemphasises the aspect of uncanny mechanicalness in a musical performance in which someone plays someone else's work, the aspect of being a marionette of the composer master's voice (cf. 1999: 477–481). For the performing musician can have various positions of subjectivity and renouncing subjectivity in the music s/he is playing. One might even take different positions simultaneously, as when I let my left hand be a marionette for the absent other's voice (for the Beethoven buried in *Kreisleriana*?) and at the same time concentrate my subjectivity on the right hand as an improvising, poeticising artist (composer Kreisler).

In fact, according to my interpretation, the creative process of the Romantic artist with its coexistence of intentionality and involuntariness is foregrounded and even thematised here in Schumann's music – and as in Hoffmann's writings, it is tinged with longing and nostalgia. The passage with the quotation of the *Appassionata* can be compared to how Hoffmann's Kreisler, combining fantasy and reflection, composes so that his left hand keeps up the stream of notes at the piano in a half-conscious manner, while the right hand writes down modulations, and makes notes of the experience (cf. Hoffmann 1989b: 81). Schumann's accented chord is at the same time both a fragment of the *Appassionata* and a commentary at a referential distance. In its double function, the chord is not only "the agent that restores sensation to us" but also "the veil that separates it from us" (Kristeva 1994/1996: 208).[16] This is characteristic

16 The reference here is to Kristeva's description of Proustian language.

of Romantic irony: the creative process is foregrounded when classical models are imitated through the distance of conscious reflection, by acknowledging imitation as imitation, recognising the loss of immediate experience (cf. Dill 1989: 179–181; Perrey 2002: 33f.).

Sound of Absence

This experience with Beethoven – marked by various divisions and distances – has helped me to expand my horizon with regard to the production of the Romantic sound, heavy with fetishized longing. Referring to the mythical, Romantic image of Beethoven of the 19th century, Roland Barthes writes: "[…] with Beethoven, the mimetic pulsion becomes orchestral; […] to *want* to play Beethoven is to project oneself as an orchestra conductor. Beethoven's oeuvre abandons the amateur and seems, initially, to summon up the new romantic deity, the interpreter" (1985: 264). Barthes italicises the word "to *want*" (*vouloir*), as if emphasising the endeavour as an impossible dream.

Even though Barthes himself situates Schumann firmly within the intimate space of the amateur, his description of the Romantic Beethoven is relevant to my interpretation of *Kreisleriana*'s fourth piece as music of absence. For this music, which is comparable to "Beethoven's deeper introductions" (Schauffler 1945/1963: 331), is intimate, but at the same time it seems to demand a reflective distance.[17] In the text entitled "Beethoven's Instrumental Music" in Hoffmann's *Kreisleriana*, the composer-conductor Kreisler, playing some modulations of Beethoven on the piano, discusses the difficulty of the instrument:

> The most refined expression of which the instrument is capable cannot bring a melody to life with the myriad nuances that the violinist's bow or the wind player's breath is able to call forth. The player struggles in vain with the insuperable difficulty of the mechanism, which by striking the strings causes them to vibrate and produce the notes. (Hoffmann 1989b: 100f.)

17 This paradox of intimacy and distance can also be understood in terms of gender. According to my interpretation, the subject of the fourth of *Kreisleriana* is a masculine Romantic artist, a composer-conductor who casts a phallic gaze (a gaze of mastery) over the composition, but who also releases feminine energies (volatility of emotion traditionally coded as feminine) in his creative process and, in a certain way, feminizes himself. On Schumann's combination of these kinds of masculine and feminine paradigms in his creativity, see Kramer's discussion of *Carnaval*, op. 9 (1993: esp. 306f.).

In spite of this, or actually exactly because of this, Kreisler regards the piano as the best instrument for bringing into being the complete sound-painting of a composer's imagination like a "good copper engraving taken from a great painting" (ibid.: 101). It is essential here that it is the indirect, abstract and illusory nature of the piano that makes it so appropriate for giving a glimpse into "the spirit-realm of the infinite" (ibid.: 98).[18] The piano, a central characteristic of which is to aspire beyond itself, is the Romantic instrument of absence and longing *par excellence*. To be the Romantic interpreter, attempting to conjure up something of the infinity of the realm of music, I need to desire the sound, to prolong the longing for the depth, which makes my arms heavier and slows down my gestures.

The tonal instability, too – the ambiguous harmonies, the open or imperfect cadences so characteristic of *Kreisleriana*'s fourth piece – can be thought of and experienced in terms of this distance of desire, reaching for an absent, impossible sonority. In the remainder of this paper, I will present two examples in both of which the impossible object of longing is represented or suggested by G minor. One of the occasions of undecided tonal oscillation is the end of Section A (see Example 7). The phrase in the bass part begins in G minor but continues unharmonised, played by the left hand alone, cadencing on a lonely B flat. Describing this as a radical experiment with tonal ambivalence, Rosen notes that melodically the phrase is rounded off by a conventional B flat major cadence (cf. 1995: 675f.), but since the dominant seventh of G minor remains unresolved, this would imply that the final Bb is to be harmonised with a G minor sixth chord. The incompleteness of the cadence is emphasised by the rests lengthened with fermatas. The openness and the long silence make

EXAMPLE 7 *Robert Schumann,* Kreisleriana, *op. 16, part 4, mm. 9–11*

18 As Rosen notes, one of the glories of the piano throughout the history of the instrument has been its ability to imitate other instruments (cf. 2002: 44). On the abstract and intellectual nature of the piano, and on the challenges and possibilities of the instrument's mechanism, cf., e.g., Neuhaus 1967: 53–55; Rosen 1995: 2; 2002: 50–58.

EXAMPLE 8 *Experiment*

the ending full of longing, stretched towards infinity (G minor?) like a question mark.

When practicing this, I try playing an A and a G on the fermatas, to arrive at G minor (see Example 8). Then I no longer play but sing them in my mind, imagining the arrival. To produce this impression, the final Bb has to be played leaving it open, not securely pressing it to the bottom.[19] To enhance the impression of reaching for infinity, I do not move my hand away from the keyboard after having played the Bb, but continue the gesture, as if feeling my way on the keyboard to the tones of A and G that will not sound (except as absent, in my mind). This is how I fill the silence with the energy of active hesitation, oscillation, with the distance of "vibratory time". The reference here is to Barthes, who develops 'oscillation' as a strategy and figure of "le Neutre" ("the Neutral", or "Neuter"). His aspiration for the Neutral – a project deeply rooted in Romanticism – is an attempt to baffle paradigmatic structures and closed systems of meaning, and to build a fragmentary system without a centre (cf. Barthes 2002: 171–175).

Another place that hovers ambivalently between G minor and Bb major is the ending of the central Section (B), the passage to the recapitulation of the opening phrase (see Example 9). There is a half cadence on the dominant of G minor – but the F# is immediately altered to a Gb and the chord to a diminished seventh. The music is about to cadence in G minor, but is, after all, turned towards Bb major again. I want to experience this oscillation and bring it forth in my playing as intensely as possible. Thus I make the most of the *ritardando* marked by Schumann and prolong the 'vibratory time' of the harmony oscillating between G minor and Bb major. Once the F#/Gb is lowered into an F, the situation is resolved to the advantage of Bb major – but before playing the F there is no need for an active intention towards that direction. The oscillation

19 Listen, for instance, to Horowitz (see 1969/1993), who leaves the cadence open, and – for comparison – to Schiff (see 1998), who arrives at the Bb firmly as if to a goal.

EXAMPLE 9 *Robert Schumann,* Kreisleriana, *op. 16, part 4, mm. 23f.*

will not happen if the treble A is played strongly, with a clear inclination towards Bb.[20]

I play with heavy fingers the G and F#, which strengthens the sense of G minor. I bring my longing for G minor to the extreme, which at a more concrete level means imagining that the chord in my hands were the seventh of G minor and would eventually be resolved to G minor. The deeper my concentration on the desire of the G minor, the stronger – paradoxically – is my expectation of Bb major. When I finally arrive at the dominant of Bb major, when the melody only barely manages to climb up to the Bb, I feel as if I had just been saved from the edge of a cliff. Through this, I feel palpably – in my hands – the impossibility of romantic love. As Kristeva puts it, to attain the impossible lost Thing of melancholy would be a paradisiacal reunion "through the nuptials of suicide" (1987/1989: 14; cf. also 12f.).

The G minor is finally achieved in the fifth piece of *Kreisleriana,* which is in that key. But this happens through an ironic mask, not from the angle of Kreisler's romantic love – which has to remain 'eternally thirsting'. As Žižek points out, even though Schumann's music addresses the Other to stretch his or her hand to us, it also involves the opposite of this entreaty: "yes, stretch out your hand, but *not too far,* keep your distance!" (1997/1999: 209). The one who is more than willing to stretch out his paw to take a firm grip on G minor is Tomcat Murr, who responds to Kreisler's ponderings on romantic longing with parodic imitation. But that is another story.

References

Abbate, Carolyn (1999). "Outside Ravel's Tomb". *Journal of the American Musicological Society* 52/3: 465–530.

20 Perahia (see 1997) plays the A with an intense inclination towards the B. For comparison, listen to Ashkenazy's (see 1992) or Lupu's (see 1995) renderings, which leave more room for oscillation.

Arnsdorf, Mary Hunter (1976). *Schumann's* Kreisleriana, *Op. 16: Analysis and Performance*. Unprinted dissertation. Columbia University Teachers College.

Ashkenazy, Vladimir (1992). *Schumann: Kreisleriana, Novelette No. 8, Sonata No. 2*. CD. Decca 425 940–2.

Barthes, Roland (1985). "Musica practica". *Responsibility of Forms*. Trans. Richard Howard. Berkeley, CA: University of California Press.

——— (2002). *Le Neutre: Cours au Collège de France (1977–1978)*. Ed. Thomas Clerc. Paris: Seuil.

Chantler, Abigail (2006). *E.T.A. Hoffmann's Musical Aesthetics*. Aldershot: Ashgate.

Charlton, David (1989a). [Introduction and prefatory remarks to *Kreisleriana*]. Charlton, ed. 23–75.

——— ed. (1989b). *E.T.A. Hoffmann's Musical Writings:* Kreisleriana, The Poet and the Composer, *Music Criticism*. Cambridge: CUP.

Dahlhaus, Carl (1978/1989). *The Idea of Absolute Music*. Trans. Roger Lustig. Chicago, IL: University of Chicago Press.

——— (1980/1989). *Nineteenth-Century Music*. Trans. Mary Whittall. Berkeley, CA: University of California Press.

Daverio, John (1997). *Robert Schumann: Herald of a 'New Poetic Age'*. New York, NY/ Oxford: OUP.

——— (2007). "Piano Works I: A World of Images". Beate Perrey, ed. *The Cambridge Companion to Schumann*. Cambridge: CUP. 65–85.

Deahl, Lora (1996). "Robert Schumann's *Kreisleriana* and Double Novel Structure". *International Journal of Musicology* 5: 131–145.

Dill, Heinz J. (1989). "Romantic Irony in the Works of Robert Schumann". *The Musical Quarterly* 73/2: 172–195.

Freud, Sigmund (1917/1981). "Mourning and Melancholia". Trans. James Strachey. *Standard Edition of the Complete Psychological Works of Sigmund Freud* 14. London: The Hogarth Press and The Institute of Psycho-analysis. 243–258.

——— (1919/1981). "The Uncanny". Trans. James Strachey. *Standard Edition of the Complete Psychological Works of Sigmund Freud* 17. London: The Hogarth Press and The Institute of Psycho-analysis. 217–256.

Goehr, Lydia (1992/2007). *The Imaginary Museum of Musical Works: An Essay in the Philosophy of Music*. Oxford: OUP.

Hoeckner, Berthold (1997). "Schumann and Romantic Distance". *Journal of the American Musicological Society* 50/11: 55–132.

Hoffmann, E.T.A. (1989a). [Review of Beethoven's *Fifth Symphony*, 1810]. Trans. Martyn Clarke. Charlton, ed. 234–251.

——— (1989b). "Kreisleriana" [1814]. Trans. Martyn Clarke. Charlton, ed. 76–165.

——— (1974). *Lebensansichten des Katers Murr nebst fragmentarischer Biographie des Kapellmeisters Johannes Kreisler in zufälligen Makulaturblättern* [1820]. Munich: Wilhelm Goldmann. (Engl. trans.: *Life and Opinions of the Tomcat Murr, together with the Fragmentary Biography of Kapellmeister Johannes Kreisler on Random Sheets of Waste Paper*. Trans. Anthea Bell. Penguin Classics. Harmondsworth: Penguin, 1999).

Horowitz, Vladimir (1969/1993). *The Complete Masterworks Recordings 1962–1973, Vol 7: Early Romantics: Chopin, Schumann*. CD. Sony Classical S2K53468.

Jones, J. Barrie (1988). "Beethoven and Schumann: Some Literary and Musical Allusions". *The Music Review* 49: 114–125.

Kautsky, Catherine (2006). "Music, Magic, and Madness: Tales of Hoffmann, Schumann, and Kreisler". *International Piano* (May/June): 44–49.

Kramer, Lawrence (1990). *Music as Cultural Practice, 1800–1900*. Berkeley, CA: University of California Press.

———(1993). "*Carnaval*, Cross-Dressing, and the Woman in the Mirror". Ruth A. Solie, ed. *Musicology and Difference: Gender and Sexuality in Music Scholarship*. Berkeley, CA: University of California Press. 305–325.

Kristeva, Julia (1987/1989). *Black Sun: Depression and Melancholia*. Trans. Leon S. Roudiez. New York, NY: Columbia UP (French orig.: *Soleil noir. Dépression et mélancolie*. Paris: Gallimard).

——— (1988/1991). *Strangers to Ourselves*. Trans. Leon S. Roudiez. New York, NY: Columbia UP (French orig.: *Étrangers à nous-mêmes*. Paris: Fayard).

———(1994/1996). *Time and Sense: Proust and the Experience of Literature*. Trans. Ross Guberman. New York, NY: Columbia UP (French orig.: *Le temps sensible: Proust et l'expérience littéraire*. Paris: Gallimard).

Lacoue-Labarthe, Philippe, Jean-Luc Nancy (1978). *L'absolu littéraire: Théorie de la littérature du romantisme allemand*. Paris: Seuil.

Loos, Helmut (2005). *Robert Schumann: Interpretationen seiner Werke. Band I*. Laaber: Laaber.

Lupu, Radu (1995). *Schumann – Kinderszenen. Kreisleriana. Humoreske*. CD. Decca 440 496–2.

Marston, Nicholas (2007). "Schumann's Heroes: Schubert, Beethoven, Bach". Beate Perrey, ed. *The Cambridge Companion to Schumann*. Cambridge, MA: CUP. 48–61.

Münch, Stephan (1992). "*Fantasiestücke in Kreislers Manier*. Robert Schumanns *Kreisleriana* op. 16 und die Musikanschauung E.T.A. Hoffmanns". *Die Musikforschung* 45/3: 255–275.

Neuhaus, Heinrich (1967). *Die Kunst des Klavierspiels*. Bergisch Gladbach: Gerig.

Novalis (1960–1988). „Das allgemeine Brouillon". Eds. Richard Samuel, Paul Kluckhohn. *Schriften*. Vol. 3. Stuttgart: W. Kohlhammer. 207–478.

Perahia, Murray (1997). *Kreisleriana. Sonata No. 1* (Schumann). CD. Sony Classical SK62786.

Perrey, Beate Julia (2002). *Schumann's* Dichterliebe *and Early Romantic Poetics: Fragmentation of Desire*. Cambrigde, MA: CUP.

Reich, Nancy B. (1985). *Clara Schumann: The Artist and the Woman*. Ithaca, NY/London: Cornell UP.

Rosen, Charles (1995). *The Romantic Generation*. Cambrigde, MA: Harvard UP.

——— (2002). *Piano Notes: The World of the Pianist*. New York, NY: The Free Press.

Schauffler, Robert Haven (1945/1963). *Florestan: The Life and Work of Robert Schumann*. New York, NY: Dover Publications.

Schiff, Andras (1998). *Schumann – Kreisleriana, Nachtstücke, Gesänge der Frühe, Geister-Variationen*. CD. Teldec 0630-14566-2.

Schoolfield, George C. (1966). *The Figure of the Musician in German Literature*. New York, NY: AMS Press.

Schumann, Robert (2004). *Kreisleriana*, Opus 16. Urtext. Munich: G. Henle.

Taylor, Timothy D. (1990). "Aesthetic and Cultural Issues in Schumann's *Kinderszenen*". *International Review of Aesthetic and Sociology of Music* 21/2: 161–178.

Todd, Larry R. (1994). "On Quotation in Schumann's Music". Larry R. Todd, ed. *Schumann and His World*. Princeton, NJ: Princeton UP. 80–112.

Vaznosyi, Bálint (1972). "Solo Piano Music – II. The Piano Cycles". Alan Walker, ed. *Robert Schumann: The Man and His Music*. London: Barrie & Jenkins. 68–92.

Välimäki, Susanna (2005). *Subject Strategies in Music: A Psychoanalytic Approach to Musical Signification*. Acta Semiotica Fennica XXII; Approaches to Musical Semiotics 9. Imatra: International Semiotics Institute.

Weingarten, Joseph (1972). "Interpreting Schumann's Piano Music". Alan Walker, ed. *Robert Schumann: The Man and His Music*. London: Barrie & Jenkins. 93–108.

Worthen, John (2007). *Robert Schumann: Life and Death of a Musician*. New Haven, CT/London: Yale UP.

Žižek, Slavoj (1997/1999). *The Plague of Fantasies*. London/New York, NY: Verso.

Mute Performances: Ekphrasis of Music, and Performative Aesthetics in Eyvind Johnson's *Romantisk berättelse*

Beate Schirrmacher

This article discusses a peculiar kind of 'mute' musical performance that features in *Romantisk berättelse* (1953, 'Romantic Tale') of the Swedish Nobel Prize Laureate Eyvind Johnson (1900–1976). Here, Beethoven's Piano Sonata No. 57, the *Appassionata*, appears not as an experience of sound but mainly as a visual experience of the pianist's moving limbs, as they are perceived by a young working-class writer, Olle. Olle sees himself excluded from a musical community; this feeling of alienation results in deliberately non-acoustic descriptions of musical performance, where it is not primarily the sound, but the performer's bodily presence that is stressed. Yet such absence of sound should not only be understood as some kind of deficit. By writing a performative 'mute' ekphrasis, Johnson deliberately questions the ideas of the transcendence of instrumental music as well as its alleged status as a universal language.

•••

In literature, intermedial references to music are a recurrent means of expression to fill a shortcoming in words. As George Steiner points out, music is one of the aesthetic means used in literature to transcend verbal communication: "One tradition finds light at the limits of language. Another, no less ancient or active in our poetry and poetics, finds music." (1967: 41) In these cases, music is perceived as one of the opposites of language, as a means of expression when words fail, and, at the same time, as a kind of universal language with a "syntax more supple, more penetrating" (ibid.: 46). The verbal pause, however, does not necessarily imply silence. Instead, it is filled by sound, or, in literature, with the evocation of sound. Acoustical foregrounding does play a vital role in many intermedial references to music in literature as has been pointed out before (cf. Wolf 1999: 74). It is one of the ways in which a literary text stresses the common ground it shares with music (see Schirrmacher 2012). Thus, the intermedial reference to music in literature in most cases implies the enhancement of the acoustical phenomena in general. That said, I will discuss a literary description of a piece of music that appears remarkably 'mute', as if the volume knob had been turned off. It occurs in *Romantisk berättelse* (1959; 'Romantic Tale'), a novel by the Swedish author Eyvind Johnson. In describing music 'silently',

 | DOI 10.1163/9789004314863_007

without the quality we first associate with it, the text points our attention to other characteristics that usually might find themselves 'drowned' in the acoustical perception of music and its description in literature.

This article thus discusses literary passages that engage with the task to describe pieces of music, what Steven Paul Scher chose to call "verbal music" (1968: 8); this term, however, is not without complications as the referential aspects are easily confused with technical aspects (cf. Wolf 1999: 59f.). Following Claus Clüver, we may call them ekphrases of music.[1] Clüver broadens the term ekphrasis in order to denote "all verbal representations of [...] text composed in a non-verbal sign system" (1997: 26). There are many different ways of representing a fictitious or factual piece of music in literature, depending on which aspect of music is to be highlighted. Johannes Odendahl distinguishes several aspects most often combined in ekphrasis of music: the *acoustical* experience, referring to such musical parameters as pitch, length or color; elements that are *causally* related to the music, such as the movement and facial expression of the performer; and verbalization of the *compositional* structure with reference to e.g. musical phrases, theme, motives. A more general means of ekphrasis operates through *contextual* references meant to trigger the reader's preconception of how a sonata, folk song, waltz, or opera might sound. Finally, the piece of music may be described by *assigning meaning*, as is the case when music is used to signify something else (and the beginning of a break, an imminent announcement, the arrival of a train is the signified), or, more often assigning meaning by individual association (cf. 2008: 15–17). The assignment of individual, associative meaning, what Wolf calls "imaginary content analogy" (1999: 63), is connected to an enhancement of the visual; such an assignment tends to verbalize the visual images triggered by the music. The important role of the visual in representing music in literature may be understood as part of the interart aesthetic to which Peter Dayan has drawn attention (see 2011).

Even when using imaginary content analogies, however, ekphrases of music by some means or other usually refer to the auditory experience; this occurs in describing the acoustical experience or using the reader's preconception of music by referring to compositional structure or social context. Even imaginary content analogies connect the vision of images with the act of listening; in some way the text indicates that the images described are inner images, that

1 An ekphrasis of music as a description of a piece of music in literature is to be distinguished from "musical ekphrasis", which Siglind Bruhn defines as "musical representation of a text first composed in another sign system" (2000: 9).

they are triggered by the act of listening. In Anthony Burgess's *A Clockwork Orange* (1962), the narrator Alex expresses the typical relation between hearing and inner vision in ekphrases of music as follows: "As I slooshied [listened], my eyes tight shut [...], I knew such lovely pictures" (1962/2000: 26f.) In the following example from Eyvind Johnson's novel *Romantisk berättelse*, however, hearing is barely referenced at all. The ekphrasis thus appears as remarkably 'mute'.

Eyvind Johnson was born in the North of Sweden. He left home at age 14 and started to earn a living as a day labourer. At 19 he began to work as a journalist, and in his early twenties he travelled on to Berlin and Paris. Of all the working-class writers who entered the literary scene during the 1920s and 1930s in Sweden, he was one of the most prolific, and in 1974, he was awarded the Nobel Prize of Literature.[2] He was also the one most influenced by modern European literature; Johnson's eloquent style is influenced by such writers as Proust, Gide, and Joyce, and he shares with Proust an interest in memories and the passing of time (cf. Orton 1972: 32–37). From Thomas Mann he picked up irony, which he turned into an even more subtle, and less scathing, form of self-irony (see Jansson 1990).

Eyvind Johnson's literary breakthrough was *Romanen om Olof* ('The Novel about Olof') in the 1930s, a (partly autobiographical) coming-of-age tetralogy. Two decades later, he picked up its threads again: in 1953, Johnson published *Romantisk berättelse*, which can be regarded as a freestanding sequel to *Romanen om Olof*. In *Romantisk berättelse*, the novel's narrator, who is named Yngve Garans and is a relatively unsuccessful writer, decides to write a novel that will look back on the 1920s in Berlin and Paris. He intends this novel to be based on his own memories, as well as those of his brother Gregor, his cousin the pianist Constance, and his friend and fellow writer Olle. Olle is the short form of Olof, and Olle has indeed the same background as the protagonist of *Romanen om Olof*. On the other hand, the well-to-do narrator Yngve is another self-ironic reflection of Johnson's own social position in the 1950s. *Romantisk berättelse* is thus a metafictional novel; it is unwieldy, and at first glance it appears like a pile of drafts, letters, diary entries that rather first ought to become a novel, which is what writer Yngve (very entertainingly for the reader) struggles with during the novel we read. Yet, as is so often the case, these more loosely structured, metafictional works reveal much about the author's poetics. *Romantisk berättelse* discusses Johnson's interest in time and in the process of writing, and his understanding of art. Further, the metafictional discussion

---

2 Johnson shared the Prize together with another influential working-class writer, Harry Martinsson.

is expressed in intermedial references (see Bernhart/Wolf, eds. 2010). Art appears personified in the narrator's cousin, the pianist Constance, nicknamed Const, which sounds exactly like *konst*, the Swedish word for 'art'. Thus music, and Johnson's relation to it, finds itself highlighted in the novel.

Due to his working-class background, Eyvind Johnson first came in contact with classical music after he left home. He never learned to play an instrument, which he sorely regretted (cf. Stenström 1978: 23). The role of music in Johnson's work has yet to be properly explored. As is the case with other autodidactic writers, e.g. Günter Grass (see Weyer 2007; Schirrmacher 2012), the fact that they did not learn either to play an instrument or to read music, somehow appears to screen the possibility of a more profound interest in or intermedial use of music. However, in the case of Johnson, Thure Stenström detects a 'passionate interaction with music'[3] in Johnson's novels. Still, it does not appear sufficient to describe Johnson as an interested amateur in music, nor to describe his interest in music only as an eloquent expression of non-professional emotional pleasure in music (cf. Stenström 1978: 22f.). Stenström places Johnson's relation to music within the Romantic tradition as a language of sentiment and feeling (cf. ibid.: 19). However, to call a novel a 'Romantic Tale' in 1953 already is a metafictional reflection on Romanticism (cf. Dahlberg 1999: 16–18); in a similar way one should expect that even the Romantic ideal of music may be found more reflected and not merely reproduced.

The central role of music in *Romantisk berättelse* is announced very early. The start of the novel is marked not by words but by musical notation that appears on the very first page, where one expects to find the unprinted flyleaves or maybe the half title and thus precedes all the publisher's peritext (see Example 1):

These are the first bars of Beethoven's Piano Sonata No. 23 in F minor, Op. 57, called *Appassionata*. At first glance, they appear quite isolated, out of context. Preceding the novel, this reference can be understood as an epigraph; however, the notation does not appear in the usual place, closest to the text, after title page and dedication (cf. Genette 1997: 149). Nor does the quotation explicitly convey information about composer or work but only refers to Beethoven if we recognize the piece and are able to read music. Even the single notes appear to have lost a part of their context, as the staff stops after the upbeat, while the notes continue. This may be a printing error, but it still leaves the notes hovering in mid-air.

3 "[…] ett lidelsefullt umgänge med musik" (Stenström 1978: 56; my translation).

EXAMPLE 1
Eyvind Johnson (1953),
Romantisk berättelse [7]

This quote of Beethoven's *Appassionata* is connected with the novel's first paragraphs which also, in an epigraphic manner, still hover on the threshold of the novel as they precede the novel's first chapter and pagination (cf. Dahlberg 1999: 30) and begin as follows:

> Begins deep down, dark, sinks back toward even greater darkness after a first attempt. Then: softly; a meld of calm and unease. Now: The melody! Glittering. A glittering climb up to the treble. Then: back deep to the left: the melody there.[4]

The words "melody" and "climb up to the treble" designate the passage as an ekphrasis of music. It is thanks to this structural description that the movement noted in the first sentence can be understood as an "iconic diagram" (Nänny 2002: 134) of a melody. Further, the reader who has noted the notation on the flyleaf will come to recognize the passage as an ekphrasis of the *Appassionata*, even before it will be explicitly established as such in the novel. The notation on the flyleaf and the initial paragraphs comment on each other and interconnect in their epigraphic function (cf. Dahlberg 1999: 42). Together they establish from the very beginning the importance of Beethoven's piano sonata for the novel. Ekphrases of the *Appassionata* will return throughout the novel in variations, as the sonata is recalled, discussed (cf. RB: 397), and played on the radio (cf. RB: 83, 500). Already in these two paratexts, some peculiarities in Johnson's way of describing the sonata attract attention. As Gavin Orton points out, the sonata is described mainly visually, in terms of light and darkness (cf. 1972: 72); only the compositional description of "melody" and

4 "Börjar långt nere, mörkt, sjunker tillbaka mot ännu mörkare efter ett första försök. Så stilla; lugn och oro blandas. Nu: melodin! Glitter. Glittervandring uppåt diskanten. Tillbaka djupt i vänster: melodin där." (Johnson 1953: [7]) All quotations from *Romantisk berättelse* (in the following abbreviated as RB) here and in the following translated by Rochelle Wright. Unfortunately the translation is as yet unpublished.

"discant" (RB: [7]) helps to interpret the visual categories of light and darkness also as an acoustical portrayal of pitch. And while in the initial paragraphs the visual is already highlighted, the acoustical recedes even more in the longest, most elaborate ekphrasis, the description of a 1923 performance (cf. RB: 353–362) to be explored in more detail below.

On "Midsummer Day 1923"[5] (i.e., June 24th), all of the novel's main protagonists are gathered at a commemoration of Walter Rathenau, one year after the German foreign minister's assassination in 1922. The narrator focalizes through Olle, who feels slightly uneasy in the high-culture atmosphere of the theatre, so unlike the cinema he knows much better. In these surroundings, only concert programmes and no sandwich papers crackle (cf. RB: 353). The situation is intimidating. Even Constance, who will perform the sonata, appears somewhat timid and nervous as she appears on the stage. Then the narrator simply states, "Constance played" (RB: 355). The following passage is explicitly marked as an ekphrasis of the piece of music performed, for in a prolepsis the narrator points out that Olle later will "try the impossible: to translate it into words; and he will not succeed" (ibid.):

> It came almost from nowhere – low and far away in the left hand in darkness. It rose upward; the music wandered across the broad, crooked, indifferent fixed smile or challenging grimace of the keyboard (he thought), up the shiny black slope of the lid – and suddenly it was there, alive, and revealed itself. The melody gleamed; you could hear it start glittering, *see* it for a few seconds before it sank back into the depths.[6]

We do find elements of imaginary content analogy in this description: the ascending of a steep hill, the shimmering as of water. Throughout the whole passage, images recur that on the one hand appear to derive from Scandinavian nature – the glitter of waves, wind blowing over a lake, the picking of berries, flower petals opening. Against this background, the musical movement described resembles that of a fish that surfaces for a second before plunging back into the lake.

---

5 "Midsommardagen 1923" (RB: 353).

6 "Det började nästan ingenstans – lågt och långt bort i vänster hand i mörkret. Det steg uppåt, musiken vandrade över klaviaturens sneda, breda, likgiltiga automatleende eller utmanande grin (tyckte han) uppför lockets svartblanka backe – och plötsligt var den där, i livet, och visade sig. Melodin glimtade, men hörde den glittra till, *såg* den några sekunder innan den sjönk tillbaka i sitt djup." (RB: 355; italics in the original).

On the other hand, as pointed out by Thure Stenström (cf. 1978: 59), this passage owes much to Marcel Proust, in particular to his description of "la petite phrase de Vinteuil" (Proust 1992: 211 et *passim*), the little phrase from a sonata for piano and violin that Swann is so very fond of in *Du côté de chez Swann* (1913), the first part of *À la recherche du temps perdu*. When Swann listens to Vinteuil's sonata, it evokes imaginary content analogies of water and moonlight, and the phrase itself is compared to the fragrance of roses (ibid.: 202). Swann then reflects on the fleetingness of musical motifs "qui par instants en emergent, à peine discernables, pour plonger aussitôt et disparaître" (ibid.).[7]

In one way, Johnson's musical ekphrasis of Beethoven nearly seems to rephrase Proust's description of Vinteuil's sonata. In another way, however, Johnson's description differs very much compared with its intertext. One closer look at Proust's ekphrastical technique will illustrate the point:

> L'année précédente, dans une soirée, il avait *entendu une œuvre musicale* exécutée au *piano et au violon*. D'abord, il n'avait goûté que la *qualité matérielle* des sons sécrétés par les instruments. Et ç'avait déjà été un grand plaisir quand au-dessous de *la petite ligne du violon* [...] il avait vu tout d'un coup [...] la masse de la *partie de piano*, multiforme, indivise, plane et entrechoquée comme la mauve agitation des flots que charme et *bémolise* le clair de lune. Mais à un moment donné, [...], il avait cherché à recueillir *la phrase ou l'harmonie* – il ne savait lui-même – qui passait [...].[8] (Proust 1992: 202; my italics)

When Swann "hears a piece of music" played he is able to "appreciate the material quality of the sound", he distinguishes the "melody" and recognizes its reappearance in a "minor key"; even if he is uncertain in their use, he is aware of musical terms such as "phrase" or "harmony". The fleetingness of musical motifs is a bodiless impression, "[u]ne impression *sine materia*" (ibid.). Mixed with the elements of imaginary content analogy, in Proust's text we find

7 "[...] which now and then emerge, barely discernible, to plunge again, and disappear and drown" (Proust online).

8 "The year before, he had *heard a piece of music* played on the *piano and violin*. At first he had appreciated only the *material quality of the sound* which those instruments secreted. And it had been a source of keen pleasure when, below the narrow ribbon of the *violin-part* [...] he had suddenly perceived [...] the mass of the *piano-part*, multiform, coherent and level, and breaking everywhere in *melody* like the deep blue tumult of the sea, silvered and charmed into a *minor key* by the moonlight. But at a given moment, [...] he had tried to collect, to treasure in his memory the *phrase or harmony* [...] that had just been played [...]." (Ibid.; my italics).

references to the acoustical experience of listening to music, appreciated by someone familiar with the conventions of classical music. The visual imagery is combined with the auditory and contextual description of the instruments and certain musical terms, in order to establish the reference to musical experience. All movement referenced is movement within the musical system. In Johnson's ekphrasis, however, hardly any musicological terms are used:

> She raised her right hand high […]. It descended, floated down, and before it reached the keys – it seemed to him – the music that had been in the hand was already there and shifted to the right hand and upward. It rose in a swirling movement according to an unknown rotation system and laws impossible to assess or even grasp. It moved far out to the right, it rose with the stiff, splayed fingers of the right hand in a quick, outward, infinitely beautiful movement that scarcely grazed the keys; while the left hand fell, hard and gentle and quick, and lifted – *scorched* – and fell again – while the swirling movement of the right hand continued at an outward angle to the right and then, quickly, gently in toward the left hand as if it was searching for something and picking it up – and it did.[9]

The movement described here is that of the hands; the notions of height and depth are located at the piano keyboard. Johnson uses nearly exclusively what Odendahl calls 'causally motivated description' (cf. 2008: 15). In Johnson's ekphrasis, what Olle perceives most is the performer's body moving. In Proust's text, the peculiar little phrase possesses a "slow and rhythmical movement", it appears agile and even elusive, "it changes direction", its return is "more rapid, multiform, melancholy", it vanishes: all movement described is musical movement:

> D'un rythme lent elle le dirigeait ici d'abord, puis là, puis ailleurs, vers un bonheur noble, intelligible et précis. Et tout d'un coup, au point où elle était arrivée et d'où il se préparait à la suivre, après une pause d'un instant,

---

9 "Hon lyfte vänsterhanden högt […]. Den föll, svävade ner och innan den hade nått tangenterna – tyckte han – var musiken, som hade funnits i handen, redan där och flyttade över till högerhanden och uppåt. Den steg i en virvelrörelse, efter ett hemligt rotationssystem och efter lagar som man inte kunde bedöma, inte ens fatta. Den rörde sig långt ut mot höger, den steg med högerhandens vitt och stelt utspärrade fingrar i en hastig, utåtgående oändligt vacker rörelse som bara snuddade tangenterna; medan vänsterhanden föll, hårt och mjukt och snabbt, och lyfte sig, *bränd* – och föll igen – medan den högra fortsatte virvelrörelsen snett utåt höger och sedan, hastigt-mjukt in mot vänster som om den sökte och tog upp något – och det gjorde den." (RB: 356; italics in the original).

> brusquement elle changeait de direction, et d'un mouvement nouveau, plus rapide, menu, mélancolique, incessant et doux, elle l'entraînait avec elle vers des perspectives inconnues. Puis elle disparut.[10] (Proust 1922: 203)

In Johnson's novel, however, Olle does not seem to follow the music in the first place; he follows it throughout Constance's movements. While Olle *sees* Constance performing, nothing is mentioned about what he *hears*. The performance, not music itself, is visualized. The contrast to Proust is not only to be found in the use of musical terms. Johnson does not follow the Western idea of music as transcending materiality. Proust stresses this idea ('an impression *sine materia*'). In Johnson's text, the musical experience does not pass beyond the performer's body. Music, in this process, finds itself named only as 'it'. This may be correct in English, in the Swedish original, however, music, *musiken*, is not referred to with the appropriate pronoun (it should be *den* not *det*) and therefore appears as an indefinite *thing*, which is passed over from the left to the right hand or the other way round.

Apparently, what is conveyed is the impression of hearing classical music without any introduction by education or experience. It is no coincidence that in Chapter 23 (cf. RB: 322–352), which precedes the *Appassionata* performance, the narrator Yngve recalls a long conversation in which Olle tells him more about his upbringing in the North of Sweden, a striking contrast with the following concert hall-scene. If, as Olle attends the performance, there is not mainly sound conveyed but movement, this is because movement is what he *sees*, what he can describe and understand. Therefore, the ekphrasis of the sonata appears mute, as if Olle were deaf, or as if we were watching a silent movie. It is not the sound of Beethoven's sonata that is evoked, but Olle watching Constance performing it: the movement of the hands is described, the arms, the shoulders, fingers spreading and closing, prompting the imaginary content analogy of a flower opening its petals. On the one hand, this is once again a reference to Vinteuil's 'little phrase', but on the other hand it refers just as much to the pianist's fingers playing the chords. More than inner images, the sonata evokes all kind of technical terms Olle has come across in his autodidactic

10 "With a slow and rhythmical movement it led him here, there, everywhere, towards a state of happiness noble, unintelligible, yet clearly indicated. And then, suddenly having reached a certain point from which he was prepared to follow it, after pausing for a moment, abruptly it changed its direction, and in a fresh movement, more rapid, multiform, melancholy, incessant, sweet, it bore him off with it towards a vista of joys unknown. Then it vanished." (Proust online).

education in the libraries' reading rooms. Classical music is just another foreign language to which he tries to gain access:

> He recalled words he had recently read in a book, a journal, the words adaptation and equalization and application, mute words you could not penetrate and force sound from, and words like die Wienermethode and Englische Methode [...], knowledge outside his reach now and perhaps always. And names. Cramer and Clementi, mute names.[11]

Here the muteness and exclusion are actually expressed verbally; classical music is part of the education Olle did not receive in his adolescence. As a consequence, classical music appears as impenetrable as the scientific use of a foreign language. In sharp contrast to the Romantic idea of music as universal language beyond words, music appears as just another foreign language one has to struggle to access. Olle's only approach is Constance's body, which he closely observes, trying to understand the physiology of playing the piano.

> And – once again – the right hand, the outward movement of the right arm, the blunt angle of the wrist and the word supination; and now the hand was brought – *wrenched* inward to pick something up, quickly (to pick some berries, the cloudberries of childhood, lingonberries, berries from a bush), pick up some nimble sounds from the keyboard; and the word pronation, which vanished and was forgotten.[12]

Supination of the arm means that the palm of the hand faces outwards or upwards, which is not very likely to take place while playing the piano. The use of anatomical terms both stresses the notion of exclusion and, on the other hand, is a means of describing the performance as bodily movement. And, indeed, in describing the outward movement of arms, wrists and shoulders during the runs, and the re-gathering of playing the chords, he does render an ekphrasis of Beethoven's sonata, seen through the performer's body.

---

11 "Han kom ihåg ord som han hade läst nyligen i en bok, en tidskrift, ord som hette adaptation och egalisering och applikation; stumma ord som man inte kunde genomtränga och få ljud ur; och ord som die Wienermethode och Englische Methode [...], en kunskap utanför hans räckvidd nu och kanske för alltid." (RB: 356).

12 "Och – åter – högerhandens, högerarmens rörelse utåt, handledens trubbiga vinkel och ordet supination; och nu fördes, *slets* handen inåt för att plocka upp något, hastigt (plocka några bär, åkerbär i barndomen, lingon, bär från en buske, plock upp några snabba ljud ur klaviaturen); och ordet pronation, som försvann och glömdes." (Ibid.; italics in the original).

Compared with Proust, Romantic ideas of musical transcendence and universal language are questioned from the perspective of Olle's working-class background. They do not appear as universal truths but rather as what they are, projections and ideological assumptions (see Schirrmacher 2014). As far as he is concerned, thinks Olle, the performance could as well be played on "painted keys"; to him it appears to be "without a sound, without a tone".[13] This might appear meaningless, and the exclusion total, but the sonata remains not totally incomprehensible to Olle. The association with painted keys offers a different approach, a different intertext than does the comparison with the well-educated M. Swann.

Painted keys on a table and another mute performance appear in *Gösta Berling's saga* (1891), Selma Lagerlöf's highly successful debut novel. Gösta Berling is a minister, deposed because of his excessive drinking. Witty, charismatic and charming, he becomes the leading spirit of the so-called squires, pensioners that have found shelter at the manor of Ekeby. However, especially in contact with beautiful women, Gösta Berling eventually becomes sorely aware that he is still a social outcast, to the extent that this makes him feel quite depressed. In the chapter "Fru Musica" ('Lady Musica'), the squires try to cheer him up; they form an orchestra and play some Haydn, without effect. One of the squires, called Lövenborg, has been slightly deranged since his fiancée drowned herself. He has

> a wooden table on which he had painted a keyboard. There he sat for hours, and let his fingers play over its black and white keys [...] and there he played Beethoven. He never played anything than Beethoven.[14] (Lagerlöf 1918: 85)

When the squires' orchestra fails to cheer Gösta Berling up, Lövenborg sets out to play on his wooden table. As the old confused man plays Beethoven on painted keys, his performance tears Gösta Berling out of his brooding.

In Johnson's musical ekphrasis of Beethoven, however, the performance appears just as incomprehensible to (at least) one person in the audience. In Selma Lagerlöf's novel, the squires and Gösta Berling attend a mute performance,

---

13 "Och han – vem? – som sitter och spelar på de målade tangenterna och inget ljud kommer, ingen ton" (RB: 357).

14 "[...] Löwenborg [har] ett stort träbord på vilket han har målat en klaviatur [...]. Där kan han sitta i timtal och låta fingrarna löpa över de svarta och vita tangenterna [...] och där spelar han sin Beethoven. Han spelar aldrig något annat än Beethoven." (Lagerlöf 1891/1986: 262).

a pantomime, which only sounds in the performer's slightly deranged head. Taken together, these mute performances deconstruct another Romantic idea, which is Beethoven as the "myth of the Romantic artist" (Seaton 2010: 318). Instead of the suffering genius who is the only one whose ears cannot hear his astonishing music, we find a slightly deranged performer who is the only one to hear the music he plays, and his grotesque performance abolishes Gösta Berling's self-pity. Likewise Olle's self-pity echoes self-irony: "You are a doomed man [...] because you never learned to play an instrument".[15] Even if the concert remains mute to Olle, even if the feeling of exclusion prevails, something is said to be "opening up" (RB: 357) as he remembers the grotesque scene in *Gösta Berlings saga*: "[...] music came out of the muteness of the wooden table – there".[16] Music does not become audible, but something else happens. Music becomes discernible as deictic adverbs start to point it out in space and time:

> And it's there at one point in the rotation, the movement of her back and arms, extended and brought together again – at one point in the field [...], at a point that lights up like a signal lamp: here, now! – the goal that is reached and immediately abandoned: here – now, it's fallen behind, it's coming back, but now is already there and not here and the movement of the upright back, the arms, the hands continues toward another here – now: now![17]

Music starts to convey meaning to Olle. It flashes like a signal lamp. Music refers to a certain point in space or time, "here, now!", in the present moment, which is "the goal that is reached and immediately abandoned".

Thus, Johnson uses the mute performance of the *Appassionata* not only to convey the sensation of exclusion, to question the idealization and especially its alleged immediacy of classical music. By describing a musical performance through the eyes of an outsider, he also withdraws the attention from the main characteristic of music as organized sound. In Johnson's ekphrasis, music neither appears as a universal language of sentiment nor, according to Hanslick's

15 "Du är en förlorad mänska [...] eftersom du aldrig lärde dig något instrument." (RB: 361).

16 "[...] raden av vitt och svartblankt öppnade sig – musiken kom ur träbordets stumhet – där!" (RB: 357; emphasis in the original).

17 "Och det finns en punkt i rotationen, hennes ryggs, hennes utbredd och återsammanförda armars rörelser – finns på en punkt i fältet påen punkt som lyser till som en signallampa: här, nu! – det målet som nås och genast överges: här – nu, det ligger bakom, det kommer tillbaka med nu är redan där och inte här och rörelsen i ryggpelaren, armarna, händerna fortsätter mot ett annat här – nu: nu!" (RB: 358f.; emphasis in the original).

famous phrase, as "tönend bewegte Formen" (1854/1911: 59), as sounding, moving forms, but rather as motion filling the present moment. This is achieved by leaving out the sound, by describing music as 'mute'. Instead of transcending it, music makes the present moment discernible as a succession of organized movements. Music does not so much appear connected with Olle's feelings, as Stenström suggests might be the role of ekphrasis of music in Johnson's texts (cf. 1978: 19). Instead, music in this passage becomes closely related to a topic increasingly of interest to Johnson: music appears related to time, its fleetingness, the fugaciousness not of things passed, as in Proust, but of the present moment.

This concern with time brings us back once again to Vinteuil's sonata. Swann too is struck and moved by the fleetingness of the music. Music for him points towards a time beyond the present. In Johnson's *Romantisk berättelse*, however, music, the *Appassionata*, is described as sheer presence. It is not transcending anything but stands for the fleetingness of the moment made visible, by the performer's movement. Thus, music is for Johnson a visualizing of the present moment of "here, now!", and therefore it is not to be severed from the moment of its performance. Music in these passages is performance highlighted, the sonata seen through the performer's body. Edward Said describes music as "an experience of the passing of time" (1991: 74), and it is in the moment of performance that the music appears most clearly as "irrecusably tied to duration or passing of time" (ibid.: 89). To Proust, the notion of the passing of time, connected with music, appears as tied to the remembrance of the Past. When Swann unexpectedly hears Vinteuil's sonata again, he involuntarily recalls and relives the moments of untroubled love with Odette (cf. Proust 1992: 326–334). In *Romantisk berättelse*, where the music is described as inseparable from its performance, the music is only evoked through the description of its performance; the stress lies on the passing of the moment, the presence. When the narrator Yngve happens to hear the *Appassionata* on the radio in the 1950s and even recognizes the recording, he does not so much remember the 1920s as he becomes aware of the present: 'I am standing, listening – now.'[18]

When Johnson chooses to describe music based on silence and abrupt ellipsis, this is not merely due to lack of musical training. On the contrary, Johnson's autodidactic background provides him with an independent, alternative perspective on music. Not being formed by musical schooling, he is able to question the Romantic idealization of music that still prevails throughout the 20th century. The autodidact's irregular approach to culture reveals itself as a challenge to the very ideas that are handed down and reproduced in education.

18 My translation. ("Jag står där och lyssnar – nu." RB: 83).

In *Romantisk berättelse*, Johnson describes an understanding of music that thwarts Romantic ideas about what classical music ought to be, instead, he highlights what is interesting to him. The mute performance thus marks, as the musical rest within a musical notation, the passing of time, of present time. The silent description of the music is therefore not to be understood as a kind a capitulation or resignation. Turning down the volume knob results in the accentuation of the performativity of music, in particular its qualities of movement in time. This understanding of music as the present moment made visible also explains why the novel is introduced with musical notation without any explanation or reference. Already Dahlberg suspects (cf. 1999: 50) that it enhances what Genette calls the "epigraph-effect", which is "due simply to its presence" (1987/1997: 160).

References

Bernhart, Walter, Werner Wolf, eds. (2010). *Self-Reference in Literature and Music*. Word and Music Studies 11. Amsterdam/New York, NY: Rodopi.

Bruhn, Siglind (2000). *Musical Ekphrasis: Composers Responding to Poetry and Painting*. Hillsdale, NY: Pendragon.

Burgess, Anthony (1962/2000). *A Clockwork Orange*. London: Penguin.

Clüver, Claus (1997). "Ekphrasis Reconsidered: On Verbal Representations of Non-Verbal Texts". Lagerroth, Britta, Hans Lund, Erik Hedling, eds. *Interart Poetics: Essays on the Interrelations of the Arts and Media*. Amsterdam/Atlanta, GA: Rodopi. 19–34.

Dahlberg, Leif (1999). *Tre romantiska berättelser*. Stockholm/Stehag: Symposion.

Dayan, Peter (2011). *Art as Music, Music as Poetry, Poetry as Art, from Whistler, Stravinsky and Beyond*. Aldershot: Ashgate.

Genette, Gérard (1987/1997). *Paratexts: Thresholds of Interpretation*. Transl. Jane E. Lewin. Cambridge: CUP.

Hanslick, Eduard (1854/1911). *Vom Musikalisch-Schönen: Ein Beitrag zur Revision der Ästhetik der Tonkunst*. Leipzig: Breitkopf & Härtel.

Jansson, Bo G. (1990). *Självironi, självbespegling och självreflexion: den metafiktiva tendensen i Eyvind Johnsons diktning*. Uppsala: Uppsala Univ. Press/Stockholm: Almqvist & Wiksell.

Johnson, Eyvind (1953). *Romantisk berättelse*. Stockholm: Bonnier.

Lagerlöf, Selma (1891/1986). *Gösta Berlings saga*. Stockholm: Bonnier.

——— (1918). *Gösta Berling's saga*. Part II. Transl. Lillie Tudeer. London: Humphrey Milford/OUP. http://archive.org/stream/gstaberlingssagoolagegoog#page/n96/mode/2up[10/01/2014].

Nänny, Max (2002). "Ikonicitet". Hans Lund, ed. *Intermedialitet: Ord, bild och ton i samspel*. Lund: Studentlitteratur. 131–138.

Odendahl, Johannes (2008). *Literarisches Musizieren: Wege des Transfers von Musik in die Literatur bei Thomas Mann*. Bielefeld: Aisthesis.

Orton, Gavin (1972). *Eyvind Johnson*. New York, NY: Twayne.

Proust, Marcel (1992). *Du côté de chez Swann: À la recherche du temps perdu*. Tome 1. Paris: Gallimard.

——— (online). *Swann's Way: Remembrance of Things Past*. Volume One. Transl. C.K. Scott Moncrieff. New York, NY: Henry Holt, 1922. http://ebooks.adelaide .edu.au/p/proust/marcel/p96s. University of Adelaide. 2012 [10/01/2014].

Said, Edward (1991). *Musical Elaborations*. New York, NY: Columbia UP.

Scher, Steven Paul (1968). *Verbal Music in German Literature*. New Haven, CT/London: Yale UP.

Schirrmacher, Beate (2012). *Musik in der Prosa von Günter Grass: Intemediale Bezüge – Transmediale Perspektiven*. Stockholm: Acta Universitatis Stockholmiensis.

——— (2014). "The Common Grounds of Music and Violence: Depicting Violence in Literature with Intermedial References to Music". Heidi Hart, Kathy Heady, Hannah Hinz, Beate Schirrmacher, eds. *Ideology in Words and Music*. Stockholm: Acta Universitatis Stockholmiensis. 141–154.

Seaton, Douglass (2010). *Ideas and Styles in Western Musical Tradition*. 4th ed. New York, NY/Oxford: OUP.

Steiner, George (1967). *Language and Silence*. New York, NY: Atheneum.

Stenström, Thure (1978). *Romantikern Eyvind Johnson*. Stockholm: Bonnier.

Weyer, Anselm (2007). *Günter Grass und die Musik*. Frankfurt am Main: Lang.

Wolf, Werner (1999). *The Musicalization of Fiction: A Study in the Theory and History of Intermediality*. Amsterdam/Atlanta, GA: Rodopi.

Silence and Music in Mallarmé's *Un coup de dés*

Mary Breatnach

1861, the date of Baudelaire's essay "Richard Wagner et *Tannhäuser* à Paris", marks the beginning of a period in France when writers sought to establish a new aesthetic based on a hearing of the music of their time. Their wish to imbue literature with musical qualities went beyond the traditional attempt to give poetry a phonetically-based musicality through rhythmic subtlety, limpidly beautiful sound patterns and the use of musical themes and images. Taking Wagner as its primary musical referent, the aesthetic is more cerebral than sensuous and proceeds from intensely analytical acts of listening. It seeks to transfer the expressive power of music to literature primarily through a purposeful manipulation of syntax. This is the aesthetic climate in which Mallarmé wrote (etc.) *Un coup de dés jamais n'abolira le hasard*. The poem is the focus of my exploration of his concept of poetry as silent music, a concept he formulated and nurtured through years of assiduous concert-going. Focusing on a series of statements from the preface to the poem, I argue that, as part of the poem's fabric, silence is at once a dynamic and a stabilizing force in a text which is demonstrably an elaborate example of the poetry Mallarmé called 'musique *par excellence*'.

• • •

"Ne trouvez-vous pas que c'est un acte de démence?"[1] (Valéry 1950: 16)

That is how Mallarmé introduced the text of *Un coup de dés jamais n'abolira le hasard* ('A Throw of Dice Will Never Abolish Chance') to his friend and disciple, Paul Valéry, in March 1897. In May of the same year a version of the work appeared in *Cosmopolis*, a multi-lingual literary review published in London between January 1896 and November 1898. The poem was preceded by a preface, written at the request of the reading committee of the review, and also by a shorter text purporting to be an editor's note. In fact, both texts were by Mallarmé.[2]

Mallarmé's premature death in September 1898 meant that an edition he was hoping to produce, with illustrations by Odile Redon, never came to fruition. In fact until 1914, when an edition was published by the *Nouvelle Revue*

1 'Don't you think it's an act of madness?' Unless otherwise stated, all translations are mine.

2 The text of this edition together with the poet's preface ("Observation relative au poème") is included in Mallarmé 1998: 391–401.

 | DOI 10.1163/9789004314863_008

française, the poem was largely ignored.[3] Furthermore, though Mallarmé had never intended the preface to be part of the finished work, his son-in-law Edmond Bonniot, who was heavily involved in the editorial process for the 1914 edition, thought it should be included. As far as he was concerned, the preface had such significance, both in the context of the poem and in relation to the thinking of which it is a summation, that its inclusion was both expedient and appropriate.

I said a moment ago that Valéry was the first person to set eyes on Mallarmé's text. Later, recounting his reactions, he described his sense of wonder:

> Il me sembla de voir la figure d'une pensée, pour la première fois placée dans notre espace […]. Ici, véritablement, l'étendue parlait, songeait, enfantait des formes temporelles. L'attente, le doute, la concentration étaient *choses visibles* [emphasis in the original]. Ma vue avait affaire à des silences qui auraient pris corps. Je contemplais à mon aise d'inappréciables instants: la fraction d'une seconde […]; l'atome de temps, […] – paraissaient enfin comme des êtres, tout environnés de leur néant rendu sensible. […] là, sur le papier même, je ne sais quelle scintillation de dernières astres tremblait infiniment pure dans le même vide interconscient où, comme une matière de nouvelle espèce, distribuée en amas, en traînées, en systèmes, *coexistait* la parole![4] (1950: 15; emphasis in the original)

Valéry's awareness of what Roger Pickering calls "the imbrication of verbal and visual" (1992: 64) in *Un coup de dés* is clear. He emphasises especially the visual aspects of the poem, and in recent times much has been made of the influence those aspects have had on the visual arts. But the poem has also inspired musical responses, and indeed when Valéry characterised the shared motivation underlying the symbolist movement as a whole, music was his point of reference. This is what he said:

---

3 Reprinted by Gallimard in 1998 to celebrate the centenary of the poet's death.

4 'It seemed to me that I was looking at the form and pattern of a thought, placed for the first time in our space […]. Here, truly, the totality spoke, dreamt, and gave birth to temporal forms. Expectation, doubt, concentration, all these were *visible things*. I was gazing at silences that seemed to take shape. For priceless moments I could contemplate at my ease: the fraction of a second […] the atom of time […] seemed in the end like beings, surrounded by their nothingness rendered palpable. […] there, on the very paper, I know not what scintillation of recent stars trembled infinitely pure in the same interconscious empty space where, like some new species of matter, dispersed in heaps, in trails, in structures, the word *coexisted*.'

> Ce qui fut baptisé le Symbolisme se résume très simplement dans l'intention commune à plusieurs familles de poètes (d'ailleurs ennemies entre elles) de 'reprendre à la Musique leur bien'. Le secret de ce mouvement n'est pas autre.[5] (1924: 105)

The key phrase, 'reprendre à la Musique', is a direct borrowing from Mallarmé and, as Valéry's words make clear, the phrase was interpreted quite differently by different individuals and groups. For Mallarmé however it had specific and, as we shall see, almost literal connotations. Indeed it is no exaggeration to say that the phrase epitomises his aesthetic. It succinctly encapsulates and articulates his aim to write 'silent Music', that is poetry in which intelligible verbal language, words that could be read silently and privately, had been, so to speak, grafted onto the same silent structure that he believed was hidden, obscured and rendered unintelligible by the sounds of conventional music. He believed the attempt to accomplish this aim was not only his duty, but that of all contemporary poets, and he was also convinced that by accomplishing it, they would succeed in restoring poetry to its rightful position as the supreme art.

The phrase also brings together several important strands of Mallarmé's experience. One is his long-standing conviction that verbal language had to be thoroughly re-created if it was to serve the needs of modern poets and poetry. Another is his crucial encounter in 1885 with the work of Richard Wagner. Early in the summer of that year, he accepted two invitations, the first to attend a concert given by the Lamoureux orchestra, the second to write an article about Wagner for the short-lived, but highly influential *Revue wagnérienne*. Until this time, Mallarmé had taken no active interest in music and, as he readily acknowledged, he had never seen or heard any of Wagner's work (cf. 2003: 1662). As a consequence of those invitations, he was plunged into new territory, and that alone might be enough to explain why, in a letter to the editor of the review, he complained that "jamais rien ne m'a semblé plus difficile" ('never has anything ever seemed more difficult to me'; ibid.). In fact, however, a reading of the article itself shows that his struggle to write stemmed from quite a different source. Unlike so many of his fellow-countrymen, Mallarmé had grave doubts and reservations about the concept of the 'Gesamtkunstwerk' or total work of art on which

5 'What was called Symbolism can be summed up very simply in the intention, common to several groups of poets (as it happens, hostile towards one another) of "taking back from Music what belonged to them". This is the secret of the entire movement.'

Wagner's entire aesthetic was founded. The difficulty he experienced in writing the article was caused by a reluctant, but undeniable lack of enthusiasm for Wagner's work which, in its turn, was patently and inextricably linked to his profound and fundamental reservations about the art of music itself and in particular about its essential dependence on 'unintelligible sounds'.

Mallarmé chose a title for his essay that points subtly, but deliberately, to two doubly-divergent perspectives. *Richard Wagner: Rêverie d'un poëte français* (2003: 153–159) refers first to a German musician and then to a French poet. These national and disciplinary differences underpin the argument that follows and lead inexorably to what Mallarmé knew very well would be controversial conclusions. Readily acknowledging Wagner's genius and making plain his awareness of the composer's achievements, Mallarmé states categorically that Wagner's art is the most all-inclusive and wide-ranging currently to exist. Furthermore, he recounts his personal misgivings and fears that he is mistaken in failing to share the wide-spread conviction that Wagner's art represents a peak that will never be surpassed and that it truly is "le terme du chemin" ('the end of the road'; ibid.: 158). Then, as if against the backdrop of the achievements with which he is confronted, a sudden illumination and validation of his aesthetic ideas occurs, he puts all his doubts aside. Provoked by the tension between Wagner's legacy and his own artistic convictions, he confidently exposes and defends his vision of a work of pure literature which, by virtue of its all-encompassing nature and its seamless unity, will be more significant and in every way superior to anything anyone, including Wagner, has achieved so far. As he says in the autobiographical letter to Verlaine (cf. 2003: 786f.), he was convinced that such a work would one day be created and would achieve everything that artists of all ages had aspired to.

It is thus to a French poet's dream of an as-yet-unrealised work of French literature that the Gesamtkunstwerk created by the German musician is compared and found wanting. Mallarmé uses the essay to pit his personal, utopian vision of literature against Wagner's 'total work of art'. As Bertrand Marchal aptly observes:

> Quelques mois avant de faire part à Verlaine, dans sa lettre autobiographique du 16 novembre, 1885, de son rêve du Livre, cet article où se nouent les réflexions sur le théâtre, la musique, la poésie et la mythologie manifestait en tout cas, en opposant l'esprit poétique, universel et abstrait, au génie wagnérien, nationaliste et mythologique, et la rêverie d'un poète français au rêve réalisé du musicien allemand, toute la dimension d'une

> utopie poétique censée refonder non pas, comme le drame wagnérien, la nation allemande, mais la Cité terrestre.[6] (1998: 1622)

The terms in which Mallarmé discussed the act of reading in the essay "Le livre, instrument spirituel" clarify and expand the nature of that vision:

> Un solitaire tacite concert se donne, par la lecture, à l'esprit qui regagne, sur une sonorité moindre, la signification: aucun moyen mental exaltant la symphonie, ne manquera, rarifié et c'est tout – du fait de la pensée. La Poésie, proche l'idée, est Musique, par excellence – ne consent pas d'infériorité.[7] (2003: 226)

By 1895, when Mallarmé wrote this essay, the centrality of music to his aesthetic thinking was well established. Equally well-established was his concept of literary language as an essentially silent and superior kind of 'music'. His engagement with Wagner's work and his attendance at concerts played an incalculable role in those developments. At a crucial point in his career, they provided him with a musical focus that not only opened his mind to the art itself, but enabled and obliged him to hone his thinking about poetry. There is however no doubt that his long-standing creative and poetic ambitions predisposed him to respond to the indivisibility of form and content that Walter Pater famously described as the 'condition of music' and everything he wrote from 1885 to the end of his life bears witness to his abiding ambition to create a verbal, and therefore intelligible, poetic language in which music's 'condition' was silently emulated. The autobiographical letter cited by Marchal is a case in point. Consider the following extract:

> [...] j'ai toujours rêvé et tenté autre chose, avec une patience d'alchimiste [...]. Quoi? c'est difficile à dire: un livre, tout bonnement, en maints tomes,

6 'A few months before recounting to Verlaine, in his autobiographical letter of 16 November, 1885, his dream of the Book, this article, in which reflections on the theatre, music, poetry and mythology are intertwined with one another, pitting the universal and abstract poetic spirit against the nationalistic and mythological genius of Wagner and contrasting the reverie of a French poet with the already accomplished dream of the German musician, had all the marks of a poetic utopia which was intended to rebuild not the German nation, as Wagnerian drama does, but the whole earthly estate.'

7 'A solitary, silent concert is given, through reading, to the mind, which regains, because of a lesser sonority, meaning: no mental means that exalts the symphony will be missing, it's rarefied and that's all – because of thought. Poetry, close to the idea, is Music, par excellence – concedes no inferiority.'

> un livre qui soit un livre, architectural et prémédité, et non un recueil des inspirations de hasard fussent-elles merveilleuses [...]. J'irai plus loin, je dirai: le Livre, persuadé qu'au fond il n'y en a qu'un, tenté à son insu par quiconque a écrit, même les génies. L'explication orphique de la Terre, qui est le seul devoir du poëte et le jeu littéraire par excellence.[8] (Ibid.)

Mallarmé's use of the adjective "orphique" in this letter has given rise to much discussion and speculation.[9] It is undeniably an allusion to the mystical dimension that, for him, epitomised the literary struggle. But it also has important musical connotations and given the recentness of his interest in concert-going and the rapidly-growing importance of music in the context of his aesthetic thinking, it seems highly probable that he had them in mind when he used it. He had long wished to create a language that would convey meaning not through description, but through suggestion. Already in 1864, aged 22, he had written to his friend Henri Cazalis telling him that he was creating a new language characterised by a capacity to conjure up impressions rather than depict or portray: "J'invente une langue", he wrote, "qui doit nécessairement jaillir d'une poétique très nouvelle, que je pourrais définir en ces deux mots: Peindre, non la chose, mais l'effet qu'elle produit"[10] (1959: 30f.). He never wavered from his belief that what constituted the difference between literature and other forms of writing was how the writer used language, and this was a theme to which he returned many times during his life. For instance in 1891, in an interview with Jules Huret, he complained that the poets of the Parnasse used a language better suited to philosophy or rhetoric than to poetry and compared them adversely to the younger generation of poets:

> Je crois que [...] les jeunes sont plus près de l'idéal poétique que les Parnassiens qui traitent encore leurs sujets à la façon des vieux philosophes et des vieux rhéteurs, en présentant les objets directement. Je pense qu'il faut, au contraire, qu'il n'y ait qu'allusion. [...]. *Nommer* un

8 'I have always dreamt of and attempted something else, with the patience of an alchemist [...]. What? It is difficult to say: quite simply a book, in many volumes, a book which might be a book, architectural and premeditated, and not a collection of chance inspirations however wonderful they might be [...]. I shall go further, I shall say: the Book, convinced that there is basically only one, attempted unwittingly by anyone who has written, even by geniuses. The orphic explanation of the World, which is the only duty of the poet and the literary game par excellence.'

9 See for example Austin 1970 and Mcgahey 1993.

10 'I am inventing a language that must necessarily flow from a very new poetic, which I could define in these simple words: To paint, not the object, but the effect it produces.'

> objet c'est supprimer les trois quarts de la jouissance du poème qui est faite du bonheur de deviner peu à peu; le suggérer, voilà le rêve.[11] (2003: 700; emphasis in the original)

By the time he was interviewed by Huret, Mallarmé had been attending the Lamoureux concert series on Sunday afternoons for several years with a quasi-religious fervour and music had become the object of his most intense analytical thinking. His daughter tells us that he talked of going "aux vêpres" (Bonniot-Mallarmé 1926: 521), but if the concert hall was his church, it was also his laboratory. Constantly, as he listened, the poet was engaged in a sophisticated and highly personal musico-poetic experiment that was inspired on the one hand by his recognition of music's power to suggest and on the other by his belief that because of the unintelligible nature of musical language, its lack of "la vaine couche suffisante d'intelligibilité" ('the vain adequate layer of intelligibility'; 2003: 230), it was incapable of authentic communication. Verbal language alone had that capacity. He was convinced that through listening he would identify the silent, structural phenomenon that he believed was the well-spring of its suggestive power and was simply obscured by musical sounds. He believed furthermore that his task was to abstract this essentially silent phenomenon from its currently audible context and find a way of using it to structure verse. He went even further, claiming that the power he felt so strongly as he listened to music had originally, and by right, belonged to poetry. So strongly did he feel this that he accused Wagner of having arrogated to himself a role that only poetry and poets were equipped to fulfil. As he says in his *Rêverie*: "Singulier défi qu'aux poëtes dont il usurpe le devoir avec la plus candide et splendide bravoure, inflige Richard Wagner!"[12] (2003: 154)

In 1893, in *La Musique et les Lettres*, the lecture he delivered to audiences at the universities of Oxford and Cambridge, Mallarmé adopts an approach to the relationship between music and literature that at first gives an impression of even-handedness. Between music and letters, he suggests, a reciprocal relationship exists:

11 'I think [...] young people have come closer to the poetic ideal than the Parnassians who deal with their subjects more in the way of the old philosophers and orators, presenting things directly. I think on the contrary one must only suggest. [...] *To name* an object is to suppress three quarters of the pleasure of the poem, which consists in the joy of deducing, little by little; to suggest, there's the dream.'

12 'What an extraordinary challenge is inflicted on poets, whose duty he usurps with the most candid and magnificent bravura, by Richard Wagner!'

> Je pose, à mes risques esthétiquement, cette conclusion [...] que la Musique et les Lettres sont la face alternative ici élargie vers l'obscur; scintillante là avec certitude, d'un phénomène, le seul, je l'appelai l'Idée.
>
> L'un des modes incline à l'autre et y disparaissant, ressort avec emprunts: deux fois se parachève, oscillant, un genre entier. Théâtralement, pour la foule qui assiste, sans conscience, à l'audition de sa grandeur: ou l'individu requiert la lucidité, du livre explicatif et familier.[13] (2003: 69)

But here too the terms of the contrast posited between the two arts tells its tale. On one side, the 'obscurity' of audible music is paired with the listeners' lack of awareness. On the other side the individual's need for coherence and rationality is met by the dazzling 'certitude' of literature. Mallarmé's partiality is beyond doubt. He spells it out more plainly in the following passage from *Crise de vers* in which, writing of instrumental sounds with barely-disguised contempt, he gives us a glimpse of himself as a listener buoyed by a profound belief in the superiority of the 'silent concert' provided by reading and motivated by an intense quest to penetrate beyond audible musical sound to the silent structure underpinning it.

> Certainement je ne m'assieds jamais aux gradins des concerts, sans percevoir parmi l'obscure sublimité telle ébauche de quelqu'un des poëmes immanents à l'humanité ou leur originel état, d'autant plus compréhensible que tu et que pour en déterminer la vaste ligne le compositeur éprouva cette facilité de suspendre jusqu'à la tentation de s'expliquer. Je me figure par un indéracinable préjugé d'écrivain, que rien ne demeurera sans être proféré; que nous en sommes là, précisément, à rechercher [...] un art d'achever la transposition, au Livre, de la symphonie ou uniment de reprendre notre bien: car, ce n'est pas de sonorités élémentaires par les cuivres, les cordes, les bois, indéniablement mais de l'intellectuelle parole à son apogée que doit avec plénitude et évidence, résulter, en tant que l'ensemble des rapports existant dans tout, la Musique.[14] (2003: 212)

---

13 'I put forward, at my own risk aesthetically, this conclusion [...]: that Music and Letters are two sides of the same coin, here extended towards obscurity; there glittering with certainty, of one phenomenon, the only one, let me call it the Idea.

One of the modes leaning towards the other and disappearing into it, re-emerges with borrowings: twice, oscillating, a whole genre is perfected. Theatrically, for the crowd who attends, without awareness, to the hearing of its own grandeur, or for the individual who requires clarity, that of the explanatory and familiar book.'

14 'Certainly, I never sit in a concert hall without becoming aware, within the obscure sublimity, of an outline of one of the poems immanent to humanity or their original form, all

The scene depicted here by the poet is described from the outside by his disciple, Valéry, whose observations provide us with some important factual information:

> On le voyait, le crayon aux doigts, qui notait ce qu'il trouvait de profitable à la poésie dans la musique, essayant d'en extraire quelques types de rapports qui pussent être transportés dans le domaine du langage. Il rêvait tout l'été à ce qu'il avait ainsi noté pendant l'hiver.[15] (1950: 71)

No-one ever knew what those notes contained, but if only because Mallarmé had no technical knowledge of music, it is safe to assume that they did not contain musicological insights. Also worth emphasising is the fact that he never sought to imitate tangible musical qualities in verse. Moreover, he was highly critical of those who attempted to do so. Take for instance the following letter written to René Ghil in 1885 in which Mallarmé faults Ghil for 'phrasing as a composer rather than as a writer':

> Je vous blâmerai d'une seule chose: c'est que dans cet acte de juste restitution, qui doit être le nôtre, de tout reprendre à la musique […] vous laissez un peu s'évanouir le vieux dogme du vers […]. Vous phrasez en compositeur, plutôt qu'en écrivain: je saisis bien votre désir exquis, ayant passé par-là, pour en revenir comme vous le ferez peut-être de vous meme.[16] (1965: 286)

---

the more comprehensible for being silent and for the fact that the composer, in order to establish its vast line, felt not the slightest temptation to expose his thoughts. I imagine, because of what is doubtless an ineradicable writer's prejudice, that nothing will remain without being uttered; that we are here, precisely, to look for […] a way of completing the transposition, to the Book, of the symphony or simply to take back what belongs to us; for it is not from the elementary sonorities of the brass, the strings, the woodwind, but, undeniably, from the intellectual word at its apogee that Music, as the totality of relationships existing in everything, must result with fullness and clarity.'

15 'He could be seen, pencil in hand, noting down things he found in music that would be useful for poetry, trying to extract some types of connections that could perhaps be carried over into the domain of language. All summer he mulled over the things he had noted down in this way during the winter.'

16 'I would criticize you for just one thing: in this act of just restitution which we must carry out – that is, to take everything back from music […] you allow the old dogma of verse to vanish somewhat […]. You phrase as a composer rather than as a writer: I'm well aware of your exquisite wishes, having been down that route myself; only to come back from it as you will perhaps of your own accord.'

On another occasion, in a letter to Dujardin, he complained about the burdensome nature of a label placed on him by Ghil in a letter in *Le Figaro*:

> Vous avez vu la lettre déplorable écrite par Ghil au *Figaro*. Je viens de lui marquer à quel point je la regrette. Symboliste instrumentiste! quel pavé, et comme on est des choses à la fois sans le savoir.[17] (1969: 133)

But then, Mallarmé was not given to making things easy. One of the great difficulties confronting those who want to understand his musico-poetic thinking is his ambiguous use of the noun itself. In Mallarmé's texts, music refers to two quite different phenomena: it can, and often does, refer simply to the art as we know it, an art of sound. Alternatively it can refer to poetry, or rather to a certain kind of poetry, the kind he wished to write, and thus, by implication, to an art from which the element of sound as it existed in conventional music was excluded. Sometimes he capitalises the word when using it in the latter sense. Often he does not. Just once, in a letter to Edmund Gosse, he made the distinction very clear. Gosse had published an article in *The Academy*, a British periodical, in which he had attempted to define the aim of Mallarmé's writing. Mallarmé's objective, he said, was "to use words in such harmonious combination as will suggest to the reader a mood or a condition *which is not mentioned in the text*, but is nevertheless paramount in the poet's mind at the moment of composition" (1998: 807; emphasis in the original). This perception went well beyond simply meeting with Mallarmé's approval: it prompted what is undoubtedly the least ambiguous account we have of what he meant when he spoke of music in a poetic context:

> Vous […] désignez la chose avec une clairvoyance de diamant. Tout est là. Je fais de la Musique, et appelle ainsi non celle qu'on peut tirer du rapprochement euphonique des mots, cette première condition va de soi; mais l'au-delà magiquement produit par certaines dispositions de la parole, où celle-ci ne reste qu'à l'état de moyen de communication matérielle avec le lecteur comme les touches du piano. Vraiment entre les lignes et au-dessus du regard cela se passe, en toute pureté, sans l'entremise de cordes à boyaux et de pistons comme à l'orchestre, qui est déjà industriel; mais c'est la même chose que l'orchestre, sauf que littérairement ou silencieusement. […] Employez *Musique* dans le sens grec, au fond signifiant

---

17 'You've seen the deplorable letter written by Ghil to the *Figaro*. I have just told him how much I regret it. Symbolist instrumentalist! What a burden, and how astonishing that one is all sorts of things at once without knowing it!'

> Idée ou rythme entre des rapports; là plus divine que dans son expression publique ou symphonique.[18] (Ibid.; emphasis in the original)

The more one reads this letter, the more one realises the complexity of the thinking underlying it. In strikingly factual terms Mallarmé describes a sequence of events that is difficult if not impossible to verify. He makes three distinct, but closely related statements. First he states quite categorically that he 'makes Music'. Second, and equally unequivocally, he declares that the Music he makes has nothing to do with sound. Finally he puts forward a definition of the phenomenon in question: 'Music is the beyond magically produced by certain dispositions of language'. Mallarmé thus reveals how this silent Music is generated, crucially portraying the fundamentally catalytic function of verbal structures in his work and thus underlining the centrality of Music to his aesthetic as a whole. Magically, mysteriously, the "rythme entre des rapports", that abstract, essentially silent structural or relational phenomenon that constitutes Mallarméan Music, is generated by means of its tangible literary counterpart, that is to say, by syntax.

The Platonic and Pythagorean overtones in what Mallarmé wrote to Gosse are unmistakeable. On the other hand, by asserting that his Music 'is the same thing as the orchestra', with the important difference that 'it occurs in a literary or silent form', he makes plain his intention to exceed the metaphorical limits often associated with such overtones. By the same token he claims a certain authenticity for his Music-making, and what lends sustainability to this claim is, more than anything else, the accuracy of his perception of the nature and workings of musical language, in particular his recognition of the identity between thought and language that characterises music, together with the contingent importance of structure.

I suggested earlier that the phrase 'reprendre à la musique notre bien' sums up Mallarmé's aesthetic as a whole. Nothing else he ever said captures his poetic convictions and motivations so succinctly. Arguably his indefatigable

18 'You describe things with such sharp insight. Everything is there. I make Music, and give that name not to the music that can be drawn from the euphonious grouping together of the words, this first kind needs no discussion, but to the beyond magically produced by certain dispositions of language, where the latter is present only as a means of material communication with the reader, like piano keys. Truly, between the lines and above the gaze this occurs, in total purity, without intervention from gut strings and valves as in the orchestra, which is already industrial; but it is the same thing as the orchestra, except that it occurs in a literary or silent form. [...] Use *Music* in the Greek sense, really meaning Idea or rhythm between the relationships; thus more divine than in its public or symphonic expression.'

efforts to imbue poetic language with music's power account in large measure for his famously idiosyncratic syntax and thus for the so-called 'difficulty' of his writing. Given his deep-seated reservations about music, the suggestion that his recognition of its power plays such a significant role in the development of his art is surely ironic. But this in no way alters the fact that for him the ultimate literary work could only be accomplished once poets had re-appropriated from music what belonged by right to them.

The musico-poetic thinking that I have outlined confirms something that is often said: Mallarmé's thinking about literature and, in particular, about the workings of poetic language, was well ahead of his time. A related matter which, as far as I am aware, has not been commented upon is the surprisingly modern nature of his insight into the way musical communication works. In some respects, rather than echoing the attitudes prevalent among musicians of his own time, Mallarmé's perceptions echo those of musicians of recent generations. Practising musicians especially would recognise from personal experience a certain similarity between Mallarmé's concept of making silent Music and the work that goes into preparing a piece for performance. To study a work in order to perform it is to embark on a sometimes slow, often arduous process of analysing its structures and their implications. This is not a matter of formal musicological analysis, though of course such analysis may play a role. It is rather a matter of what the pianist and musicologist Roy Howat calls the "task of 'reading back through'" what is written on the page. In an essay entitled "What Do We Perform?", Howat raises a pertinent question: "Can we actually 'interpret music'?", he asks. His reply is unequivocal:

> Surely not [...]. What we can interpret – indeed, can only interpret – is its notation. Since notation, to quote the ever-literal French, 'partitions' music (that is, represents or encodes it in [...] symbols, involving variable conventions and shorthands), it cannot avoid distorting it, and our task is to 'read back through' the distortions on paper, employing aural and visual awareness, skill and sensitivity. (1995: 3)

The parallel between the task described above by Howat and Mallarmé's 'Music-making' is striking. Indeed the poet himself drew that parallel in his letter to Gosse when he compared the words in a poem to the keys of a piano, going so far as to claiming parity between his Music and orchestral music – with the vital difference, carefully emphasised, that literary Music is essentially silent.

Mallarmé ends the first sentence of the preface to *Un coup de dés* with a bold claim: "Le tout", he says, referring to his text, "[est] sans nouveauté qu'un espacement de la lecture" ('apart from its spacing, the entire text [is] without novelty'; 1998: 391). He then proceeds to substantiate his remark, acknowledging at the same time the impact his use of blank space will inevitably have on the reader:

> Les 'blancs', en effet, assument l'importance, frappent d'abord; la versification en exigea, comme silence alentour, ordinairement, au point qu'un morceau, lyrique ou de peu de pieds, occupe, au milieu, le tiers environ du feuillet: je ne transgresse cette mesure, seulement la disperse.[19] (Ibid.)

This series of statements is, on a certain level, incontrovertible: no-one would deny that spacing has always played an important role in the way verse appears or is presented on the page. Yet it is difficult to accept the idea that the only thing that has happened in this particular poem is that the conventional proportion of text to silence, what he calls 'la mesure', has been broken up. Indeed, faced with what seems, even in the twenty-first century, an almost monstrously original literary work, it is hard not to balk at the idea that we are dealing with something quite as close to the conventional as Mallarmé claims. But let us put it to the test.[20]

To open the text of *Un coup de dés jamais n'abolira le hasard* is to be struck straight away by its layout. In order to read continuously to the end of the title sentence, one must turn no fewer than eight of the poem's eleven double-pages.[21] The first four words ("Un coup de dés") confront one on the right-hand side of the first double page. In order to read the fifth, ("jamais"), one must turn to the second double page. The sixth ("n'abolira") appears on the right-hand side of the fifth double page and the final two words on the right-hand side of the ninth. Thus a simple reading of the title sentence requires one to turn nine of the eleven double pages that the text consists of. It is impossible to do this without becoming aware of the patterns formed by the numerous words and phrases that spread across the double pages in many different type faces and font sizes, and of the importance of the blank space that stretches silently between them. Though this is merely the beginning of an arduous process lying ahead of any reader willing to persist in familiarising him- or herself with

---

19 'The "blanks" indeed take on importance, strike one at first; versification demanded them, as a surrounding silence, usually, so much so that a fragment, lyrical or of a few feet, occupies, in the middle, a third of the page: I do not transgress this measure, only disperse it.'

20 Given the impracticality of reproducing the text of *Un Coup de dés* in the present context, I refer readers to the published version in 1998: 366–387.

21 Drawing attention to "la vision simultanée de la Page" ('the simultaneous vision of the Page'), Mallarmé states that in the poem, this vision rather than "le Vers ou ligne parfait" ('the Verse or perfect line') is "prise pour unité" ('taken as the unit') (1998: 191).

the work, it is already enough to alert him or her to the comprehensive effects of what Mallarmé so modestly calls the dispersal of the space demanded, as he claims, by all versification, however simple and traditional it may be. Perhaps the most far-reaching and radical of those effects is that the blank space, which traditionally surrounded a poem and would therefore have been perceived as something external to the text itself, has here become a vital part of the poem itself. Mallarmé has created a text in which silence has become a visible and integral aspect of composition.

My description of reading the title sentence conveys some sense of what it is to read *Un coup de dés*. The way the reader's eye and mind are supported and compelled in equal measure by blank space enables him or her both to separate and connect in meaningful ways the myriad 'dispositions de la parole' that make up the text. To read is to consent to be drawn into this text in which the role played by silence or its literary equivalent, blank space, is as important and necessary as that played by the words and their syntactic groupings. Drawing particular attention to what he calls the 'literary' advantages of his use of blank space, Mallarmé says that it not only affects speed and movement, but also structures time and space:

> L'avantage, si j'ai droit à le dire, littéraire, de cette distance copiée qui mentalement sépare des groupes de mots ou les mots entre eux, semble d'accélérer tantôt et de ralentir le mouvement, le scandant, l'intimant même selon une vision simultanée de la Page.[22] (1998: 191)

At this point Mallarmé introduces what is perhaps the best-known passage in his preface:

> Tout se passe, par raccourci, en hypothèse; on évite le récit.
> Ajouter que de cet emploi à nu de la pensée avec retraits, prolongements, fuites, ou son dessin même, résulte, pour qui veut lire à haute voix, une partition.[23] (Ibid.)

22 'The literary advantage, if I may say so, of this duplicated distance which mentally separates groups of words or words from one another seems to be the intermittent acceleration and slowing-down of movement, scanning it, even ordering it in accordance with a simultaneous vision of the Page.'

23 'Everything happens, by means of shortening, as hypothesis; narrative is avoided. Let me add that from this unadorned use of thought with retractions, prolongations, flights, or its very design, results, for anyone who wishes to read aloud, a score.'

The phrase "à haute voix" ('aloud'), raises questions that require more discussion than is possible in this essay. Placing it in the context of Mallarméan textual aesthetics, the linguist Roy Harris makes some pertinent observations: "To suggest", he says,

> that Mallarmé is seriously thinking here of an oral delivery of his poem would miss the point of the metaphor. The score, for Mallarmé, is the paragon of a written text which presents directly, without ambiguity, what it signifies – the musical work, the composer's thoughts; whereas poets, on the contrary, are perpetually obliged to struggle against the constraints of language through which they must express themselves. (2001: 218)

One might also suggest that it is an example of Mallarmé's impish sense of humour. It often showed itself in his choice of vocabulary, and it would not be out of character for him knowingly to put his readers, as it were, off scent. Be that as it may, the word "partition" that seems indeed to relate to this idea of sound and is always interpreted as a musical reference in this particular context, also has, as Howat points out (see above), non-musical, essentially silent connotations. The *Petit Robert* dictionary offers two distinct definitions. The second – "notation d'une composition musicale" ('notation of a musical composition') – is the one that translates into English as 'score'. The first however – "PARTITION: partage d'un ensemble en parties non vides, disjointes deux à deux et dont la réunion reconstitue cet ensemble" ('division of a whole into non-empty parts, spread out two by two, the reunion of which reconstitutes this whole') – concentrates on the soundless connotations of the word. Significantly, it echoes Mallarmé's description of how the lay-out functions:

> Le papier intervient chaque fois qu'une image [...] cesse ou rentre, acceptant la succession d'autres et [...] c'est à des places variables [...] que s'impose le texte.[24] (1998: 391)

What I have called the non-musical definition of "partition" fits this account with remarkable ease. To borrow the dictionary terms, the 'non-empty' parts of the work – the text or images – are divided and spread at intervals across the empty, silent space of the double-page. Each in turn catches the reader's eye, then gives way to, or is replaced by, another.

---

24 'The paper intervenes each time an image [...] dies away or reenters, allowing others to follow and [...] it is in variable places [...] that the text stands out.'

What then of the musical definition? Its relevance is conclusively confirmed in a very Mallarméan twist. Recalling once again the process of 'making Music' that the poet described in his letter to Gosse (see above), we find a remarkable similarity between it and the process of reading that he describes here. Just as the "dispositions de la parole" referred to in the letter act as catalysts in the production of the silent, literary phenomenon that is Mallarméan Music, so the interplay between the blank space and the images or text in *Un coup de dés* result in a "partition" in the musical sense of the word. Thus the same word that makes it possible for him to refer to his startlingly bold break with traditional form in graphic terms also allows him to suggest discreetly, but clearly that he may indeed have created a work through which his readers may experience the 'solitary silent concert' he wrote of in 1895.

References

Austin, L.J. (1970). "Mallarmé et le mythe d'Orphée". *Cahiers de l'Association internationale des études françaises* 22/22: 169–180.

Bonniot-Mallarmé, Geneviève (1926). "Mallarmé par sa fille". *La Nouvelle Revue Française* 158: 517–523.

Harris, Roy (2001). *Rethinking Writing*. London: Continuum.

Howat, Roy (1995). "What Do We Perform?". John Rink, ed. *The Practice of Performance: Studies in Musical Interpretation*. Cambridge: CUP. 3–20.

Mallarmé, Stéphane (1959). *Correspondance*, I. Eds. Henri Mondor, Jean-Pierre Richard. Paris: Gallimard.

——— (1965). *Correspondance*, II. Eds. Henri Mondor, Lloyd James Austin. Paris: Gallimard.

——— (1969). *Correspondance*, III. Eds. Henri Mondor, Lloyd James Austin. Paris: Gallimard.

——— (1998). *Œuvres complètes*, I. Ed. Bertrand Marchal. Paris: Gallimard.

——— (2003). *Œuvres complètes*, II. Ed. Bertrand Marchal. Paris: Gallimard.

Mcgahey, R. (1993). "The Orphic Moment of Stéphane Mallarmé". *Nineteenth-Century French Studies* 21/3–4: 402–418.

Pickering, Robert (1992). "Writing and the Page: Rimbaud, Mallarmé, Valéry". *The Modern Language Review*: 56–71.

Valéry, Paul (1924). *Variété*. Paris: Gallimard.

——— (1950). *Écrits divers sur Stéphane Mallarmé*. Paris: Gallimard.

Silence and the Sawmill: Rainer Maria Rilke on the Nuisance of Sounding Music

Axel Englund

Addressing various passages from Rainer Maria Rilke's correspondence as well as a small selection of poems – "Musik", written in 1899, "An die Musik" from 1918, and a handful of the 1922 *Sonette an Orpheus* – the present paper attempts an interpretation of the nexus of sound and silence, poetry and music in his work. Rilke, I argue, wants to salvage the silence, privacy and integrity that he associates with his own art. This art, as he perceives it, finds its material form par excellence in the written word, produced and perceived in silence. The noisy soundscape of modernity is an obvious threat to this silence, which forces Rilke to seek solitary and isolated surroundings. But music, too, is wont to disturb: understood as actual, sounding performance, it is a public art that gives itself indiscriminately to anyone and everyone. In keeping with this notion, Rilke associates it with an inner formlessness and a tendency towards giving oneself away in all-too candid conversation. When he does speak favourably of music, he returns to notions of silence as the essential aspect of it – its mute verso is what really interests him. Hence, however compelling music may seem to Rilke at certain points in his life, it can only serve him as an idea, a projection based on the written word, but never as an actual, sounding presence.

•••

A Song of Steel

For Rainer Maria Rilke, April of 1921 was a cruel month. He was residing in the solitary Schloß Berg am Irchel, Switzerland, attempting to overcome the creative impasse from which he had been suffering for almost a decade, and which was to give way to a flood of creativity less than a year later. Writing to Marie von Thurn und Taxis on 19 November 1920, soon after his arrival, he had described the quietude of the site as the main reason for his stay:

> Ich hause allein [...] mit einer Wirtschafterin, die mich ebenso schweigsam versorgt, wie ich mich schweigsam versorgen lasse; ein verlassener Park, der gegen die stille Landschaft zu offen steht, keine Bahnstation in der Nähe und gegenwärtig obendrein lauter, wegen der

 | DOI 10.1163/9789004314863_009

> Maul- und Klauenseuche, abgesperrte Straßen – donc retraite absolue –.[1] (1950: II/186)

In April, however, these conditions changed abruptly, as a new and unwelcome element entered Rilke's quiet idyll. On the eighth of the month, he wrote in despair to his intermittent lover, the painter Baladine Klossowska:

> Pensez, on a installé une 'Scierie électrique' (ein elektrisches Sägewerk) tout en face de la sortie droite du parc, […] qui fait un bruit continuel, atroce, d'acier chantant qui attaque avec une cruauté de dentiste ce pauvre bois admirable qu'on ramène de la forêt […] mon beau beau silence! […] Diese Zerstörung des reinen Gehörs ist so fürchterlich für mich, weil mir jeder Gedanke erst wirklich wird, wenn ich ihn mir auch in klanglichen Aequivalenten darstellen kann, ihn auf eine reinste Gehörfläche projizierend; mein Gehör so fremdlings überfüllt zu finden, ist nicht anders, als sollte ich auf ein über und über bekritzeltes und beflecktes Papier schreiben –.[2] (1954: 310)

It is easy to sympathize with Rilke's vexation. What is most interesting here, however, are the terms in which he describes his predicament. Pure white paper and pure silence are the prerequisites of his poetic imagination, as if he needed to be liberated from sensual impressions of sight and sound in order for his thoughts to become real in their place.

What destroys the purity of silence, significantly, is an emblem of industrial modernity: the noisy machine. To Rilke, silence is the natural element of poetry, threatened by the evolving soundscape of the twentieth century. The sawmill severs him from the realm of pure thought and poetry. This evocation of a purity that has become inaccessible to us is quite representative of Rilke.

---

1 'I live alone […] with a housekeeper, who is as silent in attending to me as I am silent in letting myself be attended to; an abandoned park, which opens toward the quiet landscape, no train station nearby and besides that only closed streets at present, due to the foot-and-mouth disease – hence absolute seclusion –.' (Unless otherwise indicated, all translations are mine.)

2 'Imagine, an "Electric sawmill" has been installed right across the right exit from the park, […] which makes a continuous, atrocious noise of singing steel, attacking the poor admirable wood, that is taken from the forest, with the cruelty of a dentist […] my beautiful beautiful silence! […] This destruction of pure hearing is so horrible to me, because every thought is real to me only when I can represent it to myself in sounding equivalents too, projecting it on the purest surface of hearing; to find my hearing so overfull of foreign elements, is no different from writing on a paper that has been scribbled on and stained over and over –.'

Perhaps the most insistently recurrent gesture in his work is the projection of a partitioned universe, in which we have lost contact with whatever lies beyond the partition – the spiritual, eternal and mystical aspects of the world. To Rilke, this dichotomized world is a direct effect of modernity: under the dominion of instrumental reason, metropolitan anonymity, technological innovation and the accelerating pace of our lives, we no longer have access to the mystical side of existence, but remain locked within the immediately perceptible reality that surrounds us. Insofar as that reality is perceived through the sense of hearing, it is sound that prevents us from reaching beyond it – in particular sounds as obtrusive as those of noisy factories and electric saws. As a result, Rilke's evocations of silence often cast it as a vehicle of crossing the divide: like the white, unsullied paper, the utopian projection of a pure silence is the arena where poetry may reconcile us with the world beyond our senses.

Describing the sound of the sawmill, notably, Rilke uses the world "chantant" – it is a terrible song of steel that destroys both the trees and the silence. Although music and song have so often been cast as a means of reaching precisely that side of existence that Rilke perceives as lost within modernity, it is not self-evidently on the side of poetry. In his early work, music is often dismissed or disparaged, variously because it is violent, threatening, seductive or simply distracting.[3] In the late poems – written after his long period of relative unproductivity – he begins more frequently to consider music seriously as a positive force. Even then, however, his conception of music and song is typically defined in contradistinction to sounds we can actually hear. The most important work in this context is the *Sonnets to Orpheus* (*Sonette an Orpheus*), written in a feverish flow of inspiration in February 1922 and together with the *Duino Elegies* (*Duineser Elegien*), completed in the same month, typically considered the apex of Rilke's poetic achievement.

The first poem that I want to address, however, is simply entitled "Musik". It was written in 1899 and later included in his *Book of Images* (*Das Buch der Bilder*). It pits music against silence, strongly preferring the latter:

> Was spielst du, Knabe? Durch die Garten gings
> wie viele Schritte, flüsternde Befehle.
> Was spielst du, Knabe? Siehe deine Seele
> verfing sich in den Stäben der Syrinx.
>
> Was lockst du sie? Der Klang ist wie ein Kerker,
> darin sie sich versäumt und sich versehnt;

3 For an overview of such remarks, see, for instance, Schoolfield 1992.

stark ist dein Leben, doch dein Lied ist stärker,
an deine Sehnsucht schluchzend angelehnt. –

Gib ihr ein Schweigen, daß die Seele leise
heimkehre in das Flutende und Viele,
darin sie lebte, wachsend, weit und weise,
eh du sie zwangst in deine zarten Spiele.

Wie sie schon matter mit den Flügeln schlägt:
so wirst du, Träumer, ihren Flug vergeuden,
daß ihre Schwinge, vom Gesang zersägt,
sie nicht mehr über meine Mauern trägt,
wenn ich sie rufen werde zu den Freuden.
(1975: 1/379f.)

What do you play, boy? It went through the gardens
like many footsteps, like whispering commands.
What do you play, boy? Look, your soul
got caught in the syrinx's bars.

Why do you lure it? The sound is like a prison
in which it languishes and pines away;
your life is strong, but your song is stronger,
sobbingly propped on your desire. –

Give it a silence, that the soul may lightly
turn home into the flooding and fullness
in which it lived, growing, wise and spacious,
until forced into your tender playing.

How it already beats its wings more faintly:
thus will you, dreamer, waste its flight,
so that its wings, severed by the singing,
will no longer carry it over my walls
when I shall call it to the deep delights.
(1991: 29)

Silence, in this poem, is what the soul needs to take flight. It is not just any kind of silence, however, but the respite from song and music. Not only because those are the sounds evoked by the poem, but also because the word "Schweigen" (l. 9) in itself already denotes the absence of voice, speech or song. Those phenomena converge as the opposites of this poem's silence under the aegis of its title: music. The music produced by the boy is defined in various, quite curious, ways: the "viele Schritte" (l. 2) associates it with a crowd passing through the garden. The "flüsternde Befehle" (l. 2) turns it into an authoritarian force, which is developed into the notion of incarceration in the phrase "verfing sich in den Stäben" (l. 4). The word 'Stäbe', here, conflates the pipes of the pan flute with the bars of a prison: it is the concrete, physical source of the music – the syrinx – that is evoked as an image of confinement. It catches and confines the soul, and circumscribes its capacity for transcendence. The sound itself is a dungeon – "ein Kerker" (l. 5) – in which the soul will eventually perish. On the one hand, its authority is soft, consisting of whispered commands and gentle playing. On the other hand, it is ruthlessly violent: in a surprisingly brutal image, music enforces its law not only by holding the soul captive, but by sawing its wings off to prevent it from rising above the barriers that surround it, thus siding with the sawmill as a destroyer of soulful silence.

In his Florentine diaries from 1898, about a year before writing "Musik", Rilke advocates the 'separatist' view that every work in one of the arts must fulfil the task of Art with a capital A, without being combined with each other in any way. The arts are to be entirely self-sufficient: "Ein Gemälde darf keines Textes, eine Statue keiner Farbe [...] und ein Gedicht keiner Musik brauchen, vielmehr muss in jedem alles enthalten sein"[4] (qtd. Deinert 1973: 10). His own artistic medium, notably, is defined against music.

As the "viele Schritte" – a public invasion of private space associated with the boy's playing in the second line of "Musik" – suggest, Rilke perceived of music as an art that serves to make poetry public. From early on, he seems to have had a profound distaste for the public aspects of art. In the Florentine diary he speaks of the performance of poetry together with music as a concession to the mindless crowd, "das sich in seiner Trägheit am liebsten eine Kunst von der zweiten kommentieren lassen möchte"[5] (qtd. ibid.: 11). The same even goes for theatre: Rilke considers the stage itself a concession to the crowd, which really just desecrates drama (cf. ibid.).

Literature, to Rilke, is essentially silent and private, and this is one of the reasons for his reverence for the artistic medium, and for his not wanting it to get mixed up with the other, publically performed arts. Even talking to people, it appears, could at times be too public. In a 1904 letter to Clara Rilke, he makes the following remarks about having engaged in conversation:

---

4 'A painting must not need a text, a statue no colour, and a poem no music. Instead, everything must be contained within each of them'.

5 '[...] which in its dullness would prefer to have one art comment on the other'.

> Und wie schuldig fühlt man sich! Früher glaubte ich immer, es käme aus einem Bedauern, sich an nicht ganz Feine, Reife weggegeben zu haben; aber nein, es kommt einfach daher, daß Ausgeben Sünde ist, Musik ist, Hingabe ist. Im Grunde muß man sich vor seinen besten Worten zuschließen und in die Einsamkeit gehen.[6] (1950: I/95)

In this curious statement, music is aligned with communication and immorality. It is the sounding opposite of silent integrity, public and indiscriminate. The guilt is akin to the accusation levelled at the flute-playing boy in "Musik": of having yielded to music's temptation. Giving oneself out and giving oneself away is a sin: words should not be spoken, songs should not be sung. Both should be enclosed and protected by silence and solitude.

Rilke and Benvenuta: (Un)Welcome Music

This strange association between music and opening oneself up seems to echo on into, and interestingly illuminate, an episode that took place in 1914: Rilke's correspondence and encounter with a Viennese pianist by the name of Magda von Hattingberg. On 26 January, she wrote an admiring letter to Rilke, which was the beginning of an intense contact; during one month, they wrote to each other almost every day, and Rilke's letters are among the most emotional and candid in the whole body of his correspondence (see Rilke 2000).

The encounter with von Hattingberg was preceded by an increased interest in music on Rilke's part, which seems to have occurred in the two years before the outbreak of the First World War.[7] During a journey to Spain in late 1912, he read a collection of essays entitled *La musique* by the French theoretician Antoine Fabre d'Olivet (1768–1825), which he had actually purchased on behalf of a friend but found intriguing himself. He writes enthusiastically to Marie von Thurn und Taxis about Fabre d'Olivet's emphasis on "das Stumme in der Musik, [...] ihre mathematische Rückseite"[8] (1950: I/408). Rather than the

6 'And how guilty one feels! I used to believe that it came from a regret about having given oneself away to someone not quite exquisite and mature; but no, it simply comes from the fact that imparting is sin, is music, is submission. At bottom, one must close oneself before one's best words and enter into solitude.'

7 See Pasewalck 2000, who specifically addresses Rilke's changing attitudes to music in the years 1912–1914 and their relevance to a changing concept of sight and hearing in the late works.

8 '[...] the mute part of music, [...] its mathematical verso'.

polarized opposition evoked in "Musik" from 1899, silence is a part of music – the *essential* part, even:

> Hinter diesem Vor-wand [sic] von Tönen nähert sich das All, auf der einen Seite sind wir, auf der andern, durch nichts von uns abgetrennt, als durch ein bißchen gerührte Luft, aufgeregt durch uns, zittert die Neigung der Sterne.[9] (1950: 1/409)

The sounding notes are a "Vor-wand" ('pretext'). The punning hyphenation aligns itself with Rilke's idea of a partitioned universe, where we have lost contact with the other side: it suggests that the sounding notes form a wall ('Wand'), which is placed before us ('vor'), to seal us off from the cosmos. The sensually perceptible side of music, then, is little but an aural smokescreen that prevents us from gaining access to its essential aspects.[10]

However, von Hattingberg's enthusiasm about the possibility of her playing giving Rilke what his writings have already given her, seems to chime in with certain hopes of his vis-à-vis music at this time, and he gives her the name "Benvenuta". Recounting an episode from the sojourn in Spain, when he was also reading Fabre d'Olivet, he suggests the reason for her being so welcome:

> [...] plötzlich [...] wurde mir klar, dass mein Sehen überladen sei, [...] da saß ich und war wie am Ende meiner Augen, als müsste man jetzt blind werden um die eingenommenen Bilder herum, oder [...] künftig durch einen ganz anderen Sinn die Welt empfangen: Musik, Musik: das wär es gewesen.[11] (2000: 23)

After Rodin's profound influence on his poetry from the preceding decade, then, vision seemed to have lost its crucial role to him, and Rilke considers setting his hopes to the sense of hearing and the art of music: "Ihre Musik ist wie irgend eine einmal kommende Jahreszeit vor mir"[12] (ibid.: 24). It seems,

9 'Behind this pretext of notes the cosmos is approaching, we are on the one side, on the other, separated from us by nothing than some moving air upset by us, the inclination of the stars is trembling.'

10 Rilke's lack of a musical ear, to which he confessed on numerous occasions, is probably an important factor here. Cf. Schoolfield 1992: 269 and Deinert 1973: 87f.

11 '[...] suddenly [...] it was clear to me that my vision was overburdened, [...] there I was at the end of my eyes, as if one had to become blind in order to receive the images that were all around, or [...] in the future receive the world through a different sense entirely: music, music: that would have been it.'

12 'Your music lies ahead of me like some season that will once arrive'.

however, that the future is a key word. Von Hattingberg writes on 2 February: "Ja ich möchte wirklich nach Paris und garnicht mehr so klug und dumm und vorbehaltlich als 'Plan' den man hübsch erwägt und so vernünftig am Ende ausführt"[13] (ibid.: 33). Replying two days later, Rilke encourages the idea – "Meine Freundin, kämen Sie doch" ('My friend, if you would but come') (ibid.: 34). On the afternoon of the same day, however, he writes in a second letter about the difficulties of making music in his present lodgings, and adds: "Und jemehr ichs bedenke, so ist das am Ende gut, dass es *jetzt* und *hier* nicht sein kann. Ich habe manches unternommen, was ich in derselben Verfassung […] zu seinem Ausgang bringen muss, denn mit jedem Ton […] kommen andere Zeiten für andere Dinge."[14] (Ibid.: 37) He also sends a telegram the next day, saying: "Nein rufen darf ich jetzt gleich nicht nach Musik jemehr ichs bedenke"[15] (ibid.: 204). Here, as elsewhere in the correspondence, Benvenuta's person and her music merge. Together, they seem to promise Rilke a way forward. Neither seems particularly welcome as a physical presence – it cannot be *here* and *now* – but both are intriguing as mental projections or hopes for the future, encountered via the medium of the written word and read in silence and solitude.

In the end, however, he does meet her, in Berlin in February 1913. In the next months, they travel together to Paris, Switzerland and Italy. Rilke experiences a lot of music under her guidance, including regular listening lessons, and expresses his admiration for Handel, Bach and Beethoven in particular (cf. Deinert 1973: 95). After a few months, however, Rilke ends their association and returns to Paris. Writing to Lou Andreas-Salomé in a despondent mood in early July, he refers to what happened as months of suffering, and admits that in spite of the high hopes that the correspondence had awoken in him, "drei (nicht gekonnte) Monate Wirklichkeit haben etwas wie ein kaltes starkes Glas darüber gelegt"[16] (1950: 1/502). Three months of *reality*: it is the direct personal experience of both von Hattingberg's company and her music that reveals to him that neither of them can redeem the hopes that he had invested in them. Once transferred into physical presence, the intimacy found in the letters evaporates.

In late September the same year, von Hattingberg nevertheless appears to have suggested that they make a collaborative effort: a concert in Munich where Rilke would read his poetry and she would play (cf. Rilke 2000: 224).

13 'Yes I really want to come to Paris, and not at all in such a sly and stupid and reserved manner anymore, as a "plan" that one neatly considers and then in the end sensibly carries through'.

14 'And the more I think about it, it seems like a good thing in the end that it cannot happen *here* and *now*. I have undertaken much that I need to bring to a close […] in the same constitution, for with each note […] other times come for other things.'

15 'No, the more I think about it I must not call for music at this moment'.

16 '[…] three (unmanaged) months of reality have laid something like a cold strong glass over it'.

Rilke answers that he, after careful deliberation, “*nein* sagen muss, durchaus nein” (‘must say *no*, absolutely no’; ibid.: 189). From the rest of his reply, it is clear that von Hattingberg has expressed enthusiasm about the effects of music on its audience. He retorts with a revealing description of the difference between poetry and music:

> […] stell ich mir nun aber Leute vor, denen ähnlich, an denen Du so reine und heilige Wirkungen hast geschehen sehen, Hiesige, Bayern, – so möchte ich auf der Stelle zugeben, dass die große Musik etwas über ihre formlose Gefühle vermag, keineswegs aber ihnen ein Gedicht zumuthen, das seiner Natur nach allein ist, so dass der Zuhörer, davorgestellt, sich selber ganz aufzubringen hat; das Gedicht kennt ihn nicht, nimmt nicht an, dass er da sei; die Musik ist nicht unterrichteter von ihm, aber sie wird zur Luft des Raums, giebt sich ihm zu athmen und da sie überall ist, ist sie dann auch in ihm –.[17] (Ibid.; 189f.)

Music in performance lacks integrity and shape, as do the emotions of the audience it affects. Because it resounds in the room and fills the air, it intermingles with anyone and everyone at once, and is well suited to the inner formlessness of its passive listeners. Poetry, by contrast, is all integrity and self-sufficiency: it is solitary and unaware of its recipient, who must thus actively summon himself up. Its proper place is in private reading. In a public setting and framed by music, Rilke’s work would be like a fish out of water.

These extracts from Rilke’s correspondence reveal how intimately Rilke intertwined the personal relation with von Hattingberg and the art to which she was to introduce him. The idea that he had expressed to his wife a decade earlier seems to linger with him: music, in its physically experienced form, is tantamount to a careless imparting of one’s inner being or a lack of emotional contour. The intimate exchange with von Hattingberg is of immense promise to Rilke as long as it is not subjected to physical reality, and if music is to have any relevance to Rilke and his poetry, it must have nothing to do with the pretext of its sounding notes, but be consigned to a virtual existence on the silence of the page.

---

17 ‘[…] but if I imagine people akin to those in whom you have perceived such pure and holy effects, locals, Bavarians – then I will immediately admit that great music may have some power over their formless emotions, but by no means entrust to them a poem, which is by nature solitary, so that the listener who is confronted with it must summon himself completely; the poem does not know him, does not assume that he is there; music is not more instructed by him, but it turns into the air of the space, allows him to breathe it in, and because it is everywhere, it is also in him –.’

The Silence of Writing and the Orphic Machine

Rilke's increased interest in music, then, does not entail a new interest in hearing music, especially not together with poetry. A poem written in 1918, but published posthumously, can be read as an attempt to formulate an understanding of music that Rilke can endorse. It carries the same title as the Franz von Schober poem that, in Schubert's setting, came to be one of the paradigmatic instances of music and poetry merging into a sung performance – precisely the kind of intermingling against which Rilke takes such an emphatic stand:[18]

> MUSIK: Atem der Statuen. Vielleicht:
> Stille der Bilder. Du Sprache wo Sprachen
> enden. Du Zeit,
> die senkrecht steht auf der Richtung vergehender Herzen.
>
> Gefühle zu wem? O du der Gefühle
> Wandlung in was? –: in hörbare Landschaft.
> Du Fremde: Musik. Du uns entwachsener
> Herzraum. Innigstes unser,
> das, uns übersteigend, hinausdrängt, –
> heiliger Abschied:
> da uns das Innre umsteht
> als geübteste Ferne, als andre
> Seite der Luft:
> rein,
> riesig,
> nicht mehr bewohnbar.
>
> (1975: III/111)

> Music: breath of statues. Perhaps:
> silence of paintings. You language where all
> language ends. You time
> standing vertically on the motion of mortal hearts.
>
> Feelings for whom? O you the transformation
> of feelings into what? –: into audible landscape.
> You stranger: music. You heart-space

18 For further discussion of the relation between Schober's poem and Rilke's, see Kovach 1986 and Pasewalck 2000.

> grown out of us. The deepest space in us,
> which, rising above us, forces its way out, –
> holy departure:
> when the innermost point in us stands
> outside, as the most practiced distance, as the other
> side of the air:
> pure,
> boundless,
> no longer habitable.
> (1987: 147)

Music, as the object of Rilke's admiration in this poem, is consistently defined in contradistinction to its existence as empirically audible cultural practice. Employing the core gesture of interart aesthetics, the opening stanza looks to other artistic media for a definition of music: statues, images and language, implying sculpture, painting and poetry. Yet the characteristics appended to these other media are consistently beyond them. The breath of statues betokens the life that they do not possess, the silence of images implies attending to them with the sense that is typically not involved in the perception of painting, and the language is a language that speaks no more. The chief effect of these paradoxes is to emphasize the ineffability of music: the poem's voice makes a number of tentative efforts at circumscribing something that is impossible to circumscribe, thus giving less weight to the attempts themselves than to the impossibility that they serve to foreground.

Moreover, Rilke defines music against human desire. The organs lodged in our chests, every beat of which marks the passage of time and the transience of our bodily existence, are defined by directedness. The time of music makes a perpendicular stand that belies all such endeavour: it rises above desire and direction, neither moving nor fading out. From this perspective, it makes sense that the subsequent question concerning the object of emotions – the "zu wem?" (l. 5) – is left unanswered. Or, rather, that it is revised into a different question, the answer to which implies no such aim: "der Gefühle/Wandlung in was? –: in hörbare Landschaft." (ll. 5f.) The directed human emotions are transformed into a landscape, which connotes serene beauty defined by spatiality rather than temporality, as well as permanence, immobility and disinterest.

As the poem uses the word "Musik" for the second time, it is addressed as "Du Fremde" (l. 7). It is something fundamentally strange to Rilke's lyric 'we', even though, as the poem admits, the same 'we' is its point of origin. Music is constantly beyond our reach, either because it is lodged so deep within us that it cannot be grasped by our consciousness, or because it is so grand and airy that we cannot exist within it. Between these extremes lie all other aspects of music – which can be effectively summarized as its concrete practice in human culture – the eclipse of which is the tenor of Rilke's poem. It is only in this manner that music, in Rilke's view, can be appropriated by printed poetry: less audible than visible, less corporeal than spiritual, less ephemeral than permanent. Music, in other words, is dislodged from its material specificity in order to be made available to the medium of printed poetry.

Rilke's most elaborate engagement with the nexus of sound, song and silence are of course the *Sonnets to Orpheus*. This chef d'oeuvre of Rilke's late period abounds with praise for song in various constellations, but still song that is marked by silence. In the famous opening poem of the collection, creation itself is speechless:

> Da stieg ein Baum. O reine Übersteigung!
> O Orpheus singt! O hoher Baum im Ohr!
> Und alles schwieg. Doch selbst in der Verschweigung
> ging neuer Anfang, Wink und Wandlung vor.
> (1975: II/731)

> A tree sprang up. O sheer transcendence!
> O Orpheus sings! O tall tree in the ear!
> And all was still. But even in that silence
> a new beginning, hint, and change appeared.
> (1977: 85)

This tree, pure and erect, defies any sawmill. It is the phallic epitome of song, and around it, the world is silent with awe. It creates not only silence, but also creatures of silence. The poem conjures listening animals, who are themselves made from the very silence that radiates from the Orphic song: "Tiere aus Stille drangen aus dem klaren / gelösten Wald"[19] (1975: II/731). If the verb 'schweigen' has an animating quality – because it is the specific silence of a voice – this poem lets that animation enter the service of Orphic creation, breeding animals that are actually *fashioned* from silence.

In the third sonnet, a young man receives instruction about what song is and, even more importantly, what it is not:

> Dies *ists* nicht, Jüngling, daß du liebst, wenn auch
> die Stimme dann den Mund dir aufstößt, – lerne

19 "Creatures of silence crowded out of the clear / freed forest" (1977: 85).

vergessen, daß du aufsangst. Das verrinnt.
In Wahrheit singen, ist ein andrer Hauch.
Ein Hauch um nichts. Ein Wehn im Gott. Ein Wind.
(1975: II/732)

Your loving *isn't it*, even if your mouth
is pried open by your voice – learn

to forget your impulsive song. Soon it will end.
True singing is a different kind of breath.
A breath about nothing. A gust in the god. A wind.
(1977: 89)

The love that you feel and the song it engenders – that *is not it*. Here, as in "Musik", actual music is portrayed as something violent: the singing voice pushes the mouth open by force. Its opposite is the true song, which is nothing more than a divine waft.

I would like to suggest here the possibility of reading Rilke's evocations of silence as specifically related to his material medium, as a reflection on the sonnet and its physical existence as a book. While the word 'sonnet' itself has sound at its roots, it is sound in the diminutive, diminishing: ever since its beginnings, the sonnet has been an agent in the development toward silent literature: the circulation in manuscript form of Guittone d'Arezzo's and Dante's sonnet collections, in which the authors were actually involved as authorities, "marks a decisive stage in the turn of poetry from oral performance to private reading" (Kennedy 2011: 90).

The twenty-first sonnet comments playfully on this ambiguous materiality of the sonnet. It is a poem about the earth in spring, which is cast as a child who, after having studied long and hard in the school of white-bearded winter, is at last free to play and sing. It begins: "Frühling ist wiedergekommen. Die Erde / ist wie ein Kind, das Gedichte weiß"[20] (1975: II/744). What is interesting is the imagery with which Rilke describes this poetry:

O, was der Lehrer sie lehrte, das Viele,
und was gedruckt steht in Wurzeln und langen
Schwierigen Stämmen: sie singts, sie singts!
(1975: II/744)

20 "Spring has returned again. The earth / is like a child who's memorized poems" (1977: 125).

> Oh what her teacher taught her, all those things,
> and what's imprinted on the roots and long
> complicated stems: she sings it, she sings!
> (1977: 125)

Punning on plants and printed language – roots and stems – Rilke evokes the ambiguous position of the sonnet between codex culture and vocal performance. The silence of the tree is the silence of writing: the wisdom of poetry is printed in the body of nature, which starts to sing as the world turns green. Like all the sonnets to Orpheus, then, this poem is a celebration of song as a metaphor for living creation and budding nature. Here, however, Rilke's play on words in print posits the book as its ultimate origin.

Like the seasons, the song of Orpheus comes and goes. Whenever nature sings, the fifth sonnet says à propos the rose that blooms each year, it is a metamorphosis of Orpheus. It is his seasonal disappearance that guarantees our understanding of his identity:

> O wie er schwinden muß, daß ihrs begrifft!
> Und wenn ihm selbst auch bangte, daß er schwände.
> Indem sein Wort das Hiersein übertrifft,
>
> ist er schon dort, wohin ihrs nicht begleitet.
> Der Leier Gitter zwängt ihm nicht die Hände.
> Und er gehorcht, indem er überschreitet.
> (1975: II/734)

> Oh how he has to vanish so you'll know!
> Though he too were afraid of vanishing.
> Even while his word's transcending being
>
> here, he's already there, where you don't follow.
> The lyre's lattice doesn't snare his hands.
> And he obeys, even as he oversteps the bounds.
> (1977: 93)

Like the pan pipes-cum-prison bars in "Musik", the musical instrument itself, as a physical object, is what represents the confining law: "Gitter" (l. 5) refers on the one hand to the strings of the lyre and, on the other hand, to the bars of a prison that cannot hold Orpheus captive. His hands are not bound by the material world to which the musical instrument belongs, nor to the empirically audible sound that such an instrument produces. Without dissolving the opposition between sound and silence, then, Orpheus is the ultimate emblem of their coalescence.

If the projection of a divided world is fundamental to Rilke's poetry – be it a division between the visible and the invisible, the sounding and the silent, or the material and the spiritual – then its corollary is the projection of a reintegration of that which has been divided. To achieve this reintegration is indeed the ultimate task of poetry, which he entrusts to Orpheus: "Ist er ein Hiesiger? Nein, aus beiden/Reichen erwuchs seine weite Natur"[21] (1975: II/735). This does not mean that the idea of the border has become expendable to Rilke. Quite to the contrary: his poetry thrives on the existence of the very partition that Orpheus so audaciously ignores. This is the sense in which Orpheus obeys by transgressing: the partition, the grid, the ordering structure, needs to exist in order for him to fulfil the task of transcending it. The late Rilke's poetic metaphysics, then, depend less on the *affirmation* of unity and wholeness, than on the *negation* of dualism. The partition, which he evokes over and over, is the fundamental law upon which his poetic universe rests. By transgressing it, the poet-musician confirms its existence and upholds its authority.

For the human beings of modernity, however, the trick is not as easy. We are confined to the noises and distractions of perceptible reality. Surrounded by telephones, streetcars and sawmills, we are bereft of the silence that might have given us access to the other world. As a consequence, perhaps, the machine has begun to appropriate the areas associated with Orpheus:

> ALLES Erworbne bedroht die Maschine, solange
> sie sich erdreistet, im Geist, statt im Gehorchen, zu sein.
> Daß nicht der herrlichen Hand schöneres Zögern mehr prange,
> zu dem entschlossenern Bau schneidet sie steifer den Stein.
>
> Nirgends bleibt sie zurück, dass wir ihr ein Mal entrönnen
> und sie in stiller Fabrik ölend sich selber gehört.
> Sie ist das Leben, – sie meint es am besten zu können,
> die mit dem gleichen Entschluss ordnet und schafft und zerstört.
>
> Aber noch ist uns das Dasein verzaubert; an hundert
> Stellen ist es noch Ursprung. Ein Spielen von reinen
> Kräften, die keiner berührt, der nicht kniet und bewundert.

21 "Is he of this side? No, out of both/realms his wide nature grew" (1977: 95).

Worte gehen noch zart am Unsäglichen aus…
Und die Musik, immer neu, aus den bebendsten Steinen,
baut im unbrauchbaren Raum ihr vergöttlichtes Haus.
(1975: II/757)

As long as it dares to exist as spirit instead of obeying,
the machine threatens everything we've gained.
It hacks the stone starker for more determined building
so we won't be drawn by the lovelier lingering of the master-hand.

Nowhere does it stand aside so we might once escape it,
and, oiling itself in a silent factory, become its own thing.
It is life – it believes it's all-knowing,
and with the same mind makes and orders and destructs.

But for us existence is still enchanted. It's still
Beginning in a hundred places. A playing
of pure powers no one can touch and not kneel to and marvel.

Faced with the unutterable, words still disintegrate…
And ever new, out of the most quivering
stones, music builds her divine house in useless space.
(1977: 157)

Here, the classic design of the Italian sonnet, divided by a thematic shift between the octave and the sestet, is mapped over the structure of Rilke's partitioned universe. On the one side of the *volta* stands the stark noise of the machine, on the other stands the enchanted side of existence, soft words that dissolve in the face of the unsayable, and the music that emanates from trembling stones with which a divine house is built. Music is still constructing the temples of hearing: not by physically audible instruments, but by the quintessence of mute matter, that is, rock. The threat of the stone-cutting machine, however, is precisely that it does not respect the partition, but is disobedient. In other words, it imitates Orpheus. Like him, it will not stay within a restricted area, but transgresses. Like him, it is everywhere, raising claims to life and spirit. Like him, it refuses to be confined to an instrumental function. The house built by the machine and the house built by music mirror each other: the stones of the former are hard and exact, those of the latter are trembling with silent music.

The following stanzas, in a similar manner, seem to define the sound world of the machine in contradistinction to Orphic song:

Hörst du das Neue, Herr,
dröhnen und beben?
Kommen Verkündiger,
die es erheben.

Zwar ist kein Hören heil
in dem Durchtobtsein,
doch der Maschinenteil
will jetzt gelobt sein.
(1975: II/742)

Do you hear the New, Master,
droning and throbbing?
Its prophesying promoters
are advancing.

No hearing's truly keen
in all this noise;
still, now each machine
part wills its praise.
(1977: 119)

From the first line, with the prayer-like apostrophe "Herr", this poem alludes to religious language, which adheres not only to the addressed lord, but also to the machine. The cacophonic New demands worship and has its own apostles. The sounds of modernity, then, are construed as no less than blasphemy in the face of Orphic song: the imagery in which the machine is described turns it into an anti-Orpheus, which masquerades as spirit and song. This is not to say that the machine, in these poems, can simply be circumscribed as an unambiguous opposite of Orphic song. Rather, the most profound danger lies in the analogy between them. The racket of the sawmill, to which Rilke was exposed less than a year before writing the *Sonnets*, was described in similar terms: the terrible song of steel – destroyer of silence.

The opposition between the tree and the sawmill, the silent nature and noisy machine, might seem to ascribe to Rilke a deeply nostalgic response to modernity, which is essentially an extension of Romanticism into the twentieth century. Arguably, however, it situates Rilke within a specific kind of modernism, which is defined by his relation to poetry's material channels and modes of reception. The media technologies that emerged around the turn of the century exerted a decisive leverage on the self-understanding of modernist literature, by increasing its awareness of its own medial preconditions. As the phonograph made possible the recording and playback of speech, poetic writing could no longer retain its nineteenth-century illusion of having a quasi-magic connection to the human voice. Instead, it became ever more deeply entrenched in its material existence as black marks on white paper. As opposed to the Romantics, Rilke embraces voice and song *only* insofar as they can be appropriated by the silence of the book. To him, poetry depends on the silent reading of the printed book by the individual, as opposed to the sound of oral performance in front of an audience. In his despondent letter about the sawmill, Rilke fetishizes both the pure silence and the white sheet of paper. The absence that characterizes them is not empty and undefined, but harbours a specific promise: that of poetic language. The square surface, a leaf in a notebook or a single piece of paper, is there to be written upon. (And there is a compelling irony to the fact that the electric sawmill is a link in the chain of production that transforms the erect tree into the paper Rilke needs to write.) The white silence of the paper is the consecrated site where poetry might take place, where the world of the senses and the world beyond them might potentially be reconnected.

If one reads this notion as poetry's attempt at self-definition, it becomes a defence of poetry's existence as printed text. Rilke advocates the silent reading of poetry in private against its sounding performance in public – in particular in its deplorable combination with music, the art of sinful imparting and insufficient integrity. The silence that is the desirable opposite of the boy's overly public playing in "Musik", and a holy temple of hearing in the *Sonnets to Orpheus*, is not only a respite from the noisy soundscape of modernity, but also a material aspect of literature as Rilke understands it. In an acoustic environment where silence appears to be threatened by extinction, salvaging it becomes an urgent task of poetry. And in a medial landscape where the technological reproduction of sound and voice is becoming ever more widespread, the silence of the written word turns into a vital and precious quality. For Rilke, silence signifies both the solitary state in which poetry must be conceived and received, and the core characteristic of his material medium: the printed book. The most powerful amplifier of that silence, paradoxically, is music – never music as sound, but as verbally evoked idea – because the poem on the page is never perceived as so emphatically silent as when it speaks of music and song.

References

Deinert, Herbert (1973). *Rilke und die Musik*. Doct. Diss. Yale University, 1959. New Haven, CT: Yale University Library.

Kennedy, William J. (2011). "European Beginnings and Transmissions: Dante, Petrarch and the Sonnet Sequence". A.D. Cousins, Peter Howarth, eds. *The Cambridge Companion to the Sonnet*. Cambridge: CUP. 84–104.

Kovach, Tom (1986). "'Du Sprache wo Sprachen enden': Rilke's Poem 'An die Musik'". *Seminar* 22: 206–217.

Pasewalck, Silke (2000). "Die Maske der Musik: Zu Rilkes Musikauffassung im Übergang zum Spätwerk". Hans Richard Brittnacher, Stephan Porombka, Fabian Störmer, eds. *Poetik der Krise: Rilkes Rettung der Dinge in den Weltinnenraum*. Würzburg: Königshausen & Neumann. 210–229.

Rilke, Rainer Maria (1950). *Briefe*. 2 vols. Wiesbaden: Insel.

——— (1954). *Rainer Maria Rilke et Merline: Correspondance 1920–1926*. Ed. Dieter Bassermann. Zurich: Max Niehans.

——— (1975). *Sämtliche Werke*. Ed. Ernst Zinn, 12 vols. Frankfurt am Main: Insel.

——— (1977). *Duino Elegies and Sonnets to Orpheus*. Trans. A. Poulin, Jr. Boston, MA: Houghton Mifflin.

——— (1987). *The Selected Poetry of Rainer Maria Rilke*. Trans. Stephen Mitchell. London: Pan.

——— (1991). *The Book of Images*. Trans. Edward Snow. New York, NY: North Point.

——— (2000). *Briefwechsel mit Magda von Hattingberg "Benvenuta"*. Eds. Ingeborg Schnack, Renate Scharffenberg. Frankfurt am Main: Insel.

Schoolfield, George C. (1992). "Rilke and Music: A Negative View". James M. McGlathery, ed. *Music and German Literature: Their Relationship since the Middle Ages*. Columbia, SC: Camden House. 269–291.

The Inaudible Music of Dada

Peter Dayan

Dada as a performing enterprise was born in Zurich, in 1916–1919, at the Cabaret Voltaire and in the Zurich Dada soirées. It is generally thought, today, that the dominant music of those performances was percussive and tended towards the status of noise, led on by Richard Huelsenbeck's big bass drum. However, the evidence demonstrates that the vast majority of the music played was tonal, usually late Romantic or popular, much of it composed by the now forgotten Hans Heusser. Schoenberg, Debussy, and Satie were also favoured by the Dadaists. This music, and its place in the Dada movement, has been forgotten, in the first instance because the Dadaists themselves said almost nothing about it. The reasons for this silence about music are elucidated by contemporary Dada texts, notably by Savinio, Tzara, and Huelsenbeck, which show why music, for the Dadaists, must not be talked about. The music of Dada thus became surrounded by a verbal silence which has ever since prevented its sound from reaching our ears.

•••

Describing Dada is a perilous undertaking. From the very beginning, the label designated a space which deliberately allowed for rationally incompatible approaches to art to coexist. In the years after the First World War, a number of very different movements, in various cities, appropriated that label, and used it for divergent ends. However, one can at least pinpoint the origin of Dada, both geographically and chronologically. It was born in Zurich in 1916. That was where the word was first used as a designation for an artistic enterprise. It began in the Cabaret Voltaire, as a series of quite informal nightly cabaret performances in what one might describe as the back room of a pub. Then came a series of eight or nine Dada soirées, which were much more formal affairs, the first taking place in 1916 and the last in 1919. These were the first performances to be advertised under the banner of Dada. The Dada soirées were ticketed; they had programmes and entrance fees, and they happened in more or less grand rooms in the bourgeois parts of Zurich.

Since this essay purports to be about the music of Dada, it might seem logical to begin with the concrete question: what music was performed at the Cabaret Voltaire and at the Zurich Dada soirées? However, as soon as one begins to look for answers to that question, one is confronted with a very peculiar series of paradoxes. One is that there has been since the 1960s a

 | DOI 10.1163/9789004314863_010

general consensus on the subject; but that general consensus does not correspond to the evidence provided by contemporary accounts, or by the programmes of the soirées. And the second is that the Dadaists had almost nothing at all to say (on the record) about the kinds of music which, as far as we can tell, were actually dominant in the performances of the Cabaret as of the soirées, beyond simply noting their presence. The music was there; and yet those who participated in the soirées did not, it seems, want to talk about it. Furthermore, Dada criticism over the past half century has generally ignored its existence. As a result, the music which was most present in Zurich Dada has long been inaudible in the sense that when people think of or read about Zurich Dada, they do not think of or read about that music. This essay will seek to suggest that this silencing of the music of Dada is not a historical accident, but stems from the place of music at the heart of the Dada enterprise. About music, for the original Dadaists, there was nothing to be said; nothing must be said. If this leaves music shrouded in a silence which eventually leads to a general inability to perceive that it exists at all, this is a price that has to be paid.

Dada has for several decades exerted a peculiar fascination both on a close community of academics, and on quite a wide public. It is fair to say that both among the public and among the academic community, there is a generally accepted idea concerning the nature of the music that primarily characterised the Cabaret Voltaire and the Zurich Dada soirées. Dada music, it is believed, must have been a music that tended towards the status of noise, and was characterised by improvisation on untuned instruments. There are relatively few academic articles on the music of Zurich Dada; the two best-informed such articles known to me take up this received idea in their very titles. One is "The Big Drum: Boom Boom Boom Boom: The Music of Zurich Dada" by Jeanpaul Goergen (see 1996). The other is "Boomboom and Hullabaloo" by David Gascoigne (see 2010). The 'boomboom' in question refers to the sound of Richard Huelsenbeck's big bass drum. Huelsenbeck was a friend and artistic collaborator of Hugo Ball, the founder of the Cabaret Voltaire. He arrived in Zurich a few weeks after the Cabaret opened, bringing his drum with him. It is well known that he played it on more than one occasion at the Cabaret, most famously as an accompaniment to poetry. As David Gascoigne shows, his drumming was enthusiastic, loud, and soon joined by other percussive instruments; furthermore, its 'boomboom' became a favourite expression of Tristan Tzara (cf. ibid.: 198f.). However, Huelsenbeck stayed in Zurich for less than a year. He returned to Berlin in January 1917. He participated in none of the Dada soirées, and even in the Cabaret performances, the amount of time taken up by his drumming was small compared to the time devoted, as we shall see, to other kinds of music.

Did Huelsenbeck's percussive legacy inspire the music of the Dada soirées? Those soirées contained "Poésie nègre", or "Negerverse",[1] and dances which were similarly characterised as black African in style, with masks clearly inspired by African traditions. It is generally assumed that these poems and dances were accompanied (as similar poems had been in the Cabaret Voltaire) by drum-banging and other such untuned raucous sounds. "Musique et danse nègres" were, for example, performed at the "Sturm-Soirée" in April 1917, according both to the soirée programme, and to Tzara's subsequent account (cf. Tzara 1920a: 17; Bolliger/Magnaguagno/Meyer 1994: 261). However, we have, remarkably, no evidence concerning the sound of that 'musique nègre'; not even any hint of the instruments involved (if any), in accompanying this or indeed any of the dances or poetry in the soirées. The most famous of all Dada dances, "Noir cacadou", performed at the last soirée in 1919, must surely, one might have thought, have been accompanied by appropriately percussive 'primitive' or 'negro' music. Yet no contemporary or participant has anything whatever to say about this. This might seem extraordinary enough. The soirée in question was reported on at length in newspaper reviews (reproduced in Shepphard, ed. 1996: 54–57). It was described by Tristan Tzara in his own report, "Chronique zurichoise", written close to the time (see 1920a); and many of the other participants (including, for example, Suzanne Perrottet and Hans Richter) later reminisced about that soirée (cf. Perrottet 1989: 138f. and Richter 1964: 80–85); not one mentions the sounds, if any, that accompanied the dance. Why? Is it because there were none? But that in itself would have been revolutionary, and worth mentioning. In fact, this silence about music is part of a pattern. None of the participants ever had anything to say about the music of the soirées, except when it was composed music; in which case, they generally limited themselves to naming the composers. This does not mean that the music did not exist. It means that the music was not to be described.

To give the most striking example: no description of any kind has come down to us of the item which, according to the programme, opened the first Dada soirée, on 14 July 1916. The Dadaists must have liked it, because it was also played at three other soirées, on 12, 19, and 25 May 1917. It was the only item to have been performed so many times in the Zurich Dada soirées. It was a piece for solo piano appropriately entitled *Prelude*, or *Praeludium*, by the Swiss composer Hans Heusser (see 1917). Heusser was the most important musician in the Zurich Dada soirées in the sense that his music, always performed with Heusser himself at the piano, occupied far more time in the soirées than any

1 Cf., for example, the programme for the "Alte und neue Kunst" soirée in May 1917, reproduced in Bollinger/Magnaguagno/Meyer 1994: 263.

other kind of music; indeed, probably more than all other kinds of music put together. A reasonable estimate based on the soirée programmes suggests that about 20% of all the time at the soirées was taken up by Heusser's music. Yet he has been the subject of almost no academic attention. In all the extensive critical literature on Zurich Dada, there is not a single article, nor a chapter of a book, dedicated to Heusser. Indeed, it is quite apparent that no critic has ever endeavoured to find and analyse his music, though a fair amount of it, including the *Praeludium*, is accessible in the Zurich Zentralbibliothek.

A comparable critical silence surrounds the considerable amount of other composed music performed both at the Cabaret Voltaire, and at the soirées. Hugo Ball and others performed music at the Cabaret by composers including Tchaikovsky, Reger, Scriabin, Debussy, Liszt, Saint-Saëns, and Rachmaninov. In the soirées, Suzanne Perrottet played music by herself, Schoenberg, Satie, Cyril Scott, and Laban. We have incontrovertible evidence of this from contemporary accounts which there is no reason to doubt, from the surviving printed soirée programmes, and from *Die Flucht aus der Zeit*, Ball's published version of his own diary (cf. 1946: 71–82). It is clear that late Romantic music, and the avant-garde music which developed from it, were a key part of the Zurich Dada performing enterprise. It is equally clear that the piano was the instrument most often heard at the Cabaret and at the soirées, and that the great majority of the music played on it was tonal. Where it might have seemed to challenge tonality, that challenge came from the modernism of Debussy, Schoenberg, and Satie. The stereotype of Zurich Dada remains that it was a noisy movement, full of provocative shoutings, drum-bangings, inchoate clangour, and audience uproar; to the extent that it contained music at all, it would have been music veering towards the status of noise, challenging the European art and popular music traditions. But that stereotype is incompatible with the objective evidence. In fact, Zurich Dada was really full of music, music in quite a traditional sense; some of it more or less avant-garde music, but still, music that saw itself as part of the great European traditions, albeit a new development in those traditions. And yet all this music, when the Dada performances stopped, immediately became inaudible.

We have accounts of the Zurich Dada soirées from several of the participants in the movement, including Tzara, Richter, Glauser, Janco, Hugo Ball, and Suzanne Perrottet. Their accounts of the soirées are extremely varied. But there is one thing they almost all have in common. They tell us little or nothing about the music of Hans Heusser, beyond the fact that it was there. They give us no information about its character; it would be impossible to guess its style, from all the written accounts we have. Similarly, they tell us nothing about the character of the other composers, from Satie to Schoenberg, whose work was played at those soirées. And that is especially true of the Dadaists who wrote their recollections at or near the time: Tzara, Huelsenbeck, and Hugo Ball. The same generally applies to the music in the popular tradition which was a central feature of the Cabaret Voltaire, though less so in the soirées. We know largely from Ball's accounts in *Die Flucht aus der Zeit* that at the Cabaret, folk and popular music, ranging from a Russian balalaika orchestra to French and Polish songs, was from the beginning one of the core features of the cabaret. According to Ball, the star of the Cabaret, indeed, was his companion (and future wife) Emmy Hennings, an experienced cabaret singer, who also recited her own poetry. He quotes a review of the Cabaret Voltaire in the *Zürcher Post* which characterises her style:

> Der Stern dieses Kabaretts aber ist Frau Emmy Hennings. Stern wie vieler Nächte von Kabaretts und Gedichten. Wie sie vor Jahren am rauschend gelben Vorhang eines Berliner Kabaretts stand, die Arme über die Hüften emporgerundet, reich wie ein blühender Busch, so leiht sie auch heute mit immer mutiger Stirn denselben Liedern ihren Körper, seither nur wenig ausgehölt [sic] von Schmerz.[2] (Ball 1946: 89)

At the Cabaret, then, as in the soirées, the music that was most typical of the programmes was not noise, and it was not percussive. It was generally tonal, usually involved the piano, and quite often consisted of well-known songs with more or less traditional words.

We are thus faced with a paradox. The Dadaists obviously loved music; composed music, music in the traditional sense, in the great European tonal and post-tonal tradition, as well as popular, cabaret, and folk music. They almost never had a performance without it. The piano was present at all the Zurich Dada soirées except one, just as it was almost always present in the Cabaret Voltaire. In the programming of Dada events, music was always given a prominent place; and while we have echoes of many differences of opinion between the Dadaists concerning the content and organisation of those events, there is nothing whatever to suggest there was ever any argument over the music. Its place was accepted by all. And yet the Dadaists never said anything about the relationship between Dada and that music; even though they had immense

2 'But the star of this cabaret is Miss Emmy Hennings. The star as of how many nights of cabaret and of poetry. Just as years ago she stood before the rustling yellow curtain of a Berlin cabaret, her arms curved above her hips, rich as a flowering bush, so today, with ever more spirit in her countenance, she lends, to the same songs, her body, since then only slightly hollowed by pain.' (All translations are my own.)

amounts to say about so many other aspects of their relationship with various artistic traditions. Why, when so much music was performed, was so little said about it?

The clue is given by an extraordinary text entitled “Seconde origine de la voie lactée” (‘Second Origin of the Milky Way’) by Alberto Savinio, which was performed at the “alte und neue Kunst” soirée in 1917 (shortly after Heusser's *Prelude*), and later published in *Dada 3* (see Savinio 1918). It begins with a discussion of the relationship between philosophy and art, and ends thus:

> La musique, bien que de vieille souche céleste, quoiqu'apparentée à la plus ancienne noblesse planétaire – les mondes, dans leurs quadrilles, chantent merveilleusement – reliée aux ferronières platinées des étoiles... du temps déjà où Pythagore armait les p h t o n g u e s de chiffres militaires, comme des armées en manœuvre; la musique, dis-je, faisant fi de son passé illustre, s'est engluée, comme une putain tertiaire, dans les marécages floréaux!...
>
> par l'influence néfaste de certains musicofacteurs, classifiables un échelon plus bas que les semnopythèques – singes mélancholiques....
>
> (A ce point l'auteur descend brusquement de la cathèdre d'où il endoctrine les foules, d'une voix blanche il susurre:
>
> messieursdam's, aurevoir et merci!
excusez...je...je...je suis surpris...
par la colique!
>
> et s'esquive).[3]

Music, then, to be blunt, music as it has been created since the days of Pythagoras, gives Savinio diarrhoea. And this text is complemented by another,

3 ‘Music, despite her ancient and respectable celestial ancestry, despite her kinship with the nobility of the planets – the worlds, in their quadrilles, marvelously sing – bound with the platinum-plated diadems of the stars...even from those early days when Pythagoras armed his p h t o n g s with military numbers, like armies in thefield; music, say I, caring not a jot for her illustrious past, has been bogged down, like a tertiary whore, in floreal swamps!...

under the evil influence of certain musicofactors, to be classified one degree below the semnopythecus – or melancholy monkey....

(At this point the author suddenly descends from the pulpit whence he was indoctrinating the masses, in a neutral voice he murmurs:

ladies and gents, thanks and bye for now!
forgive me...I...I...find myself caught short...
by the colic!

and slips away).’

by the same author, previously published in *Dada 1*, called "Un Vomissement musical" ('A Musical Vomiting'):

> Je souligne les deux épisodes de ma vie qui provoquèrent en moi le plus intense et le plus inexprimable dégoût: le premier se rattache à mon enfance, un jour que sous l'instigation d'un marmiton sanguinaire et facétieux j'eus scié le cou à un jeune oison; le second se rapporte à mon adolescence, un soir que sous la poussée d'un allemand mélomane j'assistai à une sorte d'orgie théâtrale où les turpitudes sonores de M. Richard Strauss tenaient lieu de débauche.
>
> Au point surtout où elle en est présentement, la musique est une insulte à la dignité de n'importe quel citoyen, aristocrate, bourgeois ou prolétaire, tant soit peu honnête et propre dans son linge et dans ses affaires.
>
> Le charme de l'harmonie est la plus grave atteinte à l'honneur de l'homme libre. Parmi les principales causes de la criminalité par dégénérescence il faut placer – en premier lieu – la musique: bien avant l'alcoolisme![4]

In both these articles, Savinio aligns musical pleasure with undisciplined sexual pleasure – the last line of "Un Vomissement musical" is "post coïtum animal triste est!" – and presents that undisciplined pleasure as something disgusting, in the way that all uncontrollable and uncontrolled bodily excretory functions are disgusting. Certainly, he is here linking back to an ancient topos: wine, women and song go together, and they are opposed to dignity, honour, self-restraint, good government, and military discipline. But one might have thought that such sentiments would be totally out of place in Dada. The Dadaists had no time for military discipline, or for bourgeois notions of dignity and self-restraint. Their manifestos privilege the primitive, the spontaneous and the corporeal, against the dignified and bourgeois. They generally like the idea of art leading man back to his animalistic nature; whereas Savinio, when

---

4 'I refer to the two episodes in my life which have provoked in me the most intense and inexpressible disgust: the first, from a day in my childhood, when a blood-loving wag of a kitchen-boy induced me to saw through the neck of a young gosling; the second, from my adolescence, when, one evening, egged on by a German music-lover, I attended a sort of theatrical orgy in which the sonorous turpitudes of Richard Strauss served as an ersatz for debauchery.

Especially in her present position, music is an insult to the dignity of every citizen, whether aristocrat, bourgeois, or proletarian, who aspires to any degree of honesty and of cleanliness in matters of underwear and of commerce.

The charm of harmony is the gravest of attacks on the honour of a free man. Among the principal causes of criminality by degeneration must be placed – above all others – music: well before alcoholism!'

he likens musicians to monkeys, clearly presents the animal in art as an abomination. So what is Savinio doing in this company? Is he being ironic? No; rather, he is demonstrating what happens to music when one talks about it. Music that is talked about necessarily becomes an abomination. Only music that is not spoken of, music that remains surrounded by silence, can be worthy of its unuttered name.

Savinio leads his concept of music back to the notion, traditionally attributed to the ancient Greeks, of the music of the spheres. He associates this celestial music with military manoeuvres, and with quadrilles. Army manoeuvres and stars are, like quadrilles, *ordered* in their movements. Their order can be, and indeed has been, described in words, in thoroughly rational words. The fundamental problem with music as Savinio describes it is that it resembles quadrilles in being, like the stars or like military manoeuvres, ordered. At least ancient Greek music was dignified and aloof in its order. Modern music is worse; it is both rooted in order, and treacherously able to overwhelm our emotions and our bodies. It thus resembles the two primary enemies of Zurich Dada: modern patriotism and militarism. It is, Savinio tells us, time to fight back against this organised threat to our independence. Music, the rationally ordered art, the art of harmony, must be evacuated from the body artistic, so that we can listen instead for other, freer voices. "Le charme de l'harmonie est la plus grave atteinte à l'honneur de l'homme libre", says Savinio; if we aspire to the honour of being free men, we must not let music cast over us the spell of its numbers. Harmony, the slave of order, is the enemy of freedom.

This explains why the sexuality which Savinio associates with music is disgusting. It is not a free sexuality; it is the sexuality of slavery to the passions. Music overwhelms us like an orgy, not to allow us to express our freedom, but to enslave us to its harmonies. This loathing of the modern manifestation of the ancient concept of harmony is a fundamental tenet of Dadaism. For the Dadaist, the value of art must always escape the rational; harmony is rational; ergo, the value of art must always escape harmony, and if music is identified with harmony, then music itself ceases to be art. This principle, which is explicit in Savinio's texts, is also clearly implied (though less directly stated) in the manifestos and proclamations of the better-known Dadaists. Tzara, for example, in his "Manifeste Dada 1918", which he performed at the "Soirée Tristan Tzara" in July 1918, makes clear his loathing of harmony:

> Je hais l'objectivité grasse et la [sic] harmonie, cette science qui trouve tout en ordre.[5] (Tzara 1918)

5 'I hate greasy objectivity, and harmony, that science which finds everything in order.'

Harmony, like all science, for Tzara as for Savinio, invites us to see the world as fundamentally ordered. That, for the Dadaist, is the viewpoint of the slave, not of the free man. Dada values freedom and creativity above all; established order, science, and hence harmony are its enemies.

This seems to invite the question: can music exist without harmony? Indeed, did the music of Dada exist without harmony? The answer to the former question is certainly highly problematic; we shall shortly return to it. But the answer to the latter question is clearly no. The music of Zurich Dada was filled with harmony. Its most omnipresent sounds were tonal. The first sound heard at the first Dada soirée was the grand C major chord which opens Hans Heusser's *Prelude*. All the music by Heusser which has come down to us is tonal. So, as we have seen, was most of the other music performed at the Cabaret Voltaire as at the Dada soirées. The last piece listed on the programme of the final soirée (though it is not clear whether it was actually performed) was a piano quartet in E flat major by Heusser. But that, for Tzara as for Savinio, would have been beside the point. The question that really mattered for Dada was not: can music exist without harmony? It was: can music exist without harmony conceived of as a science, as an ordering principle? And to this latter question, they indirectly put forward the answer: yes, but only in silence.

Savinio trumpeted his hatred of music, as Tzara stated his loathing of harmony, because they could only receive music as free, hence as an art worthy of the name, if it escaped all words including their own. They fulminated against music, not in order to condemn music itself, but in order to persuade their listeners that it is disgusting, it is a betrayal, to hear music as it inevitably reaches us when it passes through words. That is why, as they decry harmony and music, they conspicuously fail to tell us which musical works, if any, might escape their fulminations. They are not condemning one musical style in order to promote another. Rather, they are condemning all music as it is received in words or by our rational faculties. That would leave the music that the Dadaists loved, that they programmed, that they listened to, free to work in its own way, and to use harmonies if it saw fit. By surrounding that beloved music with silence, by refusing to describe, discuss, or analyse it in any way, they could allow it to escape from words, from science, from harmony itself conceived as order, and thus to escape from their own fulminations. After all, harmony only becomes a science when we allow it to find all in order. It is not the harmony within any given piece of music that operates as a science; it is the concept of harmony as abstracted from music by the scientific mind, then re-applied to music to impose order upon it. The music of Dada escapes that order by refusing the scientific operation of abstraction and rational or verbal re-application; by sounding in silence.

The Dadaist, then, may well be able to enjoy music while it is being performed. Describing that enjoyment, however, writing about music in any way, creates severe problems of principle, which are most typically addressed by Dadaists through a technique that in essence goes back to the Romantics. In order for writing about music not to betray music, it must actively silence music. However much writers may adore the music they hear, when the time comes to translate music into words, it must cease to sound. Thus Tzara, in the same "Manifeste Dada 1918", evokes a silent orchestra:

> […] autorité de la baguette mystique formulée en bouquet d'orchestre-fantôme aux archets muets, graissés de philtres à base d'ammoniaque animale.[6] (1918)

In the "Proclamation sans prétention Dada 1919", which was written to be read out at the final Zurich Dada soirée and published the following year, Tzara suggests a more permanent method for silencing music than bow-greasing:

> Musiciens cassez vos instruments aveugles sur la scène.[7] (1920b)

Note that it is on stage that he is inviting musicians to break their instruments. The silencing of music is something we are to witness, like watching an orchestra with greased bows. Music is not to be forgotten; only silenced, and seen to be silenced, in words.

Tzara had intended to read out this proclamation towards the end of a soirée in which music played a particularly important and conspicuous part. Suzanne Perrottet played piano music by Schoenberg, Satie, and Cyril Scott. Hans Heusser played some of his own piano music, as usual, and there was to have been more to come: immediately after Tzara's proclamation, on the programme, as the concluding items, were more piano pieces by Heusser, and his piano quartet in E flat major, which was to have been the final sound at the final Dada soirée. But just before Tzara was due to read out his proclamation, the audience at the soirée, artfully provoked by Walter Serner, created such an uproar that, by Tzara's own account, the planned performance could not continue: "Tzara empêché de lire la PROCLAMATION DADA" (1920a: 26). Tzara's injunction to silence music was, then, itself silenced – and it was certainly not obeyed. Neither Heusser nor Perrottet broke the piano on the stage, and Tzara

6 '[…] authority of the baton mystic wand formulated as the bouquet of a phantom orchestra with silent bows, greased with philtres fabricated from animal ammoniac.'

7 'Musicians smash your unseeing instruments upon the stage.'

did not try to make them do so. Why not? It is perhaps worth pointing out that breaking pianos on stage was not, in 1919, an unknown activity in avant-garde settings. Savinio had himself impressed and inspired Apollinaire two years previously by his piano-smashing exploits (cf. Dayan 2010: 38–41). But when Savinio smashed pianos, they were not pianos that had just resounded to the composed music of Schoenberg, Scott, Satie, and Heusser.

This tangle of apparent paradoxes has its roots in the coexistence, from the beginning, in Dada, of two impulses which on the surface appear contradictory, but which in fact support each other. One is to attack any aspect of art that can be analysed as part of an ordered tradition. The other is to maintain the artistic tradition. Dada was thus always, as the title of Hans Richter's later book on the subject proclaims, 'Kunst und Antikunst' (see 1964); both art and anti-art. It is only a slight oversimplification to say that in the Zurich Dada soirées and publications, the 'anti-art' element was furnished by the manifestos and proclamations, and the 'art' was provided by the poetry, the dance, and above all the music. The aim of the 'anti-art' manifestos was not to destroy art; it was to deny us the right to say what art is. A prime target of that anti-art attack was traditional discourse on music, precisely because of all the arts, it was music, music as harmony, which seemed most open to rational analysis. But that attack on the traditional concept of music had to be accompanied by a demonstration that music can live on, once it is freed from such concepts; just as poetry can live on once it is freed from sense, and painting can live on once it is freed from representation. To silence music is to give it back its freedom.

One might describe thus the Zurich Dada technique for giving freedom to an art, without destroying it. First, one has to kill the concept of an art in words, to kill the art as something that can be defined in words, to reduce it to silence, to prevent it from speaking (and from being spoken about) with the voice of reason. When the concept of that art is dead, art as creation is free to return; and the audience, in the performing space, is free to appreciate it as creation, not as order. Thus Dada kills music as order, music as something that can be defined in words, in order for music as free creativity to return. This is what happens, both in Zurich Dada performances and in Zurich Dada publications. But for music to return, the Dadaist must be careful not to say anything about it that might be construed as resuscitating the definition in words, the conceptual definition, of that art.

So we should not be surprised to find that Tzara, in his "Chronique zurichoise", says nothing about the actual audible music of the Dada soirées beyond acknowledging its existence. The same applies to Hugo Ball, in his *Flucht aus der Zeit*. Suzanne Perrottet, in *Ein bewegtes Leben*, similarly says nothing about the music at the Dada soirées beyond stating what she actually played; she has not a word to say about the music of Hans Heusser. As for Heusser himself, I do not think we have a single printed word by him on any topic, apart from the dedications on his printed musical scores. His silence on the subject of his music is exemplary. And it has been followed by critics ever since.

It will be remembered that there was one musical instrument associated with Zurich Dada that has not been forgotten by critics, or by the interested general public: Richard Huelsenbeck's big bass drum. Now that we have seen how limited its presence was, compared especially to that of composed piano music, we should doubtless ask: why has it been remembered, as the iconic sound of Zurich Dada? The answer is that the banging of the drum, unlike Heusser's piano pieces, could come to take its place on the 'anti-art' side of Zurich Dada, which was, as we have seen, the side destined to remain audible. It was designed and received as an interruption to traditional art forms, an attempt to silence them. Like Richter forty years later, Huelsenbeck, in his seminal text on the early evolution of Dada, *En avant Dada: Eine Geschichte des Dadaismus* (see 1920), presents Dada as composed of a pro-art and an anti-art impulse. He makes it clear that the pro-art impulse was dominant in the original ideology of the Cabaret Voltaire:

> Die Energien und Ehrgeize der Mitarbeiter des Kabarett Voltaire in Zürich waren von Anfang an rein künstlerische.[8] (Ibid.: 3f.)

However, his own contribution to Dada, which began in Zurich but matured only later in Berlin, he equally clearly situates as leading towards the 'anti-art'. He explains this opposition through a contrast between "Musik" and "Bruitismus". The former he condemns, exactly as Savinio and Tzara do, by associating it with harmony, harmony conceived of as a craft accessible to reason. "Bruitismus", on the other hand, knows no such limits.

> Musik ist so oder so eine harmonische Angelegenheit, eine Kunst, eine Tätigkeit der Vernunft – Bruitismus ist das Leben selbst, das man nicht beurteilen kann wie ein Buch [...].[9] (Ibid.: 7)

8 'The energies and ambitions of those who worked together at the Cabaret Voltaire in Zurich were from the very beginning purely artistic.'

9 'Music is in any case a matter of harmony, an art, an activity of reason – Bruitism is life itself, which cannot be judged like a book [...].'

Huelsenbeck lucidly recounts how over time he developed his own brand of Dada, Berlin Dada, in which the concepts of music and of art had no place, being replaced by noise and by political action:

> In Deutschland ist der Dadaismus zu einer politischen Angelegenheit geworden, er hat die letzte Konsequenz gezogen und hat auf die Kunst ganz verzichtet.[10] (Ibid.: 24)

This political Dada, the Dada of noise, the anti-art and anti-musical Dada, existed from the beginning; it was the original Dadaists' means of attacking all verbal and rational definitions of art, and particularly of music. For the Zurich Dadaists, however, as Huelsenbeck so clearly saw, it did not destroy art. On the contrary: it created a silence within which art could flourish with a renewed freedom. What it could not do was to give the new art a politically audible voice; that would have contradicted its own first principles. The audible voice remained, and remains today, the sound of Dada as polemic, as political, as noise; the drum-beat, not the piano; Huelsenbeck, not Heusser.

The Zurich Dadaists, from Heusser and Ball to Tzara, Janco, and Arp, left a legacy of silence around the music they loved, programmed and played; a silence created by a carefully maintained absence of words, which continues to this day to make the music of Dada invisible and inaudible. Even more than the symbolists, even more than Apollinaire and the cubists, Dada projects music as the ideal of art at the same time as it rejects everything that words can say about concrete audible manifestations of music. Music has to escape our words, or it risks becoming mere harmony.

Does this mean that the music of Dada is silent? Clearly not to the extent that for the Dadaists themselves, it was (like their poetry) to be appreciated in live, sounding performance. Dada was a performing enterprise before it was a publishing one, and music was from the beginning a central part of that performing enterprise. In principle, it is in words, not in notes, that the music of Dada cannot make itself heard. Nonetheless, the exemplary rigour with which the Dadaists maintained the silence of words around their music meant that the music itself rapidly ceased to be received or perceived. When we look for the aesthetics of such a movement, we look to its words. Looking to the words of Dada, we do not find its music. Any attempt to revive that music through the medium of words would surely betray the spirit of Dada; so silent

10 'In Germany, Dada has become a matter of politics, it has followed its own logic through to the end and completely renounced art.'

it must remain; unless it becomes possible to resurrect the performance of that music in the context of a Zurich Dada soirée. I think that if this were to happen, our view of Dada would be permanently altered. Until then, its music will remain where the words of the Dadaists left it: unheard.

References

Ball, Hugo (1946). *Die Flucht aus der Zeit*. Lucerne: Verlag Josef Stocker.

Bolliger, Hans, Guido Magnaguagno, Raimund Meyer (1994). *Dada in Zürich*. Zurich: Arche.

Dayan, Peter (2010). "Apollinaire's Music". *Forum for Modern Language Studies* 47/1: 36–48.

Gascoigne, David (2010). "Boomboom and Hullaballoo: Rhythm in the Zurich Dada Revolution". *Paragraph* 33/2: 197–214.

Goergen, Jeanpaul (1996). "The Big Drum: Boom Boom Boom Boom. The Music of Zurich Dada". Brigitte Pichon, Karl Riha, eds. *Dada Zurich: A Clown's Game from Nothing*. New York, NY: G.K. Hall.153–167.

Heusser, Hans (1917). *Praeludium*. Zurich: Ad. Holzmann.

Huelsenbeck, Richard (1920). *En avant Dada: Eine Geschichte des Dadaismus*. Hannover: Paul Steegemann.

Perrottet, Suzanne (1989). *Ein bewegtes Leben*. Ed. Giorgio J. Wolfensberger. Bern: Benteli.

Richter, Hans (1964). *Dada – Kunst und Antikunst*. Cologne: M. DuMont Schauberg.

Savinio, Alberto (1917). "Un Vomissement musical". *Dada 1*. Zurich: Mouvement Dada. (Unpaginated).

——— (1918). "Seconde origine de la voie lactée". *Dada 3*. Zurich: Mouvement Dada. (Unpaginated).

Shepphard, Richard, ed. (1996). "Dada Zürich in Zeitungen". Brigitte Pichon, Karl Riha, eds. *Dada Zurich: A Clown's Game from Nothing*. New York, NY: G.K. Hall. 191–259.

Tzara, Tristan (1918). "Manifeste Dada 1918". *Dada 3*. Zurich: Mouvement Dada. (Unpaginated).

——— (1920a). "Chronique zurichoise 1915–1919". Richard Huelsenbeck, ed. *Dada Almanach*. Berlin: Erich Reiss. 10–28.

——— (1920b). "Proclamation sans prétention Dada 1919". Max Ernst, Johannes Baargeld, eds. *Die Schammade*. Cologne: Schloemilch (unpaginated).

Absence, Presence and Potentiality: John Cage's *4′33″* Revisited

Karl Katschthaler

This paper explores four performances of John Cage's famous 'silent piece' *4′33″*. The first one is the premiere performance by David Tudor, the subsequent three are performances by John Cage himself between 1973 and 1986. A discussion of the Aristotelian concept of potentiality and its interpretation by Italian philosopher Giorgio Agamben and Erika Fischer-Lichte's performance theory serve as the theoretical frame for the foregrounding of the bodily presence of the performer and the audience. In this context questions are asked like: What is a musical performance without the creation of a sound object? If we can see darkness, can we hear silence? Is silence absence of sound? What is the potentiality of silence?

•••

> Silence, yes, but what silence! For it is all very well to keep silence, but one has also to consider the kind of silence one keeps.
>
> That's not the real silence, [...] what can be said of real silence, I don't know.
>
> Samuel Beckett, *The Unnamable* (2009: 302f.; 401)

∵

Drawing on Aristotle, philosopher Giorgio Agamben distinguishes two symmetrical kinds of potentiality, the potentiality to be and the potentiality to not-be or impotence. While the first has as its object a certain act, and being-in-act means in this case a transition to a certain activity, in the second case potentiality has as its object potentiality itself. Because of the symmetry of both potentialities the passage to action cannot be brought about by the power to be alone, the power to not-be has to be transported or saved, as Aristotle says. Aristotle illustrates this symmetry of the potential to be and the potential to not-be with the example of a harpist, who equally has the potential to play and the potential to not-play. Agamben transforms the ancient harpist into a modern pianist and then elaborates his example in the following way:

> This means that, even though every pianist necessarily has the potential to play and the potential to not-play, Glenn Gould is, however, the only

 | DOI 10.1163/9789004314863_011

> one who can not not-play, and, directing his potentiality not only to the act but to his own impotence, he plays, so to speak, with his potential to not-play. While his ability simply negates and abandons his potential to not-play, his mastery conserves and exercises in the act not his potential to play (this is the position of irony that affirms the superiority of the positive potentiality over the act), but rather his potential to not-play. (1993: 35)

If we give this paragraph a superficial reading, we might conclude that a virtuoso pianist shows his power to play, whereas a real master musician to a lesser extent makes use of his power to play and rather maintains in the act of playing the virtuality, the not-playing (cf. Alloa/Lagaay, eds. 2008: 19).[1] But if we give this passage a close reading, we will soon discover some unanswered questions the most startling of which is: Why does Agamben say that Glenn Gould is *the only* pianist who directs his potentiality not only to the act but to his own impotence too? Why Glenn Gould? As Agamben does not explain his choice we can only suppose that he might think of Glenn Gould as a pianist who has played virtually all music in his repertoire in a different way than his competitors.

But there might also be another reason to champion Glenn Gould as the master in exercising his potential to not-play in the act of playing. In the communication process of music making, the perceiver may grasp Gould's potential to not-play in some of his unconventional body gestures. In his analysis of Gould's playing technique based on performances filmed by Bruno Monsaingeon, François Delalande has distinguished three different kinds of gestures: "geste effecteur", gestures that actually produce sound; "geste accompagnateur", visually perceivable body movements that are not directly linked to sound production; and "geste figuré", gestures perceived by the audience through the produced sound, but without any direct correspondence to a movement (1988: 92). In the case of a specific accompanist gesture, Gould's left hand movements when playing the piano only with his right hand, Delalande concludes that the pianist's two hands incorporate two orientations, only one of which is directed towards the production of the sound. The other, however, incarnates his reading of the score (cf. ibid.). We may also conclude that these gestures therefore do not only accompany the production of the sound object, but also make perceivable Gould's potential to not-play, to read the score and incorporate his reading in gestures which do not produce sound. In a similar way Gould's

1 This somehow simplistic reading of the Agamben text does not gain more credibility when Alloa and Lagaay refer to Aristotle's pianist [!] in the footnote of the passage in question.

humming or singing while playing the piano may not only be perceived as distraction from his piano playing, but as a gesture that produces a sound object related to the score, but not directly related to the sound object produced by the effective gestures directed on the piano.

Focusing on "the physicality of music making itself (the sight of the body's labors to produce sound)", Richard Leppert calls attention to the impact of such body gestures produced during a musical performance on the musical experience of both the performer and the observer:

> Precisely because musical sound is abstract, intangible, and ethereal – lost as soon as it is gained – the visual experience of its production is crucial to both musicians and audience alike for locating and communicating the place of music and musical sound within society and culture. [...] Music, despite its phenomenological sonoric ethereality, is an embodied practice, like dance and theater. (1995: xxf.)

In the field of theatre, Erika Fischer-Lichte has observed that with the emergence of literary theatre in the 18th century the art of acting had to be reconceived especially concerning the function of the body of the actor. In order to become a perfect vessel to physically express the meanings that the poet had contained in his text the actor had to make the audience forget about his material body:

> The actor was meant to transform his sensual body into a semiotic one which would serve as a material carrier for textual meaning. All physical aspects that exaggerated, falsified, abused, undermined, or altered its meaning in any way were to be eliminated. [...] For the body to be employed in the art of acting at all, it must be stripped of its corporeality and undergo a process of disembodiment. Any reference to the actor's bodily being-in-the-world must be exorcised from his material body in order to produce an entirely semiotic body. (2008: 78f.)

This concept of acting Fischer-Lichte calls "embodiment through disembodiment" and locates it in the realm of the mind-body dualism. In theatre praxis, however, the phenomenal body of the actor can never be excluded entirely from perception in favour of the semiotic body. In contemporary theatre therefore the "main focus lies on the moment of destabilization, in which perception switches between phenomenal body and character" (ibid.: 89). If music performance is an embodied practice, it was embodiment through disembodiment too for a long time. The musician was expected to virtually integrate his instrument as a part of his body. His extended phenomenal body had to become a perfect vessel to physically express the musical meanings that the composer had contained in his 'text' that is the score. In the second half of the 20th century, however, some composers themselves have brought the phenomenal body of the musician and its presence in musical performance to our attention. We may think here of Mauricio Kagel's instrumental theatre or Dieter Schnebel's body compositions, to name just two examples.[2]

John Cage's silent piece *4′33″* may not come to mind first in this context of music making and music perception as an embodied practice. But if we take a close look at four different performances of this piece, we may well find that the physicality of the performer plays a specific role in them and the question of the presence of the performer's phenomenal body gets addressed. First we will examine the gestures of David Tudor performing Cage's silent piece at its premiere in Woodstock in 1952.

As is well known, the premiere of *4′33″* took place within a recital of contemporary piano music. The first part of the programme of this recital at Maverick Concert Hall in Woodstock included some short experimental pieces by Cage himself, Morton Feldman, Earl Brown, and Christian Wolff. Immediately before Cage's 'silent' piece Tudor played the serialist first piano sonata by Pierre Boulez, a composer then yet unknown in the US, thus creating a contrast not only with the preceding American pieces, but even more with the following *4′33″*. The final work was Henry Cowell's *The Banshee*, a piece that has to be performed without use of the keyboard. The pianist is expected to lean into the piano body and produce the sound object by working on the strings with his hands. Whereas Cage's silent piece is a chance-generated sum of silences, the decision of placing it in the penultimate position of the recital was not determined by chance operations but was the result of David Tudor's careful consideration and even experiments with the program order (cf. Holzaepfel 2002: 174).[3]

---

2 But even a composer like György Kurtág, who articulated his rejection of body gestures several times because he thought of them as distracting from the music itself, violated his self-imposed ban on theatrical means in his *Kafka Fragments*, a work that can be characterized by its latent theatricality evoked by body gestures and in one case even proxemics composed into the score (cf. Katschthaler 2012: 84–107). For Kagel's and Schnebel's work focussing on the visual, theatrical, and corporeal in music see amongst others Schnebel 1970, Nauck 2001, Jarzina 2005, Salzman/Desi 2008, Rebstock/Roesner 2012.

3 Tudor's role in the creation process of *4′33″* must not be underestimated. He even had to persuade Cage to finish the piece because the latter had doubts about presenting a silent piece as a serious work of music.

Concerning body gestures it is obvious that there are significant differences between these subsequently performed pieces in Tudor's recital. In Boulez's sonata the performer has to direct a huge amount of different effective gestures on the keyboard of the piano because of the constantly changing dynamics and the wide pitch range of the piece. In the performance of the Cowell piece, however, effective gestures are unconventional because they are not directed to the keyboard, but directly to the strings inside the body of the piano, which results in a different posture of the player. Instead of sitting at the keyboard the performer has to stand beside the piano and bend into it, thus his effective gestures are partially hidden from the audience. From the performer's point of view, he has to execute movements, he has not been trained for and is not used to, that is, he has to meet requirements that are likely to influence his own body perception and his physical comfort. The resulting tension may quite be perceptible for the audience, too.

In a performance of Cage's silent piece, body gestures are necessarily reduced because no effective gestures are allowed on account of "the act of silencing the performer", as Douglas Kahn has put it (1997: 560). This act of silencing has tempted researchers to underestimate the physical presence and the gestures of the performer, sometimes to the extent of virtually ignoring them. Petra Maria Meyer mentions only the gesture of closing and opening the keyboard lid indicating the beginning and the end of the three movements of the piece. She then draws the conclusion that the action of the pianist turns him into an actor, who only plays his normal role in order to step out of it. The audience therefore proceeds from viewing the podium to individually listening to the sounds occurring in the auditorium (cf. Meyer 1998: 140f.). Kattrin Deufert goes even further when she states in her thesis on John Cage's theatre of presence that the audience of a performance of Cage's silent piece will not focus their attention on the performer, who only indicates the temporal beginning of the piece with the simple and obvious gesture of not playing. She also is convinced that the audience will therefore start to listen to the ambient sounds (cf. Deufert 2001: 50). This reading of Cage's composition and its performance as setting only a time-frame (cf. Meyer 1998: 143) can be traced back to a paper read by German composer Jakob Ullmann at the festival on the occasion of Cage's 80th birthday in Frankfurt in 1992, in which he states that any constellation at any time and at any location can be considered as a performance of Cage's work whenever somebody decides to listen to contingent ambient sounds (cf. 1992: 107). Michael Rebhahn on the other hand argues that in these cases a listener is using the method of Cage's piece but does not perform it, because he does not create a performance frame. The performance frame, however, is not only a time frame but requires a specific space and an audience in it expecting a musical performance. Rebhahn concludes that a performance of *4'33"* can only work in the setting of a conventional concert situation (cf. 2012: 77f.).[4]

This controversial question, whether *4'33"* requires a concert situation or not, is not easy to decide when we look at *4'33"* as a complex of different scores[5] and performances over a time frame reaching from the premiere in 1952 until 1986 taking into account performances by John Cage himself or supervised by him.[6] Thomas Maier quotes John Cage saying in 1966 that he does not need the piece anymore as we do not have to think in the category of three movements anymore. Already in 1954 Cage reported that he used to listen to the piece in the woods alone. In his Norton lectures end of the 1980s he stated: "[...] you do it either in ordinary circumstances or in extraordinary circumstances, it works very well." (Qtd. Maier 2001: 167f.) But if we look at the way David Tudor performed the piece several times, we have to agree with Michael Rebhahn that the conventional concert situation is significant. In this framing, however, the pianist's body and his gestures become significant, too.

William Fetterman has attributed a special gestural quality to Tudor's performance (cf. 1996: 75). The closing of the keyboard lid is just one element of the gestural repertoire, one that has occurred in several pieces of Cage before, amongst others in *Water Music* played in the first part of Tudor's recital in Woodstock (cf. Maier 2001: 156). But there are further gestures like sitting down in front of the piano, starting the stop watch, looking at the stop watch, stopping the stop watch, depressing one of the three pedals of the piano, according to Kenneth Silverman one different for each of the three movements (cf. 2010: 118).

---

4 For further discussion of the frame of art as one possibility of marking absence as significant see Werner Wolf's contribution in this volume.

5 According to Maier, there are in principle three different versions of the score: the lost notated score with staffs David Tudor used in Woodstock 1952; the unpublished graphical score Cage gave to Irwin Kremen as a birthday present from 1952/53; and the published linguistic "Tacet" score from 1960, published again in a revised version in 1986 (cf. 2001: 150–154). Maier does not mention, or has no knowledge of, the unpublished score Cage created for his performance of the piece in Cologne in 1986, which he glued into the guest book of the organizer with the dedication: "For Wulf Herzogenrath with friendship silently." It is a calligraphic version of the linguistic score with the timings Cage had determined by chance operations for the performance (cf. Arns/Saavedra-Lara, eds. 2012: 15).

6 David Tudor gave the premiere of *4'33"* in the Maverick Concert Hall in Woodstock on August 29th 1952. Cage himself performed the piece 1973 on Harvard Square in Cambridge, Massachusetts and on four different locations in New York City in the same year. He ultimately performed it at the opening of an art exhibition in Cologne, Germany on August 31st 1986.

The most significant gesture of David Tudor performing *4′33″*, however, is his disciplined action of reading the score and turning pages. Tudor himself has stressed the importance of this gesture: "It's important that you read the score as you're performing it, so there are these pages you use. So you wait, and then turn the page. I know it sounds very straight, but in the end it makes a difference." (Qtd. Fetterman 1996: 75) He also has described performances of the piece as a kind of meditation and as cathartic. It is evident that this is the point of view of the performer and there can be no guarantee that the audience will have a cathartic experience, too. On the one hand in his performance Tudor shows that music may come into existence by reading the score alone without playing the music. On the other hand by reading the score on the podium Tudor is not only reading it for himself. Through his physical presence as a pianist reading a score made up by empty bars, a score showing the absence of music and the potentiality of music at the same time, he is also playing this score and by playing it he communicates the music written in the score to the audience. The presence of his body, his gestures and his mimics are not only part of his performance as an actor, as Meyer sees it, but part of the music written in the score because he is reading it. From this point of view, *4′33″* can be regarded as a piece paradoxically foregrounding the corporeality of the musical performance by silencing the performer.

The second performance I will examine is one by John Cage himself. "Welcome to Harvard Square! […] Mr Cage will recreate his [!] famous performance of Woodstock in the summer of 1952" informs us a male voiceover in Nam June Paik's video *A Tribute to John Cage* from 1973. In this video, Paik documents two very different performances of *4′33″* by Cage himself. Harvard Square is a large triangular area in the centre of Cambridge, Massachusetts, the Square functioning as a commercial centre mainly for Harvard students. In Paik's video we watch some workers placing a grand piano in the centre of the square. The piano attracts a crowd of mostly young adults standing around it and waiting for the event to come. Then John Cage steps out of the crowd, sits down in front of the piano, starts the stop watch placed next to the score on the piano and closes the keyboard lid, an action he repeats two times in order to indicate the three movements of the piece. Although he does not turn pages, Cage of course does not recreate his own performance, but the premiere performance and subsequent performances by David Tudor. Therefore he is not only the composer preforming his own piece but he is to some extent also an actor who impersonates David Tudor performing *4′33″*. I don't know whether the audience on the Square had the information that John Cage would recreate the premiere of his famous piece, but even if they had it, it is quite unlikely that they knew David Tudor's way of performing it. But it must have been obvious to them that the whole event was taped by Nam June Paik. Hence they must have been aware of the fact that they were playing the audience in a film. They had not to be told so, neither had they to be told how to behave because the piano as a significant object created a specific framing of the situation. A musical instrument on the street refers to a busking situation, the fact that a grand piano is standing on the street makes it an unusual busking situation. In this case not the street musician makes people stop and listen to his playing, but the object itself. The grand piano itself turns the crowd into an audience. Because a grand piano is very strange in a busking situation, the audience gathering around this object probably did not expect John Cage to behave like a typical street musician. Some of them are surprised, as can be seen on the video, but they keep watching and listening till the end of the performance and then applaud.

The second performance of *4′33″* taped by Paik took place in New York City. Although it was also a street performance it was a quite different one. First Cage and Paik decided to perform and tape not the three movement version of the piece, which also appears in the three published versions of the score, but a four movement version. A four movement version of *4′33″* was never published in a score, but there has been reference to such a version in the program of David Tudor's recital in Woodstock, where it was listed as "4 pieces". Whether this was only a printer's error, is not clear,[7] but Paik's video shows that *4′33″* may be performed in four movements or actually rather in four pieces because every 'movement' is performed by Cage on a different location. These four locations are determined by chance operations with the help of the I Ching and a map of New York City, and they are a vacant lot overlooking the Harlem River, a spot in Times Square, one in Bleeker Street, and for the first movement 2100 3rd Avenue in Harlem. Paik's tape shows Cage standing quietly on a city sidewalk listening to the urban ambient sounds in the second, third and fourth movements. The Harlem location is different. Philip Max Gentry describes what happened and comments:

> Here, the sight of Paik's video camera and Cage's stoic stance attracted the attention of several African American teenage boys. They mug for the camera briefly, and then one turns to Cage and asks what is being taped. Cage looks briefly stricken at having to break his silence, but quickly – and nervously – smiles and explains what he is doing. It is difficult to

7 Holzaepfel comments: "Whether this was simply a printer's error (this is not as obvious as some commentators have assumed), it was an additional source of confusion for listeners already baffled by the music itself." (2002: 174).

> imagine Cage similarly breaking his silence at the Maverick, or Lincoln Center, but this is Harlem in 1973, and he is out of his comfort zone. Race matters, even for John Cage. (2008: 169)

Although Gentry refers to the performance on Harvard Square in a footnote conceding that it would be interesting to compare the two performances, he uses his short comparison only to support his argument of race and social difference as the only factor that matters in this case, when he writes:

> [...] Cage performs *4′33″* on a piano in the middle of Harvard Square, surrounded by a respectful audience of young white college students. Here, Cage is clearly much happier, and cheerfully receives his applause at the end. (Ibid.: fn. 2)

On the street in Harlem it was not possible to silence the audience and as a result the performer did not keep silence either. Of course the body of a white male standing in silence on the side walk in Harlem in 1973 functions as a social signifier and triggers reactions on behalf of the African American kids. But is it really so difficult to imagine that Cage would have broken his silence had he been asked a similar question in Harvard Square? The fact that he was not asked there cannot be explained with social difference alone. What Gentry does not take into account is the different framing of the situation generated by the presence of the piano in Harvard Square on the one hand and the absence of the piano in Harlem. In the second case there is no significant object to silence the crowd and to turn them into a watching and listening audience. In this different framing the signifying body of the performer cannot be decoded as that of a musical performer. Consequently the event cannot be decoded as a musical performance. But for the performer too it makes a difference whether he is sitting at a piano he can stare at, if he wants to avoid eye contact with the audience, or standing alone on a sidewalk. In the first case, he is communicating with his audience through the instrument, even if he does not touch the keyboard. In the second case, he meets the passers-by face to face. His inclination to answer questions will differ according to the different communication situations, and it will probably be stronger in the second one.

It is interesting in this respect to compare the performances on Harvard Square and in Harlem with a third performance Cage gave at the opening of an exhibition in the Kunstverein in Cologne on August 31st in 1986.[8] The film critic

8 Philip Max Gentry obviously has no knowledge of this performance, or if he has, he does not refer to it. He seems not to be the only one who ignores it: I have found no references to it in the literature cited in this paper.

and scholar Daniel Kothenschulte was one of the attendants and gives the following account of Cage's performance:

> Cages Uraufführung einer "Neufassung" von *4'33"* sollte die Ausstellung "Die 60er Jahre – Kölns Weg zur Kunstmetropole" eröffnen. Tatsächlich wurde das Werk bereits 1952 uraufgeführt, aber erst 1960 offiziell verlegt. Auch ich war skeptisch. Wie sollte es Cage gelingen, die in drei Sätzen geteilte Stille auf ähnliche Art zum Klingen zu bringen, wie es dem Pianisten David Tudor bei der Uraufführung möglich war, als man das unvorbereitete Publikum noch hörbar irritieren konnte? Inzwischen war es schließlich zu einer Ikone der Avantgarde geworden. Bei meiner Ankunft war der Kunstverein prall gefüllt. Nur wenige hatten Sicht auf den Komponisten, der sein Werk selbst vortragen wollte. Man wartete auf eine Vorrede, Ungeduld machte sich bemerkbar. Der Geräuschpegel im Saal war durch die Gespräche der Anwesenden inzwischen derart angestiegen, dass man ohnehin kaum eine würdige Konzertatmosphäre mehr erwarten durfte. Dann plötzlich Applaus aus der Saalmitte. Das war es gewesen. Ich hatte das Meisterwerk gehört und es nicht einmal bemerkt. Cage musste eine Vokalversion vorgetragen haben, ohne uns Hinterbänkler wenigstens informiert zu haben.[9] (2009: 10)

The framing of the exhibition opening generates different expectations than a concert situation does. It creates the expectation to listen to speeches and to watch objects and possibly performances, but not to stay silent and listen to music. Cage indicated the beginning of his performance by sitting down at a table in front of Sigmar Polke's *Schimpftuch*, one of the objects exhibited, starting the stop watch and turning an empty drinking glass upside down. This was what Kothenschulte and many others could not see. What he does not mention,

9 'Cage's first performance of a "revised version" of *4'33"* was to open the exhibition "The 60s – Cologne's path to art metropolis". In fact, the work was already premiered in 1952, but was not officially published until 1960. I was sceptical. How should Cage succeed in presenting the three movements of silence in a similar way pianist David Tudor managed to do it at the premiere when it was still possible to audibly irritate the unprepared audience? By now it had eventually become an icon of the avant-garde. On my arrival, the Art Association location was packed to capacity. Few had sight of the composer, who wanted to present his work himself. We waited for an opening speech, impatience was noticeable. In the meantime the noise level in the hall caused by the conversations of those present had risen to such extent that one could hardly anymore expect a decent concert atmosphere. Then suddenly applause from the middle of the hall. That was it. I had heard the masterpiece and had not even realized it. Cage must have presented a vocal version without even informing us backbenchers about it.' (My translation).

probably because he does not remember it, is an attempt by Wulf Herzogenrath, the organizer of the event, to mark the beginning of the performance and to silence the audience. When Cage had taken his place at the table and before he started his stop watch, Herzogenrath shouted: "Bitte Ruhe! Danke!"[10] But the silencing of the audience does not work, after short laughing the conversation goes on. A significant part of the audience does not listen to the music of ambient sounds because they do not even notice the performance of the music. They do not notice it because they cannot see the performer's signifying body and his gestures. On the one hand the Cologne performance of *4′33″* by John Cage, therefore, can also be regarded as the ultimate demonstration of the essential role of the visual in music performance. On the other hand it again raises the question if we are able to perceive silence and what silence is.

If the potentiality of sight is seeing darkness, then the potentiality of hearing must be hearing silence, as Giorgio Agamben suggests interpreting Aristotle:

> When we do not see (that is, when our vision is potential), we nevertheless distinguish darkness from light; *we see darkness*. [...] if potentiality were, for example, only the potentiality for vision and if it existed only as such in the actuality of light, we could never experience darkness (nor hear silence, in the case of the potentiality to hear). But human beings can, instead, see shadows (*to skotos*), they can experience darkness: they have the *potential* not to see, the *possibility of privation*. (1999: 180f.)

According to Agamben we human beings are different from all other animals because we know privation, because we are capable of our own impotentiality (cf. ibid.: 182). We can close our eyes and see darkness, but we cannot close our ears to hear silence. Even if we clap our hands over our ears we rather perform a gesture expressing our wish not to hear something or anything, but we are not able to block sounds from our ears in this way, except very quiet ones. Conditions of absolute silence can only be approached by elaborate technology, in a room built to absorb and block sound reflections. In 1951 or 1952, Cage visited such an anechoic chamber at Harvard University and to his own surprise he did not hear silence, but two different sounds:

> It was after I got to Boston that I went into the anechoic chamber at Harvard University. Anybody who knows me knows this story. I am constantly telling it. Anyway, in that silent room, I heard two sounds, one high and

10 'Silence please! Thank you!' (My translation).

> one low. Afterward I asked the engineer in charge why, if the room was so silent, I had heard two sounds. He said, "Describe them." I did. He said, "The high one was your nervous system in operation. The low one was your blood in circulation." (Cage 1969: 134)

This experience told Cage that there is no silence in terms of absolute absence of sound.[11] As a consequence, his intention with *4'33"* was not to show us the absence of music as the presence of silence, but rather to make us hear a whole world of sounds, which are absent when we listen to the presence of music.[12]

Nevertheless there obviously is a potentiality of silence. Just like sound, silence too has the potential to be and the potential to not-be. Silence has the potential to be even when there is sound. This kind of silence occurs when nobody is listening. It is the absence of the perception of sound. In Woodstock in 1952, people do not listen to the ambient sounds of nature but regard *4'33"* a bad joke. In Harlem in 1973, teenagers do not listen to the urban soundscape but break the silence and ask questions. Finally, in Cologne in 1986, the people at the exhibition opening do not even realize that there could have been something to listen to. Silence in terms of not-listening occurs in all these performances of Cage's silent piece. Probably against his intentions John Cage did not only show us that there is *no* silence, he also showed us that there *is* silence.

References

Agamben, Giorgio (1993). *The Coming Community*. Minneapolis, MN: University of Minnesota Press.

——— (1999). *Potentialities: Collected Essays in Philosophy*. Stanford, CA: Stanford UP.

Alloa, Emmanuel, Alice Lagaay, eds. (2008). *Nicht(s) sagen: Strategien der Sprachabwendung im 20. Jahrhundert*. Bielefeld: transcript.

Arns, Inke, Fabian Saavedra-Lara, eds. (2012). *Sounds Like Silence: Exhibition Guide. Cage/4'33"/Silence 1912–1952–2012*. Dortmund: Hartware MedienKunstVerein.

11 Cages anechoic chamber experience shows that there is no silence in psychoacoustic terms. This does not mean, however, that there cannot be silence in psychological terms. If somebody, for example, has been to a deep cave (alone or in silent, non-moving company) and has stopped there for a while he may have discerned the almost complete absence of sound there as silence. (I thank Werner Wolf for pointing this out to me.)

12 For a more elaborated discussion of the impact of Cage's anechoic chamber experience on the genesis of *4'33"* cf. Gann 2010: 160–166.

Beckett, Samuel (2009). *Three Novels:* Molloy, Malone Dies, The Unnamable. New York, NY: Grove Press.

Cage, John (1969). *A Year from Monday*. Middletown, CT: Wesleyan UP.

Delalande, Françoise (1988). "La Gestique de Gould: Élements Pour Une Sémiologie Du Geste Musical". Ghyslaine Guertin, ed. *Glenn Gould Pluriel*. Québec: Louise Courteau. 85–111.

Deufert, Kattrin (2001). *John Cages Theater der Präsenz*. Norderstedt: Books on Demand.

Fetterman, William (1996). *John Cage's Theatre Piece : Notations and Performances*. Amsterdam et al.: Harwood Academic Publ.

Fischer-Lichte, Erika (2008). *The Transformative Power of Performance: A New Aesthetics*. New York, NY: Routledge.

Gann, Kyle (2010). *No Such Thing as Silence: John Cage's 4'33"*. New Haven, CT: Yale UP.

Gentry, Philip Max (2008). "The Age of Anxiety: Music, Politics, and McCarthyism, 1948–1954". Ph. D. Thesis, UCLA.

Holzaepfel, John (2002). "Cage and Tudor". David Nicholls, ed. *The Cambridge Companion to John Cage*. Cambridge/New York, NY: CUP: 169–185.

Jarzina, Asja (2005). *Gestische Musik und musikalische Gesten: Dieter Schnebels Visible Music: Analyse musikalischer Ausdrucksgesten am Beispiel von* Abfälle I,2., für einen Dirigenten und einen Instrumentalisten, *und* Nostalgie, Solo für einen Dirigenten. Körper, Zeichen, Kultur 14. Berlin: Weidler.

Kahn, Douglas (1997). "John Cage: Silence and Silencing". *The Musical Quarterly* 81/4: 556–598.

Katschthaler, Karl (2012). *Latente Theatralität und Offenheit: Zum Verhältnis von Text, Musik und Szene in Werken von Alban Berg, Franz Schubert und György Kurtág*. Frankfurt/Main: Peter Lang.

Kothenschulte, Daniel (2009). "Viereinhalb Minuten mit John Cage: Erinnerung an eine Kölner Aufführung von *4'33"* – und warum man in der Musik noch längst nicht kennt, was man schon weiß". *ON – Neue Musik Köln* 2/09: 10–11.

Leppert, Richard (1995). *The Sight of Sound: Music, Representation, and the History of the Body*. Berkeley, CA et al.: University of California Press.

Maier, Thomas E. (2001). *Ausdruck der Zeit: Ein Weg zu John Cages stillem Stück* 4'33". Saarbrücken: Pfau.

Meyer, Petra Maria (1998). "Als das Theater aus dem Rahmen fiel". Erika Fischer-Lichte, Friedemann Kreuder, Isabel Pflug, eds. *Theater seit den 60er Jahren: Grenzgänge der Neo-Avantgarde*. Tübingen: Francke: 135–195.

Nauck, Gisela (2001). *Dieter Schnebel: Lesegänge durch Leben und Werk*. Mainz: Schott.

Rebhahn, Michael (2012). *"We must arrange everything": Erfahrung, Rahmung und Spiel bei John Cage*. Saarbrücken: Pfau.

Rebstock, Matthias, David Roesner (2012). *Composed Theatre Aesthetics, Practices, Processes*. Bristol: Intellect.

Salzman, Eric, Thomas Desi (2008). *The New Music Theater: Seeing the Voice, Hearing the Body*. Oxford/New York, NY: OUP.

Schnebel, Dieter (1970). *Mauricio Kagel: Musik, Theater, Film*. Cologne: DuMont Schauberg.

Silverman, Kenneth (2010). *Begin Again: A Biography of John Cage*. New York, NY: Alfred A. Knopf.

Ullmann, Jakob (1992). "Im Bergwerk des Geistes". *John Cage: Anarchic Harmony. Ein Buch der Frankfurter Feste ´92/Alte Oper Frankfurt; ein Festival zum 80. Geburtstag*. Stefan Schädler/Walter Zimmermann, eds. Mainz: Schott. 105–107.

The Silence of an Elephant: Luigi Nono's *Al Gran Sole Carico d'Amore* (1975)

Bernhard Kuhn

This article studies the text, music, and performance of Luigi Nono's *Al gran sole carico d'amore* (1975) with particular attention to the significance of silence and absence of textual, musical, and scenic elements. It argues that the function of the absence of conventionally significant elements from this azione scenica is not only to underscore its political meaning, but also to elicit a reflection on contemporary music theater and art in general. While metareferences are recognizable in text and score, the potential of actual recognition depends to a large degree on the performance. Successful in this respect is the production directed by Katie Mitchell, which incorporates a second level of visual presentation in the form of filmic projections. While such a visually dominant performance influences the relationship between stage, text, and music, it also highlights the absence of elements and the significance of silence. Mitchell's interpretation thus not only invites the audience to reflect on the revolutionary moments of the past, but also elicits a reflection on the work itself and implicitly on the role of art and media in the 20th and 21st centuries.

• • •

Luigi Nono's *Al gran sole*[1] was composed between 1972 and 1974 and was first performed on April 4, 1975 at the Teatro Piccolo of La Scala in Milan. Some years later, Nono described his azione scenica[2] as "ein großer Elefant der Mittel"[3] (Stenzl 1998: 90; Stenzl 2012: 29). In this article, I will show that many conventional components of music theater are actually absent from this work and that silence has a significant function in *Al gran sole*.

Silence becomes a major component in Nono's later works, for example in his string quartet *Fragmente – Stille, An Diotima* (1980), which explicitly alludes to silence already in the title,[4] or *Prometeo* (1984). While the literature has so

1 In this article, I refer to *Al gran sole carico d'amore* in its short form, *Al gran sole*.

2 Nono defined *Al gran sole*, like his first theatrical work, *Intolleranza* (1960), as "azione scenica", which literally translated means 'stage action'.

3 "[...] a big elephant of components" (my translation).

4 The English translation of "Stille" is 'silence'. *Fragmente – Stille, An Diotima* was first performed in 1980 at Bonn-Bad Godesberg by the LaSalle Quartet.

 | DOI 10.1163/9789004314863_012

far not paid much attention to Nono's prior use of silence, this article seeks to fill this research gap with respect to *Al gran sole*.[5] While *Al gran sole* can be seen as a synthesis of Nono's earlier works, Nono himself saw it also as test for new perspectives (cf. Stenzl 1998: 84). Silence is one such new element that plays a pertinent role in *Al gran sole* and gets further developed in Nono's later works.

The theoretical focus of this article is on meaningful forms of absence in the plurimedial art form of musical theater by reflecting on absences in text, music, and scene. Of particular interest is the interaction between moments of absence or silence in one medium, for example music, with the other media involved, such as the text or the nonmusical performance on stage. Due to the multitude of media involved in a plurimedial work of art, it is possible that one means of expression is suppressed by another and thus de facto silenced. In addition to highlighting several forms of absence in Nono's azione scenica, it is therefore the goal of this article to analyze the realization of silence and silencing in the work performed on stage. Of particular interest in this regard is Katie Mitchell's production of *Al gran sole*, which was first presented 2009 in Salzburg and then 2012 in Berlin.

Iconicity of Absence

In order to reflect on the function of the fragmentary nature of the libretto and in particular of the absent elements within Nono's azione scenica, the categories Werner Wolf has defined in an article on the literary iconicity of absence prove useful (see 2005).[6] While my focus is not only on the iconicity of absence in one single medium, I believe that several of Wolf's distinctions can be productively used to describe artistic forms of absence in plurimedial art forms, such as musical theater. In particular, two distinctions are relevant for our purpose. The first is the distinction between supplemented signifying blanks and non-supplemented signifying blanks (cf. ibid.: 115). This distinction means that for example aural blanks during a theater performance, such as pauses, can be supplemented by gestures underscoring the silence and its iconic significance,

5 Stenzl divides Nono's works into three phases: Nono's early years and first phase, which ends with Nono's first azione scenica, *Intolleranza* (1960); a second phase, ending with *Al gran sole*; and a third phase with *Prometeo* (1984) as the major work (see Stenzl 1998).

6 See also Werner Wolf's contribution to this volume.

or not. The function of the signs supplementing the blank is to highlight the blank and thus have the potential to trigger a cognitive awareness of the blank and/or its iconic meaning.[7]

The second relevant distinction concerns the positioning of the blank. According to Wolf, textual gaps can appear as internal or intratextual blanks if they are inside a text, or as external if they are outside the text, thus framing the text (cf. ibid.: 115). This distinction can easily be applied to other media as well.

Text Fragments

Al gran sole is not a traditional opera and the libretto does not provide a typical opera plot nor a linear story line.[8] There is very little dialogue and no real development of characters. The libretto consists of a series of text fragments referring to revolutionary moments in the 19th and 20th centuries, all of which failed. The main characters are women who are connected with the uprisings. All events take place in the past, but they are presented from a contemporary point of view.

The first part of the azione scenica takes place during the period of the Paris Commune in 1871 when workers took power for a short while until order was restored through military violence. This historical moment is connected with the events taking place about 80 years later in Bolivia and Cuba when Che Guevara and others fought against the power of the military juntas in Latin America. The main characters in the first part are Louise Michel, who actively fought during the days of the Paris Commune, and Tania Bunke, a woman from East Berlin who helped create the communist state in Cuba and fought in the guerilla war in Bolivia, where she was killed in 1967.

The second part begins with a reference to the Russian revolution of 1905, and then shifts to worker issues in Turin during the late 1940s and 1950s. Included are also brief references to the Vietnam War in the early 1970s. The historical moments of the second part are represented by and large through literary figures, such as the mother from Maxim Gorki's novel entitled *The*

---

7 As can be expected in plurimedial performance works, blanks of one medium are frequently accompanied with signifying signs of another medium unrelated to the blank. These unrelated accompanying signs, which don't foreground the blank, cause the opposite result by making the blank and its potential iconic meaning unrecognizable.

8 The libretto is quoted after Nono 2012.

Mother and Deola, a prostitute thematized in Cesare Pavese's poems. Excerpts of these texts are included in the libretto.

The fragmentary nature of the libretto is apparent from the beginning. The azione scenica starts with a prelude consisting of two parts, entitled "A: La belleza no está reñida con la revolución"[9] and "B: Lotta ieri e oggi".[10] The text of part A includes Ernesto Che Guevara's title quote "La belleza no está reñida con la revolución" and four lines from a 1888 song written by Jules Jouy, entitled *Louise Michel*, which is associated with the Paris Commune. The text of Part B consists exclusively of a quote in Italian by Karl Marx from his *The Civil War in France* (1871), which also refers to the Commune. The prelude therefore connects three different text fragments in different languages – Spanish, French, and Italian – from three different time periods and cultural contexts, but all referring to revolutionary moments. The libretto then continues in a similar manner, by weaving heterogeneous text fragments together. Most of the fragments from the first part refer to the Paris Commune,[11] but they also include quotes referring to the Russian revolution and fictional quotes referring to the war in Bolivia. While it is not the purpose of this article to offer a detailed analysis of all references and quotes, the above-mentioned fragments of the prelude already demonstrate how Nono spins his textual web in his azione scenica.[12] Throughout the libretto he thus confronts his audience with a montage of quotations of heterogeneous text fragments such as aphorisms, poetic texts, dramas, political texts, biographical literature, diary entries, and political song lyrics.

Compared to traditional 19th-century opera, the libretto of *Al gran sole* is quite different, and its fragmentary nature indicates distance from traditional opera. However, as we know from Albert Gier's seminal study on the libretto, libretti characteristically incorporate a contrast structure and typically consist of a series of rather static moments, which relate to each other not only in a linear manner but primarily on the paradigmatic level, which then creates the

9 "A: Beauty and revolution are no contradiction" (my translation).

10 "B: Struggle yesterday and today" (my translation).

11 The first part includes several intertextual references to the Commune, such as quotes from Bertolt Brecht's *Die Tage der Kommune*, Lenin's text entitled *In Memory of the Commune*, Arthur Rimbaud's poem *Les mains de Jeanne-Marie*, which includes the line that gave *Al gran sol carico d'amore* its title, or Louise Michel's memoirs.

12 Vieira de Carvalho analyzes textual and musical quotations in many of Nono's works. He concludes that the fragmentary use of quotations in *Al gran sole* illustrates Nono's technique of montage. According to Vieira de Carvalho, the "*delinearization* of history" corresponds to Nono's "*delinearization* of dramaturgy" (1999: 64; emphases in the original).

meaning of the libretto (cf. 1998: 6–14). While *Al gran sole* neither includes a linear story nor a real contrast structure, the fragments from different historical periods, although certainly linked in an unusual and radical manner, are all connected with the theme of failed revolution. Even within each of the two parts, a series of texts relate to a topic, such as the Paris Commune or the Russian revolution of 1905. On a formal level, the libretto of *Al gran sole* thus represents a radicalization of the libretto form (cf. ibid.: 232).

Adopting Wolf's terminology, it can be established that fragments – since they are by definition incomplete – are framed by blanks (see 2005). Furthermore, the text of *Al gran sole* incorporates framing blanks, which are of iconic significance. Since the fragments point to other texts, as intertextual references they invite the reader to recognize the quotes and their context, and thus to fill in the blanks. The majority of the quotations point to a certain moment in history, specifically failed revolutions, and the fragmentary character of the text underscores the incompleteness of history. The fragments of the libretto are thus part of Nono's attempt to create a 'theater of consciousness', which tells not only a story, but by reflecting on the history of the 19th and 20th centuries demands that the audience make the connections between the texts and the historical reality of the past and the present (see Stenzl 2001).

Musical Fragments

The score of *Al gran sole* is also of fragmentary nature.[13] Similar to the use of different literary quotes in the text, in the score, Nono incorporates a variety of heterogeneous musical pieces. According to Vogt, the score of *Al gran sole* is like a mosaic of smaller units, which is quasi connected in a discontinuous way (cf. 1984/1985: 132). Nono includes many references to his previous works, sometimes only very short elements of a few measures or less. Different from the literary quotations in the text, Nono typically doesn't incorporate them in their original form but modifies them, for example by connecting the musical excerpt with a new text or by recomposing a piece for a different arrangement. The score for "Schieramento della macchina repressiva" (Nono 1978: Secondo tempo, mm. 268–274), for example, is adapted with only minor transpositions from Nono's first azione scenica, *Intolleranza*, where this orchestral piece referred to moments of terror and fear. In *Al gran sole*, its function is similar since it repeatedly characterizes soldiers and other organs

13 The score is quoted after Nono 1978.

of repression (cf. Vogt 1984/1985: 132). Nono also incorporates elements from his *Canti di vita e d'amore*, in particular the part entitled "Sul ponte di Hiroshima", a cantata referring to the victims of Hiroshima. In *Al gran sole*, this part is connected with Louise Michel and the Paris Commune. In the second part, Nono incorporates references to *Ein Gespenst geht um die Welt*, including direct quotations of the corresponding text referring to the communist manifesto. In addition to self-quotations, Nono integrates popular political songs, such as the *Internationale*, *Bandiera Rossa*, the Russian revolutionary song *Dubinuska*, or Cuban or Chinese political songs.[14] Nono reworked these songs by transposing them from their tonal nature to the atonal system and frequently combining direct musical quotations with a contrapuntal orchestra.[15] Other modifications include change of rhythm through stretching of the tone length, as is the case with a brief quotation of the *Internationale* at the end of the azione scenica (cf. Vogt 1984/1985: 134).

Considering the heterogeneous musical material, on a formal level the structure of the score is quite comparable to the way the heterogeneous text fragments are connected in the libretto. It is further remarkable that each segment of the score requires a different musical arrangement and seems separated from the next segment. The score thus combines and frequently contrasts taped recordings, big and small choruses, solo voices and a full orchestra.

The function of the intermusical references is similar to the function of the intertextualities in that they point to other musical pieces and their historical and political context. The context is similar to the one of text fragments since many of the musical references point to revolutionary events or to moments of political violence. Similar to the function of the blanks framing the intertextual references, the fragmentary nature of the intermusical references points in an iconic way to the incompleteness of history. While they thus elicit the actualization of a particular historical moment or underscore the concept of violence in general, additional meaning is created through transformation of the presented musical material, in particular when musical elements are absent.

---

14 Nono had previously used some of these songs in earlier compositions, for example the *Internationale* and *Bandiera Rossa* in *Ein Gespenst geht um die Welt* (cf. Vogt 1984/1985: 134).

15 One example is the *Dubinuska* in the second part. The melody appears first in the timpani. Then the song is transformed in a contrapuntal manner by two flutes. Finally, the *Dubinuska* is sung without words by the chorus of the workers (cf. Fearn 2007: 37).

Musical Blanks: Explicit and Implicit Silence

The musical blanks in *Al gran sole* can be distinguished between explicit and implicit moments of silence. Explicit silence describes moments of no sound. Comparable to textual blanks, explicit silences or musical blanks may either appear within a musical piece – as an intramusical blank – or outside, thus framing the music. The first moment of silence in *Al gran sole* is one of intramusical silence in the prelude, which starts with sounds on tape.[16] On the tape, we hear first a loud mechanical sound, which is immediately followed by several seconds of recognizable silence. A framing moment of silence appears at the beginning of the part entitled "Schieramento della macchina repressiva" in the last scene before the finale. This moment is explicitly marked in the score with the words "in silenzio". During the first three measures, the orchestra is silent and only the chorus sings "piano" the vowel "a" (Nono 1978: Secondo tempo, mm. 637–639).[17]

The primary function of both of these moments of silence is to create space for reflection. Both of these moments are presented at critical moments in the azione scenica. The first takes place at the beginning, right after the first sound, and the second right before the piece referring to the forceful repression of the revolutionary movement.

There are other framing moments of explicit silence in the score, in particular before the beginning of a new musical segment. Before the *Dubinusca*, for example, the score includes a blank measure, but, in contrast to the framing silence of the "Schieramento" piece, the aural blank is not explicitly highlighted as such. This and other similar moments of silence framing a particular musical segment ought not to be considered as iconic per se since they merely point to and underscore the fragmentary nature of the score. These brief segmentary blanks therefore primarily serve the structural function of separating one particular piece from the rest of the score.

In contrast to explicit silence, implicit silence describes moments leading up to silence, when for example the score requires a reduction to pianissimo often until almost reaching silence. The conductor Ingo Metzmacher points to the strong contrasts presented in the score, in particular between the potent

---

16 In the score the length of the tape is established as ca. 55 seconds (cf. Nono 1978: 1).

17 In addition to underscoring the contrast between silence and the following full orchestra, the soft human voice of the chorus supplements the orchestral silence with semantically meaningless vowels.

orchestra and the solo voices, and underscores the power of the female voice: "Im Zentrum der Aufmerksamkeit stehen die Frauen und ihr Gesang. Gegen das gewaltige Orchester behaupten sie sich in all ihrer Zerbrechlichkeit. Schaffen Inseln der Stille inmitten entfesselter Kräfte"[18] (2012: 16). Those 'islands of silence' are created primarily through a combination of silence of the orchestra and the tender and very high soprano voices.

In instances of solo soprano, another phenomenon becomes relevant, which I suggest defining as silencing of words. In those moments, words are unrecognizable and only vowels or single syllables are identifiable in a way that the text is de facto silenced by the music. This phenomenon is of course not unusual for the musical theater in general and not limited to Luigi Nono or his use of solo voices.[19] In general, this form of silencing is also not of iconic significance since the unrecognizability of words is part of operatic conventions. Following Metzmacher's observation, however, I would argue that the silencing of text in the solo voices in *Al gran sole* takes on a particular meaning. The Chinese philosopher Lik Kuen Tong wrote that silence should "not be conceived as the mere absence of speech, but rather as its transcendence" (1976: 169). In our case, the voices seem to move away from textual communication towards an exclusively musical meaning by creating a space beyond a world describable with words.

One example is Tania's part from the first scene, entitled "Interrogativi di Tania la guerrigliera", where she asks the question: "Nada será mi nombre alguna vez?"[20] (see Example 1). The solo voice alternates between pp and ppp and ends with the vowels "a" and "u". Frequently those instances of solo voices are connected with death, the ultimate silence, as is also the case with Tania's quote reflecting on her remembrance after death.

Since *Al gran sole* is a plurimedial work of art, in addition to recognizable explicit or implicit moments of silence in the score, silence, or rather moments of absence, of one medium are frequently accompanied by signifying elements of another medium. These moments can either be what Wolf defines, as already referred to, as "supplemented blanks" when the present element points to the blank of the other medium, or they can negate the blank by overwriting or filling it (cf. 2005: 115).

---

18 'Women and their voices are at the center of attention. Against the powerful orchestra, they hold their ground in all their fragility. They create islands of silence in the middle of unleashed forces' (my translation).

19 Michael Halliwell reflects on the phenomenon of textual silencing in his contribution to this volume.

20 'Will my name at one point be nothing?' (my translation).

EXAMPLE 1 *Al gran sole,* mm. 136–151: "Interrogativi di Tania la guerrigliera" (Nono 1978: 29)[21]

21

Al gran sole includes several instances of supplemented blanks. There is already a first example of a supplemented textual silence in the prelude, specifically in Section B entitled "Lotta ieri e oggi". It is a sequence for orchestra and tape without voice. The printed score, however, includes words in the orchestral lines, not to be pronounced and therefore not destined for the audience to be heard. The space between the printed lines thus supplements the unpronounced words. In mm. 59f., the timpani score is accompanied by the line in parenthesis, "Che tu, borghese, schiacciasti nel sangue", in mm. 84–88 "non più gruppi isolati divisi ma la gran classe dei lavoratori", and in mm. 122f. "alto la bandiera rossa". These words derive from the revolutionary song entitled *La Comune di Parigi*.[22] The technical function seems to communicate to the orchestra and in particular the timpani to sing it silently and to play according to the rhythm of the song. The text provides a semantic link to the narrative content of the first part of *Al gran sole* since it also refers to the Paris Commune. While the missing words between the silent quotations can formally be defined as a supplemented intratextual blank, the semantically significant and partly missing element is the actual song, which is performed only rhythmically by the timpani. Although the intermusical link and the absent aural text and melody are marked only for the musicians and the audience familiar with the score, this moment not only iconically underscores the incompleteness of history, but also triggers a reflection on the aesthetic significance of a song without text and melody.

The score also includes an iconic form of aural blanks, which is connected with a specific semantic meaning of the text. The verb 'continuare', in English 'to continue', can be used as a transitive and intransitive verb. In the finale of the first part, the mother uses this verb in a transitive way: "Le rivoluzioni russe del 1905 e del 1917 continuano in situazioni differenti, in altre condizioni, l'opera della Comune."[23] (Nono 1978: Primo tempo, mm. 783–806) The part is sung primarily by the contralto interpreting the lines of the mother.[24] By separating

22 The first lines of *La Comune di Parigi* are: "Non siam più la Comune di Parigi/che tu, borghese, schiacciasti nel sangue/non più gruppi isolati e divisi/ma la gran classe dei lavoratori." ('We are no longer the Paris Commune/that you, bourgeois, crushed in blood/no longer isolated and separate groups/but the great class of workers.') The translation of "alto la bandiera rossa", is 'up the red flag' (my translations).

23 'The Russian revolutions from 1905 and 1917 continue in different situations under different circumstances the work of the Commune." (My translation). The quotation is from Lenin's *The State and Revolution* (1917). For an analysis of the relationship between this quote and *Al gran sole*, cf. Schomerus 2000: 276f.

24 Parts of the line are sung by the sopranos. The words "del 1905 e del 1917" are sung by the chorus.

verb and object with the modal attributes "in situazioni differenti" ('under different circumstances'), the listener does not know until the end of the sentence whether the meaning is that revolutions continue or, in fact, the revolutions continue the work of the Commune. This double meaning is reinforced by the score, which to accompany this line incorporates a total of 22 measures (mm. 783–805) and includes a rest of one measure in the voice line before pronouncing the direct object, "l'opera della Comune" (m. 802). While the text refers to past revolutions in Paris and Russia, the aural blank potentially triggers the intransitive meaning of the verb 'continuare' and thus implicitly points to a continuation of the revolutions in the future. Considering further the ending of *Al gran sole* and the last lines of the libretto, "Non piú servi né padroni./Su lottiamo!"[25] (Nono 2012: 68) from the *Internationale*, the continuation of the fight for a revolution ought to be considered as the central political message of Nono's azione scenica.

Al gran sole carico d'amore on Stage

Considering the plurimediality of *Al gran sole* during a performance, another iconic form of silence, namely 'silencing', becomes apparent in the voices of most of the female characters. According to the score, there is no physical relationship between the characters on stage and their voices, since the voice of most of them is sung by more than one person. Louise Michel's voice, for example, is typically presented by four sopranos and some of her expressions are sung by the whole chorus, which means that there is no unity between body and voice. The only person generally performed by only one voice is the mother, sung in the contralto voice.

Separation of body and voice is created also at several other moments by the use of loudspeakers and tape recordings. The text of Karl Marx's *Civil War in France* spoken during the prelude, for example, is played from tape. Furthermore, frequently voices or orchestral music are transmitted via microphone and loudspeakers, which further separates singer and voice and even orchestra and sound.

While the separation of body and voice, and especially when represented by more than one voice, elicits a reflection on the relationship between the individual and the collective, these moments of silencing create a sense of

25 'No more servants and masters./Come, let's fight!' (my translation).

alienation. Comparable to the above discussed elements of absence, including the fragmentary nature of libretto and score as well as moments of silence and signifying blanks in text and score, they have the potential to trigger alertness and reflectiveness in the audience. While the reflectiveness is certainly directed towards the thematic subject of the azione scenica, the revolution and the fight for a better world, at the same time, in particular by incorporating elements distancing the work from traditional opera, *Al gran sole* has potential to question the form and social role of the musical theater in general. Whether such a metareflection is successful depends, however, on the realization of Nono's work on stage.

The first performance of *Al gran sole*[26] in 1975 at the Teatro Lirico took place under the direction of Jurij Ljubimov, the founder of the Russian Taganka Theater. Of major importance in this performance was the presentation of space, which similar to the Taganka theater should not be limited to stage decorations. At the same time, technical elements, such as light fixtures, should be visible. The goal was to create a maximum of expressivity and intensity by limiting the production to the bare essentials: space, light, and bodies. Since the chorus is musically highly significant, in this production, it became also visually dominant by fixing its members to five movable platforms which were present on stage during the whole first part. With different height and angle combinations of the platforms and in combination with changing light effects, they created a dynamic and highly expressive theatrical space (see Aulenti 1977 and Pestalozza 1977). While a detailed analysis of this performance is not the purpose of this article, these brief remarks underscore that Ljubimov together with Nono chose a non-naturalistic, rather abstract approach, which intentionally leaves lots of room for active viewer interpretation.

The most recent interpretation of *Al gran sole* is Katie Mitchell's production, which premiered 2009 at the Felsenreitschule of the Salzburg festival and was presented in 2012 in Berlin.[27] The Berlin performance took place in the Kraftwerk Mitte, a former heating plant, in which the Staatsoper had constructed an opera house with an enormous stage and orchestra pit and 970 seats for the audience. In this production, the stage is divided into five cubicles. During the performance a video film is projected onto a big screen above the cubicles. The chorus sits on the side of the stage. The solo singers are positioned on the front part of the stage. In front of them is a display similar to a

26 All performances of *Al gran sole* are very different since Nono's score includes only minimal stage instructions.

27 This article concentrates on the Berlin performance. For an analysis of the Salzburg production, see Schläder 2010.

display in a museum containing objects, symbolizing the main characters and historical moments portrayed. By setting the action in a museum, the following scenes present the textual and musical fragments referring to past revolutions de facto as flash-back.

While the singers, the chorus, and the orchestra perform Nono's score, in the cubicles, women representing the main female characters present mostly domestic scenes and to some degree are connected with the revolution, by either helping with tasks or suffering, for example, the death of a son. In addition to the main characters, cameramen are on stage filming the women in the cubicles. The filmed images are synchronically projected onto the screen above. Mitchell also includes additional previously recorded video footage, which is intercut with the live footage.[28]

By contrast to Ljubimov's rather abstract interpretation, Mitchell thus provides a concrete narrative to Nono's music and establishes a rather dominant visual element by screening film clips above stage.[29] Rebecca Schmid from National Public Radio commented that the video images provide an "accessible context" for Nono's azione scenica, but criticized that the images were "more distracting than illuminating" (2012). While this might be the case and seems a logical first interpretation, it misses the point of Mitchell's production.

An exclusive focus on the video images and the music could easily lead to a superficial misinterpretation of the work as a story of women connected with revolutionary moments told by the images and accompanied by music. In doing so, one would ignore the simultaneous performance and filming on stage, the separation of acting and singing, the incorporation of previously filmed material, and above all the significance and beauty of the music performed in this unique performance space. Furthermore, the video images are not a real film with a conclusion but, comparable to Nono's libretto and score, consist primarily of fragments, which thus leave many questions open. Mitchell's production, therefore, does more than simply replace Nono's azione scenica with a silent film spectacle. Instead, the production foregrounds the reflection on silence and silencing central to *Al gran sole* on the level of content as well as on the level of form. In a highly noticeable manner, this production highlights the separation of body and voice not only musically, but explicitly on stage. Since the main characters acting in the cubicles are projected onto the big screen, it becomes obvious that they are not singing.

---

28 For an analysis of the filmic materials and their montage, see Schläder 2010.

29 In Salzburg, the screen was not directly above but at the side of the stage so that the visual experience of the audience could be compared to watching a tennis match.

Furthermore, from the audience's point of view, it is extremely difficult to simultaneously watch the scenes performed on stage and screened images, considering further that at times more than one scene is performed on stage and that previously filmed video material is included.[30] On the visual level, it is therefore appropriate to speak of visual silencing of the stage acting through the video images.

On the political level, Katie Mitchell is updating Nono's message. While the call for a communist revolution of the working class would probably seem outdated to some members of the audience in the 21st century, fighting for a better world by means of art is still a viable cause to many. In contrast to the Ljubimov production, where only the voices of the women are heard, Mitchell portrays also their bodies and underscores their voicelessness by means of the video images. Although this certainly foregrounds the feminist perspective of Nono's work,[31] it also points to many people who in today's society don't have a voice. By connecting voiceless women to Nono's music and singers' voices, Mitchell also highlights in a metareferential manner the societal role of the musical theater, and art in general, to 'voice' and critically reflect on political and social aspects of our world.[32]

Furthermore, by means of the different media employed, Mitchell thematizes the role of musical theater within today's media reality. The primary element triggering such a metareflection in the attentive audience is the live broadcast of scenes performed on stage and the combination of the live footage with previously filmed scenes. In addition to questioning the authenticity

30 Schläder defines the plurimediality of Mitchell's production as a carefully structured media program, which consists of constantly changing combinations of space, light, sound, performers, stage props, composed text, and filmic narration (cf. 2010: 110).

31 For a feminist reading of Nono's *Al gran sole*, see Kutschke 2008.

32 While in the 1970s intellectuals and engaged artists like Nono actively participated in public discourse with their art, already in 1962 Nono thought about the creation of a new musical theater. In his reflections, entitled "Possibilità e necessità di un nuovo teatro musicale", he outlined some of his ideas for a new form of musical theater. Such a theater should be closely allied with the great struggle for a new human and social condition, which for Nono meant communism. The new theater should further be committed politically, linguistically, and socially, and be a theater of conscience, which doesn't limit the audience to a passive presence at a ritual and instead actively involves them in order to provoke them to make necessary choices (see 1977). Raymond Fearn sees *Al gran sole* as an attempt to create such a new musical theater (see 2007). While it might be problematic to consider this azione scenica as absolute fulfillment of Nono's 1962 ideas regarding such a new theater, major elements are certainly recognizable, in particular in Mitchell's production.

of the filmed image[33] in the age of digital technology, or recordings in general, it elicits questions about the relationship between musical theater and film in today's world. While technology, such as video and film, offers many possibilities for stage performances, and with the use of high definition technology for instance we have today the possibility of watching operas simultaneously on screen all over the world, we are still not able to successfully do this with Nono's azioni sceniche, which require a particular space in order to aurally be successful. While the Ljubimov production has been broadcast on Italian television,[34] it is impossible to record the atmosphere and sound created in the space of the Kraftwerk Mitte and the nuances created by the distribution of sound through loudspeakers located at specific places in the audience.

Al gran sole is a politically committed work of art which aesthetically has the power to elicit a critical reflection on this work and contemporary reality. This is the case primarily thanks to elements of absence in libretto, score, and, possibly, scenic performance. Katie Mitchell's production brings Nono's azione scenica into the 21st century and, particularly with the incorporation of live video, has the potential to trigger significant reflections about our political and artistic realities today.

References

Al gran sole carico d'amore. Luigi Nono (2012). Berlin: Staatsoper im Schillertheater. Performance Booklet.

Aulenti, Gae (1977). "Appunti sulla messa in scena". Degrada, ed. 64–70.

Degrada, Francesco, ed. (1977). Al gran sole carico d'amore*: Nono Ljubimov Borovskij Abbado Degrada Aulenti Pestalozza: Per un nuovo teatro musicale.* Milano: Ricordi.

Fearn, Raymond (2007). "Prometheus or Icarus? Idea and Ideology in Nono's *Al gran sole carico d'amore*". *Tempo* 61/239: 28–39.

Gier, Albert (1998). *Das Libretto: Theorie und Geschichte einer musikoliterarischen Gattung*. Darmstadt: Wissenschaftliche Buchgesellschaft.

Kutschke, Beate (2008). "'Le donne in rivolta o la rivolta femminile?': Luigi Nonos *Al gran sole carico d'amore* und die italienische Frauenbewegung". Beate Kutschke, ed. *Musikkulturen in der Revolte*. Stuttgart: Franz Steiner. 142–152.

---

33 Schläder interprets the parallel representation of stage spectacle and film as reflection on the individual perception of reality (cf. 2010: 122).

34 Nono participated in this television production. A DVD of this production is available at the Archivio Luigi Nono in Venice.

Lik Kuen Tong (1976). "The Meaning of Philosophical Silence: Some Reflections on the Use of Language in Chinese Thought". *Journal of Chinese Philosophy* 3: 169–183.

Metzmacher, Ingo (2012). "Der großen Sonne entgegen". *Al gran sole carico d'amore.* 15f.

Nono, Luigi (1977). "Possibilità e necessità di un nuovo teatro musicale". Degrada, ed. 9–14.

——— (1978). *Al gran sole carico d'amore. Au grand soleil d'amour chargé. Azione scenica in due tempi. Partitura. Nuova versione.* Milano: Ricordi.

——— (2012). "Al gran sole carico d'amore: Azione scenica in zwei Teilen. Libretto". *Al gran sole carico d'amore.* 46–68.

Pestalozza, Luigi (1977). "Luigi Nono e Luigi Pestalozza a proposito di *Al gran sole carico d'amore*". Degrada, ed. 71–77.

Schläder, Jürgen (2010). "Intermediale Wirklichkeit: Zur komplexen Verschränkung von Fiktion und Virtualität in Katie Mitchells *Al gran sole carico d'amore*". Jürgen Schläder, Franziska Weber, eds. *Performing Intermediality: Mediale Wechselwirkungen im experimentellen Theater der Gegenwart.* Leipzig: Henschel. 84–129.

Schmid, Rebecca (2012). "Industrial Revolution: Staatsoper Berlin Stages Premiere At The Kraftwerk". NPR. March 7, 2012. http://www.npr.org/blogs/nprberlinblog/2012/03/06/148053709/industrial-revolution-staatsoper-berlin-stages-premiere-at-the-kraftwerk. [1/28/2016].

Schomerus, Ute (2000). "'Lenin 71–17': Zur Verknüpfung historischer Kontexte in Luigi Nonos *Al gran sole cario d'amore*". Constantin Floros, Friedrich Geiger, Thomas Schäfer, eds. *Komposition als Kommunikation: Zur Musik des 20. Jahrhunderts.* Frankfurt am Main: Peter Lang. 259–277.

Stenzl, Jürg (1998). *Luigi Nono.* Reinbek bei Hamburg: Rowohlt.

——— (2001). "Stories: Luigi Nono's 'theatre of consciousness' *Al gran sole carico d'amore*". *Luigi Nono: Al gran sole carico d'amore.* Teldec. CD booklet. 26–33.

——— (2012). "Ein großer Elefant: Luigi Nonos *Azione scenica Al gran sole carico d'amore*". *Al gran sole carico d'amore.* 29–32.

Vieira de Carvalho, Mário (1999). "Towards Dialectic Listening: Quotation and *Montage* in the Work of Luigi Nono". *Contemporary Music Review* 18/2: 37–85.

Vogt, Harry (1984/1985). "'Al gran sole' carico d'autocitazione – oder: Zwischen Patchwork und Pasticcio. Zur dramaturgisch-musikalischen Gestaltung der 2. Szenischen Aktion *Al gran sole carico d'amore* von Luigi Nono". *Neuland: Ansätze zur Musik der Gegenwart* 5: 125–139.

Wolf, Werner (2005). "Non-supplemented Blanks in Works of Literature as Forms of 'Iconicity of Absence'". Costantino Maeder, Olga Fischer, William J. Herlofsky, eds. *Outside-In – Inside-Out.* Iconicity in Language and Literature 4. Amsterdam/Philadelphia, PA: Benjamins. 113–132.

The Sound of Silence: A Tale of Two Operatic *Tempests*

Michael Halliwell

Sound and silence are central to the meaning of Shakespeare's *Tempest*. "Be not afear'd; the isle is full of noises" insists Caliban to the interlopers, while Prospero renounces his power: "I'll break my staff, / Bury it certain fathoms in the earth, / And deeper than did ever plummet sound I'll drown my book." Sound from a variety of sources as well as music function as a thematic thread throughout the work, and opera as a 'sounding' art form must meet these challenges on its own generic terms in any adaptation. Indeed, adaptation itself can be seen as a form of 'silencing' of the source work which itself then is an absence. There is a silence and a refusal to speak at the heart of *The Tempest*, particularly as reflected in the arch manipulator Prospero. His characterisation as well as that of the two indigenous inhabitants of the island, Caliban and Ariel, has evolved much in recent times, as revealed in many intermedial rewordings where frequently the potency of language and its silencing has been central. The language of the play is profoundly musical, constantly invoking the art of music, yet Shakespeare's text can be an obstacle in adaptation. This paper considers two recent operas which grapple with these issues in very different ways. In Lee Hoiby's (1986) version the original text is used with modification and shortening, but still exerting clear dramaturgical imperatives. Thomas Adès's (2004) opera completely reworks the original text: the libretto controversially silences much of the power and richness of Shakespeare's text through an effective blend of heightened contemporary colloquial language redolent with occasional echoes of the original: a linguistic strategy engendering a creative tension in the response of the audience. There is thus both presence and absence in both these operatic texts.

•••

> He collected absences. For him they were as intense, haunting and real as the presences that they shadowed. And so, on this day late in August of 1911, he had intentionally arrived that little bit late to join the queue, this slight boy-man of 28 with his friend Max, heightening the anticipation [...].
>
> When they eventually entered the Louvre's Salon Carré, senses heightened by the delay, they approached the spot where the Mona Lisa had been displayed for generations [...]. Taking his friend by the shoulder Max pushed to the very front, and they gazed at the wall in astonishment, as other onlookers paused to deposit flowers on the floor beneath, with notes of remembrance tied in silk ribbons.

 | DOI 10.1163/9789004314863_013

> He stood in front of the wall, rapt, those obsidian eyes staring. The painting, of course, was gone. That's why he was there. It had been stolen a week before, and the Museum had only just reopened to the public. The crowd had come expressly to see where it used to be, and now wasn't. For Franz Kafka, the Mona Lisa was in the process of joining that internal collection of what he called his 'invisible curiosities': sights, monuments, and works of art that he had missed seeing. (Gekoski 2011)

In the adaptation of a source work into a different genre a frequent regret is what has been left out – an absence that often continues to resonate in the new work. This occurs most frequently in the adaptation of works of fiction into film, where, due to the nature of the new medium, much of the source material has to be shortened, excised or re-configured. A more radical approach – an appropriation, where the source work serves as a point of departure – engenders both absence and a form of silencing of the original work. In operatic adaptation this process is even often more extreme than in film. Music can and often does silence text, and many of the conventions of the genre such as vocal and choral ensembles intensify this process. Opera is the site of a constant struggle where language attempts to assert, defend or even extricate itself from the silencing effect of music. In texted music it is not only the instrumental accompaniment that is a factor, but also the range and often extreme demands that the vocal line places on the intelligibility of the words. However, one might argue that the task of the librettist in opera is deliberately to create ellipses and absences in the text which must be filled-out and expanded by the music. In this essay I look at two contemporary operatic versions of *The Tempest* from the perspective of language and its silencing, both in terms of strategies adopted in the construction of the libretti, but also in the musical characterisation of the character of Ariel, focusing on a particular performative moment: Ariel's song "Full fathom five", and Caliban's speech "Be not afeard" – one an actual performative song, and the other an extended lyrical passage.

A common view of *The Tempest* is that it is the kind of play eminently suitable for translation into another medium. Indeed, it is "an extraordinarily obliging work of art. It will lend itself to almost any interpretation, any set of meanings imposed upon it: it will even make them shine".[1] David Lindley

1 Ann Barton (Shakespeare 1968: 22). Christine Dymkowski remarks that the play's "protean nature" finds "ever new ways to voice contemporary social, political and cultural concerns and to voice them powerfully" (2000: 93).

observes that the play's "concentrated spareness [...] joined to its teasing allusiveness, positively requires its readers or audiences to supply contexts in which it might define itself" (Shakespeare 2002: 53). The play has probably attracted more operatic adaptations than any of Shakespeare's other plays. Julie Sanders argues that the dramatic form "encourages persistent reworking and imagining. Performance is an inherently adaptive art; each staging is a collaborative interpretation, one which often reworks a play script to acknowledge contemporary concerns or issues". The movement "into a different generic mode can encourage a reading of the Shakespearean text from a new or revised point of view" and the "transfocalization which is part of this process is often the impetus for adaptation" (2005: 48f.).[2] Of course Shakespeare, pre-eminently among all dramatists, has always proven a popular source for operatic adaptors. I suggest that W.H. Auden's long poem, *The Sea and the Mirror*, his meditation on the play, is a pervasive presence in both adaptations.

The Tempest is suffused with music, both 'phenomenal' as well as its use as a trope.[3] But its music is not unproblematic. Auden argues that

> it is not one of the plays in which, in a symbolic sense, harmony and concord finally triumph over dissonant disaster [...]. Justice has triumphed over injustice, not because it is more harmonious, but because it commands superior force; one might even say because it is louder. (1975: 526)

Despite the double plot there is a clarity of character depiction as well as situation, a fundamental aspect of operatic dramaturgy, and the play's characters suggest archetypal patterns in their representation. It can be regarded as a 'revenge play' – a persistent sub-genre in operatic representation. There is a stern, yet loving father protective of an impressionable daughter being pursued by a passionate young man – another persistent operatic trope.[4] Other characteristic operatic situations include a king surrounded by scheming and disloyal courtiers as well as some disreputable comic characters who would not be out of place in the *opera buffa* tradition; both genres emerge from the

---

2 Peter Greenaway's film, *Prospero's Books* (1991) and Julie Taymor's recent film version of the play (2010) spring to mind, both engaging in a radical way with the source text.

3 I use the term 'phenomenal' in the sense that Carolyn Abbate (cf. 1991: 119) uses it to suggest discrete performances embedded in the larger performance; for example, a character self-consciously singing a song in opera.

4 Father-daughter relationships are the stuff of opera. One needs only to think of many such relationships described in the operas of Verdi. Indeed, Verdi himself considered the possibility of an operatic version of *The Tempest*.

Italian *Commedia*. There is a pervasive supernatural element embodied in Prospero's magic and made manifest in the figure of Ariel, and allied to this is the deployment of spectacle, particularly in the feast and the masque scenes in the play – something that opera does very well. This is one of the few plays of Shakespeare's that almost completely observe the classical Aristotelian unities of place and time, and its dramaturgy is relatively straightforward to incorporate into a swiftly-flowing, coherent operatic action. In addition, both *The Tempest* and *Othello* are "traditional paradigms for any postcolonial scholar or writer; their presence operates as a musical refrain in itself, although one rewritten and recontextualized at every turn" (Sanders 2005: 54).

However, the play's suitability for operatic adaptation is problematic to which the paucity of operatic versions of *The Tempest* in the current repertory attests, and Shakespeare's plays in general can be seen as both a fruitful source as well as potential disaster for the aspiring librettist and composer. Opera critic Bernard Holland warns:

> For the opera composer, *The Tempest* is both enticement and trap. Its irresistible ingredients include familial betrayal, violence among the upper classes, sweeping fantasy, the power of magic, and above all the musical imagery that Shakespeare gives to speech. 'Set my words', Shakespeare seems to say. 'Turn them into melody and harmony.' (1994)

Peter Wynne notes that the "depths and shoals of the lyric stage are littered with hulks that once flew Shakespeare's banner" (1994: 54). Early musical adaptations focused on incorporating the characteristic features of the masque popular in the 17th century, and there is evidence to suggest that Mozart was toying with a libretto based on the play just before his death – some would say that his *Magic Flute* can be seen as a version of the play (cf. Schmidgall 1990: 284). Beethoven contemplated an opera based on it; Mendelssohn actually considered two libretti based on the play before rejecting both, while the Verdi Archives contain a finished libretto dated 1866 (cf. ibid.: 283). The attractions of the play did not diminish in the early 20th century, with several operatic versions possibly hampered by not being able to shake off the all-pervasive musical and dramaturgical influence of Wagner. Modernist trends in opera later in the century did not prevent versions emerging during the period before and after the Second World War: Swiss composer Frank Martin's severely modernist version, *Der Sturm* (1954), is highly regarded by some. However, the modernist idiom might be seen as problematic in adapting Shakespeare in general.[5]

---

5 Winton Dean maintains that Martin's opera "fails because it attempts the impossible. Such a literal and unadorned setting, apart from reducing the pace to a crawl, sets up an impossible

Despite the play apparently being problematic as an operatic source it has lost none of its attraction in recent years with versions by Americans John Eaton appearing in 1985, Lee Hoiby in 1986, Peter Westergaard in 1994; the first employing extensive use of electronic music, the second written in a lushly neo-romantic idiom, and the third employing a severely modernist musical language but with more traditional structures.[6] However, the versions that seem most likely to sustain a place in the repertory are those by Hoiby (1926–2011) and by British composer, Thomas Adès (born 1971). Premiered to great acclaim at the Royal Opera, Covent Garden in 2004, Adès's opera has received several other productions around the world including a revival in 2007 at Covent Garden as well as a sumptuous new production at the Metropolitan Opera in 2012 – a performance seen around the world as a High Definition broadcast to cinemas. Director Robert La Page set the opera within a theatre – not just any theatre, but Milan's La Scala where Prospero, as Duke of Milan in the play, doubles as stage manager and director.[7] La Page self-reflexively transposes the connection between the uninhabited island and the bare stage of Shakespeare's theatre, staging a meta-referential meditation on the nature of opera as an art form where the stage of the opera house is magically peopled by Prospero the director.[8]

Although Hoiby's version has not been taken up by major opera companies apart from a nationally broadcast Dallas Opera production in 1996, it is consistently staged by regional American companies not daunted by the challenges posed by this large-scale work. Hoiby was one of the most successful lyrical voices in contemporary American opera, never really departing from his tonal roots, an unpopular approach in regard to the dominant modernist aesthetic in the immediate post-war decades. However, like several other notable American composers, his style has over the last twenty years found itself back in the art music mainstream.[9]

---

challenge to the poetry. Sprechgesang and a parlando delivery, so far from adding anything to 'Be not afeard' and 'Our revels now are ended', only confirm that music is superfluous. Nor does Martin re-create the lyrical and magic elements of the plot in musical terms; the love of Ferdinand and Miranda remains cold and Prospero becomes a droning bore. The best music occurs in Ariel's songs, especially 'Full fathom five' with its rhythmically varied refrain." (1964: 814).

6 The year 2000 saw the publication of a version by Australian composer, Peter Tahourdin, also characterised by the use of extensive electronic resources, but it still awaits a first performance.

7 The first act is on the theatre stage looking out to the auditorium, the second act is backstage, while the third is set on the floor of the auditorium with the characters facing the stage. This production was awarded the 2013 Grammy for classical music.

8 Interestingly the recent film adaptation of *Anna Karenina* similarly takes place within a theatre.

9 Other notable opera composers who could be included here are Gian Carlo Menotti, Samuel Barber, Carlyle Floyd and Dominick Argento. Hoiby's final work, an adaptation of *Romeo and Juliet*, has not yet received a fully staged performance.

Auden starts his playful, yet moving appropriation of Shakespeare with the Stage Manager's address to the audience, tapping into the deep silence at the heart of the play.

> Well, who in his own backyard
> Has not opened his heart to the smiling
> Secret he cannot quote?
> Which goes to show that the Bard
> Was sober when he wrote
> That this world of fact we love
> Is unsubstantial stuff:
> All the rest is silence
> On the other side of the wall;
> And the silence ripeness,
> And the ripeness all.
> (2003: 60)

Shakespeare's language is perhaps one of the major pitfalls in adapting Shakespeare in English and a problem that Verdi, most notably, managed to avoid when adapting Shakespeare.[10] The richly allusive language as well as its acknowledged difficulty for contemporary audiences to comprehend poses what some would see as almost insuperable problems. It is an operatic cliché, but the existential question is almost always asked of a proposed musical adaptation of a literary work: is the music going to add anything to the original? If not, why bother! The most effective opera libretti often consist of language pared down to essential elements but still 'poetic' on their own more limited, terms. If too much of the 'music' of the original text is retained, what can 'real' music effectively add?

Unlike the most successful twentieth century 'English' Shakespeare opera, Britten's *A Midsummer Night's Dream*, Adès's libretto by Australian playwright Meredith Oakes is a blend of heightened contemporary colloquial language embedded with shards and echoes of Shakespeare's original text, creating an element of tension for the listener. This strategy simplifies and updates the archaic language of Shakespeare, often a barrier for play as well as opera audiences, where textual intelligibility is always an issue. It allows more immediate accessibility but also provides freedom for the composer to 'deconstruct'

10 Verdi's final two masterpieces, *Otello* and *Falstaff*, are among the most highly regarded operas in all the repertoire. Arrigo Boito's libretti are outstanding examples of a librettist engaging creatively with Shakespeare's text, simplifying, re-arranging and modernizing it, but creating a comparable richness of texture and poetic possibilities.

the text and create something evocative and contemporary.[11] "The greater the text, the greater the tension can be between linguistic meaning and the influence on perceived meaning that a musical setting can have", argues Leon Botstein (2013: 12). But this is not the whole truth. Auden, as librettist, maintained:

> The verses which the librettist writes are not addressed to the public but are really a private letter to the composer. They have their moment of glory, the moment in which they are as expendable as infantry is to a Chinese general: they must efface themselves and cease to care what happens to them [...]. I believe that, in listening to song (as distinct from chant), we hear, not words, but syllables [...]. The poetic value of the words may provoke a composer's imagination, but it is their syllabic values which determine the kind of vocal line he writes. In song, poetry is expendable, syllables are not. (1975: 473)

Essentially, Auden the librettist is recognising and even endorsing the 'silencing' of much of the semantic element of the text in its musicalization.

For most audiences Shakespeare seems full of keenly-anticipated quotations, and in the imaginative reworking of the original text librettist Oakes has had her cake and eaten it! Her text displays enough resemblance to the original that the well-known lines are recognisable if sounding slightly strange; there is a sense of the original text 'lurking' behind the modern demotic text. Yet the text also has a distancing effect, particularly in the use of deliberately banal rhymes and half-rhymes, the repeated use of assonance and alliteration and frequent amusing and abrupt verbal turns of phrase. This has the effect of drawing attention to the text while estranging it – appropriate in an adaptation of a play so deeply and self-consciously concerned with language. This libretto reduces many of the semantic difficulties of the play while simultaneously restructuring the narrative sequence; a combination of both presence and absence.[12]

---

11 Andrew Clements's review of the premiere observed that Adès and Oakes's adaptive strategy "is not a reworking of Shakespeare's play, not an exercise in filleting, and not a commentary upon it either. It is best described as a paraphrase, a condensation of its extraordinary poetry into a language that is still rich, but is much more grounded in modern demotic. Memories of the original constantly break through." (2004).

12 The premiere of the opera occasioned a substantial amount of comment on the text – most appropriate for a version of play in which the power and the abuses of language are of such thematic importance.

But the language of Oakes's libretto does contribute considerably to the musical aspects of the work, echoing the music of the original text while avoiding some obvious operatic disadvantages. Adès describes the purpose of this textual strategy as "to be all the more faithful and concentrate the drama" (2003b). This highly stylised text allows space for musical development without obstructing melodic complexity, gradually building up a verbal rhythmic expectation which demands a musical response. Oakes herself comments in Audenesque terms:

> The opera *The Tempest* is inspired by Shakespeare's play, rather than literally being based on every aspect of it. There are key images from the play as well as new material. From among the play's many themes and possible interpretations, the opera focuses on the difficulty, and the necessity, of mercy. The libretto uses contemporary vocabulary. Its lines are short, rhythmic and rhymed or semi-rhymed, echoing Shakespeare's strophic songs more than his blank verse. This choice reflects the play's magical, ritual, childlike elements, and acknowledges the traditional power of incantation in song. The operatic Prospero is the passionately vengeful man seen in the play, more than the wise disconnected actor also seen there. Despite his near-omnipotence, he finds things out as he goes along, and experiences contradictory emotions to the end. (2003)

Alex Ross observed that he was

> distressed to find that "Full fathom five," three of my favourite words in the language, had become "Five fathoms deep" – but veterans of contemporary premieres will be relieved to find that for once a librettist and a composer have taken charge of a sacred text and made it their own. Too often these days, we get Cliff Notes operas that effortfully string together one famous literary line after another. This libretto is designed to be sung – "full fathom five" is, on close inspection, short on long vowels – and Adès makes the most of it. (2004)

Sanders observes that appropriation is "frequently involved in a process of reading between the lines, offering analogues or supplements to what is available in a source text, and drawing attention to its gaps and absences" (2005: 60). Hoiby's librettist, Mark Schulgasser, notes that the "lovely thing about a libretto is that it is never finished…it's designed to be incomplete. In fact, one might say my task was to unfinish *The Tempest*, to deconstruct it, so that it might be finished again by Lee [the composer]" (qtd. Schmidgall 1986: 12). He changes textual sequence and reassigns dialogue, but it is difficult to radically alter characterization as revealed through the soliloquy and dialogue of the source text. This is perhaps where Shakespeare exerts a stranglehold on adaptors who are too 'faithful' – a loaded term in adaptation studies; it is not the richness of the poetry, but the deeper structure and characterisation as it emerges in the source that profoundly influences any English-language adaptation. As Verdi observed when adapting Shakespeare: "one must take the bull by the horns" (qtd. Schmidgall 1990: 283). Adès and Oakes allow themselves more freedom; they delete characters, the masque disappears; they both shift and invent incident and intensify the confrontations between characters, and the two plots often merge. The whole of the Naples court is on the island, thus allowing the use of a full chorus with all its wide-ranging sonority. They also expand the way characters are presented: for example, giving Antonio elements of interiority through 'invented' soliloquy by creating dialogue absent in Shakespeare; a particularly potent example occurs at the end of the opera when Antonio realizes he has been outmanoeuvred by Prospero and vents his frustration in an 'invented' aria, revealing much of his character. Gavin Plumley describes how "reported action becomes action proper and the central dispute between Naples and Milan plays out in a series of vignettes, dialogues, and confrontations. Such a dichotomy can be heard in the very text the characters sing, where simple couplets often underline conflict and resolution alike" (2012: 43). There is a 'freedom', perhaps even 'silencing' of the source which could find parallels with some Shakespearean adaptations / appropriations for the musical theatre such as the Rogers and Hart reworking of *The Comedy of Errors*: *The Boys from Syracuse*, and the Bernstein and Sondheim version of *Romeo and Juliet*: *West Side Story*. In this vein, the Cole Porter version of *The Taming of the Shrew*: *Kiss me Kate*, has a bet both ways with the presence of Shakespeare's text explained by a 'performance' of Shakespeare's play embedded in the larger action. In all three of these musicals there is much less 'reverence' for the original than most operatic adaptations which perhaps explains some of the enduring success of the Porter and Bernstein works and the 'failure' of many 'faithful' operatic reworkings. Operatic structures and traditions are prominent in both *Tempest* operas with ensembles conflating text and actual scenes; both also use musical dance forms reflecting the baroque period of the play – and there are many aria-like moments, all suggesting an intertextual dialogue with other adaptations.

Gary Schmidgall draws the parallel between Shakespeare's theatre and opera: both being what he calls the 'theatres of virtuosity'; both genres having voice as their fundamental element (cf. 1990: 283). Auden noted that

> Ariel *is* song; when he is truly himself, he sings […]. Yet Ariel […] cannot express any human feelings because he has none. The kind of voice he requires is exactly the kind that opera does not want, a voice which is lacking in the personal and the erotic as like an instrument as possible. (1957: 524)

This role is cast with a high coloratura soprano who, in each opera, has music of great virtuosity to sing, lying high in the range with florid melismas and extended vocalisations. These are moments when actual text recedes, or even disappears, which highlights the constant tension between words and music in opera, but also illustrate how the source text is 'silenced' both literally and metaphorically in these operas. This is analogous with what Michel Poizat has described as the conflict between reason and emotion where one feels a "radical antagonism between letting yourself be swept away by the emotion and applying yourself to the meaning of each word as it is sung" (1992: 36). The power of the actual material sound of the voice in opera, stripped of verbal signification, is significant, and florid vocal forms where sound obliterates text are disturbing because the sonority of the voice, as Carolyn Abbate reminds, "pointedly focuses our sense of the singing voice as one that can compel *without* benefit of words" (1991: 4).[13] Here the otherworldly nature of the character is emphasised; in both operas the representation of the character reflects the sonic world of the play where sound in various forms is omnipresent, much of it instigated by Ariel who tends more towards disembodied sound than word. This is something that Prospero seems to long for in Auden's poem:

> But now all these heavy books are no use to me any more, for
> Where I go, words carry no weight: it is best,
> Then, I surrender their fascinating counsel
> To the silent dissolution of the sea.
> (2003: 44)

This is echoed in Adès's opera through the words of Alonzo who, lamenting the apparent death of his son, cries out in his grief, "Words, words, words can't cure

---

13 Paul Robinson misses the point where he observes that "the crucial thing about high notes is that these altitudinous, incomprehensible tones occur precisely at the moments of greatest dramatic significance, when the text, in theory, ought to matter most […]. Opera, in other words, grows inarticulate just when it seeks to say the most important things." (1988: 334) These 'important things' are being articulated by the voices, in fact.

it" (2003a: 139). If in the play the trajectory is towards an ultimate silence, in the opera the ending is disembodied sound and 'silent' words.

The most 'powerful' and potent voices in opera are female; most florid music in opera is sung by female singers, erasing text – the melismas in particular in the vocal line often render words unintelligible. Jacqueline Fox-Good argues that Shakespeare 'feminises' his singers: music "gathers subversive energy" from the fact that

> it *is* music, given the way in which music's substance and meaning have been so consistently constructed in the Western tradition [...] for song and music are themselves thought to be a "feminine nature." [...] Western music shares with women a social construction of "irrationality" and the either divine (ineffable) and/or bestial (mad, unreasonable, or unreasoning) status which that irrationality confers. Such irrationality, of course, is irrevocably bound to the body, making music, like women, dangerously erotic and seductive. (1996: 254f.)

Shakespeare's plays are full of phenomenal songs used for particular dramatic and thematic purposes.[14] Ariel's "Full fathom five" can be seen as a *mise en abyme* and read as a "virtual epitaph for the play, a summary of Shakespeare's chief thematic preoccupations, with suffering, change, rebirth" (ibid.: 250).[15] Auden distinguishes between the two kinds of song in Shakespeare's plays:

> A called-for song is a song which is sung by one character at the request of another who wishes to hear music, so that action and speech are halted until the song is over. [...] On the stage, this means that the character

14 As Mark W. Booth notes: "A song set in a play, but set out of the play too by its music, facilitates our indulgence in feelings that may be undercut before and after the music plays." (1981: 118).

15 Fox-Good analyses the original version of the song by Robert Johnson which might have been used in the first production of the play, and argues that the song's words "emphasize death, intensify and beautify its finality; its music enacts transformation, change, possibility". The song inhabits "a middle realm, in neither air nor earth, but in the sea Ariel is singing about – a liminal, fluid, shifting medium with continuous potential for change and rebirth." (1996: 253) Auden notes that the song, which is sung by Ariel to Ferdinand, has the "effect of instrumental music [...] direct, positive, magical". The effect of the song on Ferdinand is "not to lessen his feeling of loss, but to change his attitude towards his grief from one of rebellion [...] to one of awe and reverent acceptance [...]. Thanks to the music, Ferdinand is able to accept the past, symbolized by his father, as past, and at once there stands before him his future, Miranda." (1975: 525f.).

> called upon to sing ceases to be himself and becomes a performer; the audience is not interested in him but in the quality of his singing. The songs, it must be remembered, are interludes embedded in a play written in verse or prose which is spoken; they are not arias in an opera where the dramatic medium itself is song, so that we forget that the singers are performers just as we forget that the actor speaking blank verse is an actor. (1975: 511)

According to Auden the second kind of singer is the 'impromptu singer' who

> stops speaking and breaks into song, not because anyone else has asked him to sing or is listening, but to relieve his feelings in a way that speech cannot so or to help him in some action. An impromptu song is not art but a form of personal behaviour. It reveals, as the called-for song cannot, something about the singer. (Ibid.: 522)

Ariel's song, "Full fathom five", would fall into Auden's 'called-for' song category. As in most operatic adaptations, the vocal casting can provide significant insights into the perspective on the play taken by composer and librettist, and the vocal distribution is of crucial importance in regard to the ultimate 'meaning' of the opera. In Hoiby's opera much of the casting is predictable, while in Adès's work there is some casting 'against the grain'.

Ariel in Adès's opera is called upon to sing music of the utmost virtuosity at the upper extreme of the vocal range. In the first half of the opera the words are all but unintelligible, provoking one critic to label the role "homicidal" (Ross 2004: 98)! At times the singing is deliberately excruciating to listen to, and surely to perform, but the vocal range gradually becomes less extreme with the words increasingly intelligible, adding to the poignancy and even 'humanity' of this character. This vocal casting embodies much of what Auden sees as the fundamental nature of the character. In this sense both operas depersonalise, de-eroticise and even de-gender the character through the nature of their music with its lack of human vocal warmth and in Adès's case in particular, 'inhuman' demands. Even operatically-trained voices at this extreme range lack warmth and beauty in the timbre, a quality prized in most operatic singing, but this strategy as it is used here is both a metaphorical as well as literal silencing of the character.

In "Full fathom five", Hoiby incorporates the dialogue from the play between Prospero and Miranda into Ariel's 'performance' of the song, using the formality inherent in the Shakespeare song to create a much larger structure using text from later in the scene to emphasise this sense of formality while still continuing to advance the action.[16] Adès makes very different choices; the quarrel between Prospero and Ariel is accompanied by jagged, violent music and angular vocal lines. Prospero commands Ariel to "bring me Ferdinand! Sing!" and Ariel's song emerges from the D that both sing in unison, but then he has a leap of more than an octave to a high E (this pitch seems to be almost the median in Ariel's early music in the opera – illustrative of the extremely high range of the part). In contrast to Hoiby's treatment of the song, Adès has no other voices and the song stands alone as it would in the play. Significantly, the echoes of the original words of the song are stronger here than in the rest of the libretto:

Full fathom five thy father lies;	Five fathoms deep / Your father lies
Of his bones are coral made;	Those are pearls / That were his eyes
Those are pearls that were his eyes;	Nothing of him / That was mortal
Nothing of him that doth fade	Is the same / His bones are coral
But doth suffer a sea-change	He has suffered / A sea change
Into something rich and strange.	Into something / Rich and strange
Sea-nymphs hourly ring his knell:	Sea-nymphs hourly / Ring his knell
[Burden: Ding-dong.]	I can hear them / Ding dong bell.
Hark! now I hear them – Ding-dong bell.	(Adès 2003a: 57–59)
(Shakespeare 2002: 122; 1.2, 396–403)	

The use of this extreme vocal line in both operas suggests the otherworldly nature of this spirit being, but, in Adès, through the very evident vocal effort required, the cruel imprisonment and even 'torture' of the character by the arch manipulator Prospero. He 'silences' any verbal resistance from Ariel by making the words unintelligible, and this enormous vocal exertion is a manifestation of the control he has over all the inhabitants of the island. The very materiality of the sound of the soprano voice under extreme pressure, and the particular qualities that the singer brings to it, add a very definite layer of significance to the opera, only fully revealed in performance. Here the operatic realisation of the character appears somewhat to contradict Auden's conception of the character in the play; Prospero 'silences' language and thus strips the character of his humanity who struggles through 'inhuman' vocal effort to assert himself. His command to 'sing' contradicts his silencing of their words, but it is perhaps the Barthesian "Grain of the Voice" (see 1977) here which is

16 Caliban only enters after this, as opposed to the play – the violence which characterises his entrance is unexpected!

most significant, not semantic meaning. However, as Prospero gradually loses control over the other characters, perhaps most importantly his daughter, he achieves some insight into their suffering, including that of Ariel, who 'regains' intelligible voice as this occurs.[17] When Ariel approaches humanity – "Your heart would soften / Mine would, were I human" (Adès 2003a: 223) – significantly, the vocal line suddenly descends right into the lowest and most intelligible register of the soprano voice.

Caliban is cast as a tenor in both operas, unusual if he is to be seen as a 'villain' as this character-type is usually the property of the lower voices. This vocal range can be seen as that of the hero, but this view is problematic. In Hoiby's opera the role requires a dramatic tenor and the vocal demands of the role are considerable. This results in aspects of the aggressive side of the character being more prominent by the very nature of the 'heroic' vocal exertions required, and could almost be seen as a more 'traditional' interpretation of the character when compared with the way the character has been presented on the spoken stage in recent years. He frequently appears vocally as more than a match for Prospero, primarily in the sense that his vocal weight and heft matches and often surpasses that of Prospero.

---

17 Of course, these are not the only songs in Shakespeare's *Tempest*, but those sung by Ariel differ substantially in intention and effect from those sung by the other characters. As Lindley notes: "[…] one of the most striking difference between them and the later songs of Stephano and Caliban is not merely their different musical vocabulary, but the fact that the first-person pronoun does not figure in their lyrics, so that, unlike the popular songs, they do not invite us to adopt the position of the singer, but place us passively as recipients of their address and observers of their effect. However much the music itself speaks to us as an aesthetic event and involves us in its emotional affect, it reaches us in a fashion quite distinct from the immediate, impromptu singing of the low-life characters. There is a world of difference, then, not only between the vocabulary and instrumentation of these opposed music, but between the fundamental nature of the relationship they set up between song and theatre audience." (2006: 226) Lindley further observes of the performance of Ariel's songs in the play that he is "singing airs which are neither scripted nor chosen by himself, but by Prospero. Throughout the play he is the magician's agent and executant; the nature of the investment that Ariel himself brings to his singing is therefore ill-defined […] many recent productions have seen [Prospero and Ariel's] relationship as one of tension, and have influenced in a variety of ways Ariel's reluctant servitude […] the effect on his musical performances is further to detach them from the performer and to emphasize their instrumentality in the prosecution of Prospero's designs. This is in accord with the general turn in *Tempest* criticism over the last thirty-five years or so, which, concentrating on the politics of the play, has converted Prospero from benign magus to imperialist despot." (Ibid.: 227).

In contrast, the role in Adès's opera requires a sweet-voiced lyric tenor with a good top register, and the potentially 'heroic' character of the tenor voice is undercut by making his music a mixture of lyricism and rhythmically harsh and jagged lines with large interval leaps. As opposed to the silencing of Ariel, he is en-voiced. Musically, he is often a deliberate mirror of Prospero: his mood changes can be as abrupt and unexpected as those of Prospero. There is no suggestion that he attempted to rape Miranda as in the play; thus our harsh judgment of his subjection and ill treatment by Prospero becomes even more pronounced in Adès's opera, and further emphasises the critical representation of Prospero established throughout the opera. The text that Caliban sings, as in the play, is just as or even more linguistically inventive compared with the other characters, and is cast in the same linguistic register, suggesting a complexity to the character and adding to his positive portrayal.

The view of Caliban and Ariel as a reflection of Prospero has been prominent in more recent criticism of the play with, in crude terms, Caliban representative of the flesh and Ariel of the mind (cf. Lindley 2006: 64). One could argue that something approaching this conception occurs in Adès's opera in the musical characterisation of these three characters. In their vocal lines, all three characters frequently mirror each other, with both Ariel and Caliban sometimes echoing different facets of Prospero's vocal delivery. At times he has the jagged and extreme vocal mode of Ariel while at others he approaches the lyricism and eroticism of Caliban's music in his more contemplative moments.[18] In Hoiby's opera the musical characterisation of each of these characters remains more distinctly separate with each character essentially retaining their vocal identity throughout.

As might be expected, some of the most effective 'stand-alone' numbers in both operas emerge from soliloquies rather than songs as such, and it is not surprising that it is Caliban's "Be not affear'd" from the play – a speech which directly addresses the music thematic of the play – which elicits the most lyrical response from both composers. Many reviews of Adès's opera singled out this moment for special praise, and the similar moment in Hoiby's work has become a popular solo concert piece.[19] Hoiby has the 'aria' arising out of the

18 One could see this strategy as an echo of what Verdi does in *Otello* where the vocal characterization of the three central characters varies between the extreme lyricism of Desdemona and the jagged, quasi-spoken delivery of Iago, with Otello wrenched between the two poles of this spectrum according to the dramatic and emotional situation.

19 The composer envisaged the potential popularity of this piece and wrote an alternative concert ending as an appendix in his score. Soon after the premiere of the opera it was 'appropriated' by the great soprano, Leontyne Price, and sung as a stand-alone aria

scene in which Caliban tempts Stephano and Trinculo with the prospect of usurping Prospero's power and the possibility of possession of his daughter. The scene is interrupted by an invisible Ariel, with 'tabor and pipe', imitating Trinculo's voice. Out of a mainly recitative-like scene the aria comes as a moment of great lyricism with a smoothly-descending vocal line over an undulating string accompaniment. Some way into the aria an off-stage female chorus provides an aural equivalent of the "thousand twangling instruments will hum about mine ears" (Hoiby 1986: 198f.). In effect the aria is divided into two verses and the choral accompaniment becomes more prominent in the second verse as both Caliban and the sopranos rise in unison to a sustained high A natural as the key changes from D major to A major (the key of the finale). The aria ends quietly with a soft high F for Caliban with two bars of the opening undulating accompaniment in the strings. The structure of the aria, with its repetition and build-up to a climax, gives it a formal quality and it is very much a vocal set piece, mirroring in some ways the spoken 'aria' for Caliban from the play.

> CALIBAN (with distant voices):
> Be not afear'd; the isle is full of noises, sounds and sweet airs, that give delight and hurt not. Sometimes a thousand twangling instruments will hum about mine ears; and sometime voices, that, if I then had wak'd after long sleep, will make me sleep again; and then, in dreaming, the clouds methought would open, and show riches ready to drop upon me; that, when I wak'd, I cried to dream again. (Ibid.: 3.2.136–144)

Adès develops a similar moment in his opera. Several of Caliban's scenes are played out in front of the whole court in act two. A quarrel between Antonio and Sebastian occurs after a choral introduction to the act and Antonio turns bitterly on all around him as he perceives that he is blamed for the disaster which has met their voyage. His bitter tirade is interrupted by Ariel imitating his voice and a frantic, high-lying ensemble ensues which has Ariel soaring at the top his range above the 'confusion' of the other voices. At the peak of the ensemble Caliban enters and his wonder at this strange new sight is mocked by the court who murmur: "A monster…a local" (Adès 2003a:106). Stephano and Trinculo, in a grotesquely comic duet (the combination in duet between counter tenor and bass is inherently comic), taunt him and then ply him with

---

in concert (see http://articles.philly.com/1988-01-25/news/26283234_1_david-garvey-songs-arias).

brandy against the advice from Gonzalo. Caliban's vocal line becomes increasingly animated as he generously, but drunkenly, promises the assembled company that he will show them the secrets and delights of the island. This develops into a large ensemble, again with Ariel soaring above. As the court becomes aware of the strange sound of this almost disembodied voice it causes consternation and the ensemble is interrupted by Caliban's aria. Suddenly the jagged chromaticism and violent rhythm of the preceding ensemble is 'silenced' by Caliban's high A and the aria is accompanied by shimmering strings in a clear A major. His vocal line is smoothly lyrical and slow-moving and is a strong aural contrast with what has gone before. Although it is not formally structurally demarcated as Hoiby's equivalent aria, there is still enough of the feeling of a set piece, mainly in terms of the harmonic, rhythmic and instrumental separation of this moment from the rest of the discourse, and the aria ends with an octave descent from high A to a *piano* sustained low A. It is one of the most magical moments in the opera and is only rivalled in this by the reconciliation quintet at the end of the opera.

CALIBAN:
Friends don't fear
The island's full of noises
Sounds and voices
It's the spirits

Sometimes they come
After I've slept
And hum me
Back to sleep
With a twanging
And a sweetness
Like playing
A thousand instruments
Then I dream I'm seeing heaven
It's as if
The clouds had opened.

I see riches
Raining from them
Then I wake
And cry to dream again.
(Ibid.: 125–127)

Both composers return to unambiguous tonality in the finale of both works: music functions here as a metaphor for harmony and reconciliation. At this moment, music seen as an expression of the ineffable, silences language with its limited capacity for transcendence. Hoiby's finale is one of the most effective moments in the whole score and incorporates all the vocal forces at his command. The great moment of reconciliation is achieved in music of ravishing beauty, much like the equivalent moment in Adès's opera. Hoiby leads into this with the final lines of Ariel's song: "Where the bee sucks", ending on a high B which is taken up by the female chorus as what had been a vividly chromatic passage modulates into an ethereal A major. The melody that is woven through the finale is first heard in sustained strings and it gradually is taken up with variations by the various voices. Miranda's "brave new world" occurs at the musical highpoint of the ensemble, and the finale is unashamedly 'romantic' in idiom and sustains the A major key, similar to Adès's sudden movement into a clear C major for the equivalent moment in his opera.[20] There is even an echo in Hoiby of the great reconciliation moments in Mozart's *Figaro* and *Così* with the tempo changing abruptly from *lento* to *allegro* where different voice groups alternate, much as would happen in a Mozart finale. However, the tempo moderates back to *lento* to set up the final leave-taking between Ariel and Prospero.

As all the voices die away, they are isolated by the lighting and the stage direction indicates: "Prospero and Ariel regard each other; with a small gesture Prospero releases Ariel, who receives his freedom with a sudden amazed enlivenment" (Hoiby 1986: 319f.). Here Hoiby's interpretation differs radically from that of Adès. The final moment is described in the stage directions as: "Ariel departs slowly, tasting his freedom, and with a loving glance towards Prospero" (Ibid.: 320). This is accompanied by soft, sustained strings, still in the 'reconciliation' key of A major with echoes of the opening A major chords of the opera, and Ariel vanishes to a rapid harp arpeggio. There is little sense of any conflict remaining, with the island returning to its primal state. Hoiby does not have Shakespeare's epilogue as spoken by Prospero although it is printed at this point in the vocal score.[21] The moment of reconciliation and forgiveness in Adès occurs as the harmony briefly moves into C major and he develops a lyrical diatonic melody sung by Prospero and then a form of canon as each character sings variations of this melody. In these large ensembles it is music rather than text that carries the emotional charge and meaning; text, in large ensembles is virtually silenced.

---

20 One could argue that this is a rather obvious musical gesture, yet its effectiveness at a similar dramatic moment in both operas cannot be disputed.

21 In an insert to the score Hoiby notes that it is not to be performed.

Adès's opera has a final scene not in Shakespeare with Caliban alone yet 'accompanied' by the offstage voice of Ariel in a wordless vocalise sounding out variations on the notes in his characteristic chord – variations of an E-B-C sharp pattern established earlier. Prospero pleads in vain with Ariel to stay; he has freed Ariel although he has also attempted to 'silence' him in the final moments of the opera. The scene ends with Caliban 'reclaiming' his 'kingdom' before all dissolves into silence with the haunting sound of the now 'disembodied', and unaccompanied – yet still 'powerful' voice of Ariel – truly a spirit of air: acousmatic sound encompassing physical absence but sonic presence – a final acknowledgement of the visceral power of the voice without any need of signification through text.

The last word Caliban sings is his own name – through his 'naming' of himself he has reclaimed what was stolen from him. He echoes Ariel's E-B-C sharp pattern, once the sounds of silencing but now of freedom for both.[22]

> CALIBAN: Who was here?
> Have they disappeared?
> Were there others?
> Were we brothers?
> Did we feast?
> And give gifts?
> Were there fires
> And ships?
> They were human seeming
> I was dreaming
> In the gleam of the sand
> ARIEL: (*offstage*) A-i-e
> CALIBAN: Caliban
> In the hiss of the spray
> In the deep of the bay
> In the gulf in the swell
> Caliban.
> ARIEL: (*offstage*) A-i-e
> (Adès 2003a: 243–245)

22 Fox-Good maintains of the play that "although Caliban has learned Prospero's language [...] it is not only within the discourse of colonialism that Caliban can speak. He possesses an(other) language of his own, as well: music. It is Caliban's distinctive sound, the grain of his voice, that empowers him in ways even Prospero cannot subjugate." (1996: 261).

The postscript of Auden's poem, with Ariel's vocalization suggesting Auden's 'evaporating sigh', has similar echoes:

> Never hope to say farewell,
> For our lethargy is such
> Heaven's kindness cannot touch
> Nor earth's frankly brutal drum;
> This was long ago decided,
> Both of us know why,
> Can, alas, foretell,
> When our falsehoods are divided,
> What we shall become,
> One evaporating sigh
> … *I*
>
> (Auden 2003: 45)

Caliban's is the last voice we both hear and 'see' in the opera. The two characters are musically irrevocably linked; isolated, yet free together on their island. Adès suggests that, freed from Prospero, and through the power and 'authenticity' of his own voice, Caliban has reclaimed his kingdom while Ariel has moved into the desired free and ethereal state. Caliban, by echoing Ariel's music is 're-learning' authentic language which endows his freedom.[23] He has defied Prospero's earlier accusation: "Creature, you have no future." (Adès 2003a: 220) One can interpret this representation as suggesting the ephemeral nature and ultimate failure and, indeed, final silencing of the colonial project. The wordless sound of Ariel's voice is symbolic of Prospero's relinquishing of control and Ariel's freedom – finally freed from the 'curse' of language.[24]

---

23 In the play Fox-Good argues that Caliban's "distinctive *sound* is one he possessed when he was 'his own king' and that he does not relinquish even when he *knows* Prospero's language, which he then uses in order to curse his master […]. When Prospero is destroyed, music shall remain." (Ibid.).

24 Adès does not use Ariel's final song, "Where the bee sucks". As Lindley notes, this song has proven problematic for stage directors of the play. The song accompanies Prospero's putting on his ducal robes but "seems a strange ditty to assist in the moment of Prospero's triumph. Where the song speaks of a life of hedonistic idleness, Prospero is about to resume the cares of ducal authority in Milan; where the narrative is focused upon Prospero's action, the lyric speaks entirely of Ariel. The apparent collision between action and song has often prompted directors to move the song elsewhere in the play, or else to have Ariel perform it without reference to Prospero […]. 'Where the bee sucks', from another perspective, offers a clear sense of the implication and consequence of Prospero's

Auden likens Prospero to the Duke in *Measure for Measure*: "The victory of Justice which he brings about seems rather a duty than a source of joy to himself." His tone is that of a man who "longs for a place where silence shall be all" (2003: 67). Adès's opera ends seemingly unresolved, disappearing into a resonant silence.[25] In a recent commentary Adès famously described Wagner as a 'fungus', yet his work is suffused with Wagner – not the least in the emergence of Prospero as a disgruntled, disillusioned and increasingly vulnerable Wotan-like figure, lacking the overwhelming power of his counterpart in the play, and covered in a series of body markings eerily suggestive of the runes of Wotan's spear.[26]

These two adaptations thus reveal a very different approach to the source. Hoiby's opera might be considered as *Literaturoper* while Adès's is more an appropriation of the source. Hoiby, by using the original text and retaining much of the action and dramaturgical shape of the play, suggests a more 'traditional' conception, culminating in resolution, reconciliation and forgiveness. Adès, while also interrogating the idea of forgiveness and mercy, sees the play as a starting point for a meditation on opera itself. His opera emphasizes the pervasive self-referentiality of the play, particularly its problematising of language and theatre, and by using a theatre as the setting the Metropolitan Opera production imaginatively responds in a meta-theatrical fashion using a wide range of visual resources which expose the inner-workings of the opera house, thus drawing attention to the inherently self-conscious artificiality of the operatic art form itself. Consciously or not, both Adès and La Page seem to be in dialogue with Auden's poem as well.

---

abjuration of magic. Once his 'art' is abandoned, then Prospero must lose control of Ariel and of his singing […]. Ariel sings in his own insouciant voice, [and] he does so in an entirely solipsistic song […]. When Ariel finally sings for himself, the self-indulgence of his lyric opens up the possibility that music itself is morally neutral, that its effects ultimately depend upon the uses to which it is put." (2006: 230–232) What Adès does in his reconfiguring of the source is to suggest this freeing of Ariel in his wordless vocalise which ends the opera.

25 Lindley notes that after this song in the play "there is no more music. Indeed, of all the late plays this is the one whose ending is most provisional" (2006: 232).

26 Adès: "I don't find Wagner's an organic, necessary art. Wagner's music is fungal. I think Wagner is a fungus. It's a sort of unnatural growth. It's parasitic in a sense – on its models, on its material. His material doesn't grow symphonically – it doesn't grow through a musical logic – it grows parasitically. It has a laboratory atmosphere." (2012) As Gavin Plumley notes: "If in Shakespeare's play Prospero is the origin of poetry and imagination, in the opera – as with Wagner's Wotan – he is a source of darkness and despair." (2012: 43) There is an interesting absence in Adès's latest work, *Totentanz*, premiered in 2013 at the Proms. It is a setting of a text which accompanied a now absent frieze that was destroyed when Lübeck's Marienkirche was bombed in WW 2.

> Sing, Ariel, sing,
> Sweetly, dangerously
> Out of the sour
> And shiftless water,
> Lucidly out
> Of the dozing tree,
> Entrancing, rebuking
> The raging heart
> With a smoother song
> Than this rough world,
> Unfeeling god.
>
> O brilliantly, lightly,
> Of separation,
> Of bodies and death,
> Unanxious one, sing
> To man, meaning me,
> As now, meaning always,
> In love or out,
> Whatever that means,
> Trembling he takes
> The silent passage
> Into discomfort.
> (Auden 2003: 69)

Schmigall sagely observed, "what a particular actor, director, scholar, or composer finds in a Shakespeare play will tell more about the finder than about the play itself" (1990: 259), a comment certainly born out by these two very different works. While both operas engage with the source work in inventive ways, it is Adès's opera which directly addresses issues of language and silence in a most creative manner. His opera offers a postcolonial perspective; Prospero becomes a much more authoritarian figure, emblematic of the colonial invader and oppressor, while the representation of Caliban, largely through the 'softening' of the character through the lyrical and extremely beautiful music he is given to sing, is more sympathetic than in 'traditional', older productions of the play. In the final moments of the opera the audience is left with the sound of Caliban and Ariel's voices rather than those of the seemingly more powerful characters – there is no epilogue for Prospero – he has been 'silenced'. Mary Ann Smart describes how the orchestra in Lucia's mad scene ultimately silences her voice (cf. 1992: 140), but here the opposite occurs, and it is Ariel's voice that silences the orchestra that, with Prospero, might be regarded as a symbol of colonial oppression. Unlike the case in many operatic mad scenes and other similar moments, where prior musical material is recalled in the orchestra, here it is the character themself who summons up the music they had previously performed. It is ultimately the 'text-free', 'silent' voice that completes the meaning of this opera.

Perhaps it is too early to say whether these operas will dispell the perception that *The Tempest*, despite many attempts, defies effective operatic representation. It might appear to be a shoal upon which are 'littered many hulks', to misquote a previous comment, yet both operas provide strikingly different, but highly engaging responses to Shakespeare's play; only time will tell how seaworthy they are, but the seas are calm and the gales auspicious!

References

Abbate, Carolyn (1991). *Unsung Voices: Opera and Musical Discourse in the Nineteenth Century*. Princeton, NJ: Princeton UP.

Adès, Thomas (2003a). *The Tempest: An Opera in Three Acts*. Vocal Score. London: Faber Music.

——— (2003b). http://thomasades.com/compositions/tempest_the [02/01/2014].

——— (2012). [Interview with Tom Service]. *The Guardian*, 29 September. http://www.theguardian.com/books/2012/sep/28/composer-thomas-ades [04/01/2014].

Auden, W.H. (1975). *The Dyer's Hand and Other Essays*. London: Faber and Faber.

——— (2003). *The Sea and the Mirror: A Commentary on Shakespeare's* The Tempest. Princeton, NJ: Princeton UP.

Barthes, Roland (1977). "The Grain of the Voice". *Image – Music – Text*. Transl. Stephen Heath. New York, NY: Fontana. 179–189.

Booth, Mark W. (1981). *The Experience of Songs*. New Haven, CT/London: Yale UP.

Botstein, Leon (2013). "Words and Music: The Legacy of Dietrich Fischer-Dieskau (1925–2012)". http://mq.oxfordjournals.org/content/early/2013/07/31/musqtl.gdt008 [06/01/2014].

Clements, Andrew (2004). "The Tempest". http://www.theguardian.com/music/2004/feb/11/classicalmusicandopera [06/01/2014].

Dean, Winton (1964). "What is a Musical Drama?" *The Musical Times* 105/1461: 810–814.

Dymkowski, Christine (2000). *The Tempest*. Cambridge: CUP.

Fox-Good, Jacquelyn (1996). "Other Voices: The Sweet, Dangerous Air(s) of Shakespeare's *Tempest*". *Shakespeare Studies* 24. Madison, NJ: Fairleigh Dickinson UP. 241–274.

Gekoski, Rick (2011). "Fact-check Fears". http://www.theguardian.com/books/2011/sep/09/fact-check-rick-gekoski [07/01/2014].

Hoiby, Lee (1986). *The Tempest: An Opera in Three Acts*. Vocal Score. New York, NY: G. Schirmer.

Holland, Bernard (1994). "New Musical 'Tempest': Servant of Shakespeare". http://www.nytimes.com/1994/07/18/arts/opera-review-new-musical-tempest-servant-of-shakespeare.html [06/01/2014].

Lindley, David (2006). *Shakespeare and Music*. Tunbridge Wells: Arden Shakespeare.

Oakes, Meredith (2003). http://thomasades.com/compositions/tempest_the [02/01/2014].

Plumley, Gavin (2012). *The Tempest*. Metropolitan Opera Program. 43–45. http://www.metoperafamily.org/uploadedFiles/MetOpera/7_season/911_playbill/6_Tempest/Nov%2010%20Tempest.pdf [04/01/2014].

Poizat, Michel (1992). *The Angel's Cry: Beyond the Pleasure Principle in Opera*. Trans. Arthur Denner. Ithaca, NY: Cornell UP.

Robinson, Paul (1988). "A Deconstructive Postscript: Reading Libretti and Misreading Opera". Arthur Groos, Roger Parker, eds. *Reading Opera*. Princeton, NJ: Princeton UP. 328–346.

Ross, Alex (2004). "Rich and Strange: Thomas Adès' *Tempest*". *The New Yorker*, March 1. http://www.therestisnoise.com/2004/04/thomas_ads_temp.html [02/01/2014].

Sanders, Julie (2005). *Adaptation and Appropriation*. New York, NY: Routledge.

Schmidgall, Gary (1986). "A Long Voyage". *Opera News* 50: 10–13.

——— (1990). *Shakespeare and Opera*. Oxford: OUP.

Shakespeare, William (1968). *The Tempest*. Ed. Anne Barton. Harmondsworth: New Penguin Shakespeare.

——— (2002). *The Tempest*. Ed. David Lindley. Cambridge: CUP.

Smart, Mary Ann (1992). "The Silencing of Lucia". *Cambridge Opera Journal* 4/2: 119–141.

Wynne, Peter (1994). "A Midsummer's Night Tempest". *Opera News* 58. June. http://search.proquest.com.ezproxy2.library.usyd.edu.au/docview/224223040/fulltextPDF/142CBC81492EEF1D96/53?accountid=14757 [03/01/2014].

Word and Music Studies: Surveying the Field

∵

The Film Musical as a Subject for Word and Music Studies

Emily Petermann

The film musical with its reliance on a frequent blending of the non-diegetic music track and the diegetic sound track and its alternation between speech and song provides a special case of word-music(-image) relations that have yet to be theorized in a Word and Music Studies context. The often fluid transition from dialog to musical number marks not a change in diegesis, but another mode of expression within the storyworld – musical numbers are instrumental in furthering the plot, yet serve different functions from dialog. Drawing on Possible Worlds Theory, this paper demonstrates that the less realistic mode of representation found in the musical numbers allows the musical film to construct a separate ontological realm of dream, fantasy, hypnosis, or performance which is characterized by song and contrasts both with the actual world of the viewers and with the textual actual world of the characters, which is characterized by speech.

•••

Though word and music studies have made great progress in defining a number of relevant fields of study, the filmic and theatrical arts – with the notable exception of opera – have to date been somewhat undertheorized within this framework. In contrast to opera, the musical is characterized less by the blending of dialog and music than by an uneasy balance between them, with spoken dialog (i.e., the 'book') alternating with sung 'numbers'.[1] 'Book' is the term used in musical theater for "the script of a musical, excluding the lyrics of the songs" (Shepherd et al., eds. 2003: 632), while the songs are referred to as 'numbers', or "item[s] (song, dance, instrumental) in a program of musical entertainment" (ibid.: 637).

1 Through-sung musicals such as some by Stephen Sondheim or Andrew Lloyd Webber are a significant exception to this practice and can be seen as a gesture towards operatic form and style. Of course, opera, too, possesses such a distinction between the aria and the recitative, which is related to but not identical with that of number vs. book in the musical. As this paper will show, the more marked contrast between the presence or absence of diegetic music heightens the contrast between such sections and establishes different possible worlds within the musical that are characterized by song vs. speech.

 | DOI 10.1163/9789004314863_014

In the case of the *film* musical, there is yet another tension between the patterns of speech and song as they also occur on the stage, on the one hand, and traditional uses of non-diegetic music in the film, on the other. I will thus examine the film musical as a fruitful field of intermedial interaction between words and music. First, a note on my material: for pragmatic reasons, I will restrict myself to film rather than stage musicals, though my examples are actually all film adaptations of previous Broadway successes. I will examine a few well-known, classical musicals from the 1950s – *Singin' in the Rain* (1952) and *Oklahoma!* (1955) – and one contemporary hit – *Chicago* (2002). These are all 'integrated' musicals, a term that was coined to distinguish them from revues or other vaudeville-inspired formats from which the musical developed. Integration in this sense means that the songs are not mere ornamentation but are fully integrated into or central to the plot of the film.[2]

In the following, I begin by considering some of the traditional functions of film music in non-musical films, with an eye to extending these observations to the special case of the musical. I will then argue that the musical's distinction between book and numbers can be reexamined in terms of a frequent assignation of music and speech to separate ontological realms. To do so, I will draw on concepts from Possible Worlds Theory as it has been used in literary criticism by Marie-Laure Ryan (see 1992) and others to discuss distinctions between the real world of the film, which is characterized by speech, and the ideal world that is characterized by song and dance.

Film Music in Non-musical Films

Studies of film music have traditionally focused on non-diegetic music, examining the soundtrack and its contribution to atmosphere, pace, or characterization. These studies have explicitly excluded the film musical, recognizing that its music operates in a very different and multifaceted manner, to which

---

2 But see McMillan 2006 for a powerful critique of the concept of integration and an argument instead for a view of the musical as characterized by the difference between book and number. He suggests the term "coherence" rather than "integration" as the ideal to which the musical aspires (ibid.: 73; 208f.). Though he speaks primarily of the stage musical, his observations hold true for the film musical as well. Non-integrated musicals such as several early 'backstage' musicals or biopics on the lives of musicians would also be fascinating in this context, but the relationship between the book and numbers is quite different and so I will exclude this type from my present discussion.

I will return in a moment. Typical functions of film music include contributing to the establishment of a setting in a particular time and place and to the characterization of a figure or that figure's mental or emotional state, reinforcing the mood or atmosphere of a scene (cf. Phillips 2009: 172), and helping to "elicit feelings and moods that are difficult or impossible to explain in words" (ibid.: 175). I will briefly touch upon three of these aspects of film music in general that are important for my examination of music in the film musical: the use of non-diegetic music to underscore the narrative or what happens in the diegesis; film music's connections to the emotions; and the way different approaches to sound design within a film can help distinguish different realms.

Typically, film music serves to underscore the film's narrative, which involves a parallel conception of music and images, in which the images are generally seen as dictating the music that accompanies them, rather than vice versa. According to Siegfried Kracauer in *Theory of Film*, music "restates, in a language of its own, certain tendencies, or meanings of the pictures it accompanies" (qtd. Larsen 2005: 42). I will ignore for the moment this relatively simplistic conception of musical meaning and focus instead on the idea of the sound track as underscoring or supporting the image track, which reflects a traditional understanding of the relationship between these components of a film. This parallelism, however, is not the only approach. Indeed, film music can also be conceived as a counterpoint to the images, contrasting with and complementing the narrative they convey with an additional story of its own. In the 1933 film *Deserter*, the composer Vsevolod Pudovkin chose to break with the "monotonous parallelism" of most film music, instead using uplifting marching music to contrast with the images of a workers' rebellion being put down. He was striving for "the objective representation of reality in the image and the revelation of the profound inner content of reality in the sound" (Pudovkin 1960: 310f.; qtd. Larsen 2005: 82f.), such that the drive towards victory remains literally audible even in a scene of temporary defeat.[3]

The ideal of counterpoint in film music is important when we look at the way segments dominated by music – the musical numbers – often serve as a counterpoint to the narrative conveyed in the non-musical segments of the book. As with Pudovkin's distinction between outer and inner realities, the musical tends to ally speech with realism and external reality, while the musical numbers express an inner reality connected with dreams, longings, and emotions.

3 But cf. Larsen's observation that audiences may not have appreciated the particular nuances of meaning Pudovkin was aiming for (2005: 82f.).

Bernard Herrmann, presumably best known for his composition of scores for several Hitchcock films, emphasized this role of film music in expressing emotional content alongside its function in shaping the narrative and determining tempo. He speaks of music's ability to "invest a scene with terror, grandeur, gaiety, or misery", but also to "seek out and intensify the inner thoughts of the characters" (Herrmann 1945: 27; qtd. Larsen 2005: 140), expressing "what the actor can't show or tell" (Gilling 1971–1972: 37; qtd. ibid.). Alfred Hitchcock, too, asserted that film music can "express the unspoken" (Watts 1933–1934: 82; qtd. ibid.: 232 n19).

Music's ability to represent emotion is of course disputed, with a wide range of positions taken by composers, critics, and philosophers of music. Without going into this debate here, it seems safe to say that music cannot generally represent anything specific, telling a story in a narrow sense. Nonetheless, its associations for listeners with basic emotions and moods are hard to ignore, even if these associations are seen as culturally conditioned rather than inherent in the music (cf. Larsen 2005: 71; 74). In the context of the present examination of the way music and words interact in the film musical, it is significant that discussions of music's ability to express emotion often emphasize the contrast between such expression and the different mode of expression found in language. As I will argue, the musical exploits this difference by assigning particular types of content to the musical numbers as opposed to non-musical speech. Very often this is emotional content that is in some way repressed or censored by the characters' conscious selves and is dependent upon the emotional release of song and dance.

Not only musicals, but also non-musical films may employ contrasting sound design concepts to distinguish different realms. In his discussion of different approaches to sound design, James Buhler (see 2001) explores the opposition between diegetic and non-diegetic music in films such as *The Jazz Singer* (1927) and *King Kong* (1933). While the former is considered the first sound film, only the musical numbers in fact employ synchronized sound, using for the rest of the narrative an approach to sound design drawn from silent films – with asynchronous musical accompaniment. This status of the numbers as special and as distinct from the narrative will set a pattern that remains intact for a large number of musicals even after entire films are synchronized from the late 1920s on. Buhler's other examples, though, show that sound design can also help to structure a non-musical film. The King Kong, 1933 version of *King Kong*, for example, reserves music in the soundtrack for the portion of the action set on Skull Island, marking this as a fantastic place apart from the ordinary and music-less scenes set in New York (cf. Buhler 2001: 56). As we will see, musical numbers similarly provide a whiff of unreality or fantasy, distinguishing them from the prevailing realism (more or less) of the rest of the film.

Roles of Film Music in Musicals

The combination of music with non-musical speech is a defining characteristic of the musical, whether on stage or screen. The division of a musical into narrative portions and song-and-dance numbers is such an obvious feature that this element of its structure has received a lot of attention. It is both a large part of what appeals to fans of the genre and, at the same time, what its critics disparage for its lack of realism.

Part of the way songs are integrated into the plot is to find some way of motivating them within the storyworld of the film. The most obvious form of motivation for musical numbers is a plot that centers on show business, such as in the backstage musical, which requires little in the way of a transition between narrative and number: the performance of songs fits within the realistic frame of the story if characters are professional singers and dancers.[4] When this is not the case, however, the musical requires some other device to plausibly link song and dialog. The lack of realism in characters singing and dancing means that what happens in the numbers is generally in some kind of an imaginary sphere – whether the fantasy world of performance, of dreams and desires, of memory, of hypnosis, or set in a world that is a fairy-tale domain altogether (*The Wizard of Oz*, *Brigadoon*, many Disney fairy-tale musicals, etc.). In addition to the question of realism, on a structural level the transition from speech to song in the film musical requires some kind of a bridge: "Song as a special domain would be opposed to the hum-drum world of dialog but this would constitute a naked opposition, an all-or-nothing alternative between two antithetical realms [as in the stage musical, cf. Altman 1987: 66]. The film introduces a diegetic source of music [...] to break down the absoluteness of that opposition" (ibid.: 67). Altman argues that the sudden presence of an orchestra playing during the numbers is an established convention in the stage musical and needs no such bridging device, but that with their more complex sound tracks film musicals work to mix and link these disparate modes more

4 Many of the songs of a show or backstage musical can be compared to what Carolyn Abbate in opera studies has labeled "phenomenal music", in contrast to the "noumenal" music that pervades characters' lives and that they are seemingly unaware of as music (1991: 119). For a discussion of this distinction, cf. Halliwell 2005: 56–58.

subtly. He has termed this transition an "audio dissolve" – a reversal of the traditional hierarchy between image and sound, such that events in the image track are often dictated by what happens in the music track, as when people begin moving to the rhythm. He explains the audio dissolve as follows:

> At first the image track calls forth musical accompaniment by means of an audio dissolve (sound is motivated, naturally and thematically, by the diegesis/image). Once this progression is complete, the reversal can take place: *the movement which we see on screen is now an accompaniment to the music track*. A new mode of causality now appears, a simultaneous mode wherein the image is 'caused' by the music rather than by some previous image. In short, the normally dominant image track now keeps time to the music track, instead of simply being accompanied by it. The music and its rhythm now initiate movement rather than vice versa. (Ibid.: 69; italics in the original)

Examples for such transitions include the rhythmic walking and other everyday movements Fred Astaire uses as lead-ins to dance numbers (a shoe-shine, a toy drum, or simply walking could suddenly be a tap dance feature), the way he and other musical stars move "from diegetic conversation to diegetic song" "by rhythmifying and melodizing his voice patterns" (ibid.: 67), as well as humming or other diegetic sounds that evoke related supra-diegetic music, such as a music box in the Elvis movie *Blue Hawaii* (1961) or a robin singing outside the window during "A Spoonful of Sugar" in *Mary Poppins* (1964). The diegetic sound is supplemented by a non-diegetic orchestra, making of the whole performance a supra-diegetic music, partly outside, partly inside the diegesis.[5]

As this shows, the levels of diegetic and non-diegetic sound in the musical film are thoroughly complicated in a way that is not typical of non-musical films.[6]

---

5 *Supra-diegetic* is Altman's term for music in a film musical that hovers somewhere between purely diegetic and purely non-diegetic music. A fairly rare phenomenon outside of the musical, the supra-diegetic music of the audio dissolve is central to the switch between book and number sections of the musical film, as the music transitions from being apparently only audible to the audience to being sung or performed by characters in the film or vice versa. It generally does not become entirely diegetic, however, as an off-screen orchestral accompaniment usually heightens the musical experience in an in-between, supra-diegetic manner.

6 There are also cases of audio dissolves occurring in non-musical films, such as when the song "Non Nobis Domine" is sung by Henry's army in *Henry V* (1989) and serves as a bridge between diegetic and non-diegetic music. But because such diegetic music is relatively infrequent in non-musical films, however, the audio dissolve is a minor phenomenon there compared to its role in the musical (cf. Buhler 2001: 40f.).

It is important to note that the transition from dialog to number thus marks not so much a change in diegesis, but another mode of expression within the storyworld – no mere ornamentation, musical numbers (in integrated musicals) are instrumental in furthering the plot, yet serve different functions from dialog. Very often, what cannot be said can be sung, as exemplified by the love song as expression of emotion.

Picking up on music's traditional association with the emotions, as mentioned earlier, the love song is a typical example of how song opens up an ideal realm that contrasts with non-musical dialog. In *Oklahoma!*, for example, Laurey and Curly are not willing to acknowledge their feelings for one another, yet beginning with the song "The Surrey with the Fringe on the Top" they use duets as an unreal space for exploring romantic fantasies. In this scene, Curly tries to convince Laurey to be his date to the barn dance that evening, describing in this song the beautiful horses and carriage he would use to bring her there. Seduced by his vision, Laurey dreams along with him.

When the song is interrupted, Curly admits he "made the whole thing up", upon which she accuses him of lying: "Aunt Eller, make him get hisself outta here, tellin' me lies!", which emphasizes not only the dream-like quality of the song but also her inability in spoken conversation to admit that she is attracted to Curly. He begins singing again, prefaced with the words, "don't you wish there was such a rig, though? I can picture the whole thing". His soothing lullaby-esque tone and rocking motion while singing the last verse calm Laurey and she lays her head on his shoulder to the sound of lyrics revolving around dreams, demonstrating the way the sound track determines what happens on the image track, an example of the audio dissolve as discussed above. At the close of the song, the contrast between song and speech is again emphasized when Laurey insists "only there ain't no such rig. Whydya come around here with your stories and your lies, gettin' me all worked up that way?" Laurey's un-spoken desire for Curly and the romance he sings of is clearly visible to outsiders, even if she won't yet admit it to herself. Aunt Eller responds: "Why don't you grab her and kiss her when she acts that way, Curly? She's just achin' for you to, I bet." To which Laurey retorts: "I won't even speak to him, let alone allow him to kiss me", which forms quite a contrast to her loving motions and facial expressions during the song.

The later song "People Will Say We're in Love" fulfills a similar function. In lyrics such as "Don't take my arm too much / Don't keep your hand in mine / Your hand feels so grand in mine / People will say we're in love!" Curly and Laurey use a tactic of indirection to acknowledge and deny their feelings at the same time. This fits with Altman's description of the ideal world that musicals explore through dreams, make-believe, or the unreal world of performance. Altman has coined the term "personality dissolve" (1987: 80f.) to explain the way characters can try on the repressed sides of their personality in modes such as dream, hypnosis, or make-believe, where they do not have to take responsibility for their feelings or actions. What he implies but does not explicitly state, is that this 'ideal' world is characterized by song, while the 'real' world is one of speech. An even more marked example of this use of music as a safe space is the dream ballet within the same film, in which Laurey works through her feelings for Curly and for his rival, Jud Fry, in a dream sequence that is clearly set apart from the textual actual world of the rest of the film. At the beginning of the scene, after Laurey takes a potion that is intended to help her make up her mind, she falls asleep. Soon after, Laurey, played by Shirley Jones, passes the role over to her dream double, the dancer Bambi Linn. In addition to the use of dance doubles for Laurey and Curly, the unreality or even surreality of this dream world is evident in features such as the more abstract and minimalist sets and the use of narrative dance in the absence of dialog or even song lyrics.[7]

Oklahoma! offers examples of musical numbers as make-believe, as flirtation without commitment, and as the exploration of hopes and fears in the safe world of a dream. Other types of unreal or intermediate worlds where characters can try out feelings that are inexpressible in dialog include hypnosis, wishes or desires, or other mental actions that yield possible worlds that are somehow at variance with the actual world represented by the film. I am here using Marie-Laure Ryan's terminology from Possible Worlds Theory (PWT), in which the main diegesis of the film is understood as the "textual actual world" (TAW), which is separate from our own actual world (AW) and is also connected to a variety of possible worlds (PW) created by characters' mental activities such as "wish worlds, obligation worlds, belief worlds, intention worlds (goals and plans), mock-belief worlds (fake representations used in order to deceive), and fantasy worlds (dreams or fictional stories told within the story)" (Ryan 1992: 543). In each of these cases, the world is possible and yet has not been actualized; Ryan asserts that the "general goal of characters is to resolve conflicts by aligning all of their private worlds on TAW [the textual actual world]" (ibid.: 544).

In the case of the film musical, the possible worlds of make-believe and dreams allow the exploration of possibilities that have not yet been realized within the textual actual world itself, leading to an awareness by the characters of those possibilities and their potential integration into the textual actual world. Though songs like "People Will Say We're in Love" ostensibly deny Laurey's and Curly's feelings for one another, they also make the two aware of how mutual those feelings in fact are. It is a short leap from Laurey's dream

7 For an analysis of the dream ballet, see Petermann 2015.

of marrying Curly (in the dream ballet "Laurey Makes Up Her Mind") to their actual marriage later in the film. Possible worlds of wishing and dreaming may – though not always – be reconciled with the actual world within the film.

This resolution of the possible and textual actual worlds also occurs in *The Pirate* (1948), which offers additional examples of how the 'safe' mode of song is used to express 'repressed' desires. *The Pirate* is set in an exotic and fantastic Caribbean village, where Judy Garland plays the young upper-class woman Manuela, who is engaged to the staid and unattractive mayor Don Pedro but dreams of romance with the infamous pirate Macoco. The film opens with Manuela reading to an intra-diegetic audience of other young women, expressing her fantasy of this pirate as a romantic figure that contrasts with her mundane life. This introduction is in a way paralleled by the actor Serafin's (played by Gene Kelly) first appearance soon after with the song "Niña", in which he imagines making love to every girl he meets – although the fantasy-quality of his number is less apparent, since all of this actor's life seems to take place in the fantasy world of the stage. When he meets Manuela,[8] he suddenly only has eyes for her, but despite his attempts to seduce her and the obvious fascination he holds for her as well, Manuela refuses to acknowledge him. It is not until he hypnotizes her during a performance of his acting troupe that she can admit her passionate desires. Though these desires are explicitly directed at the imagined Macoco, her song and dance performance while under hypnosis also features erotic dancing with a crew of male dancers, paralleling Serafin's "Niña" earlier, and culminates in an intense kiss between Manuela and Serafin as he attempts to wake her from her hypnosis. Although her conscious self denies this attraction and would certainly censor such actions, her subconscious, when given free reign, is able to express intense emotion. Significantly, such freedom in musicals nearly only happens when characters sing or dance.

It is no accident in *The Pirate* that the character who draws Manuela out of her accustomed reserve is a performer by trade. At the conclusion of the film Manuela has abandoned her bourgeois lifestyle to join Serafin and his acting troupe, with the two performing a reprise of his song "Be a Clown". In the musical,

8 The meeting of Manuela and Serafin is a very interesting scene; he admits his feelings immediately, declaring love with almost no preliminaries – probably because, as an actor, he already lives in a make-believe world and lacks the internal censor that Manuela has. He mentions that Americans marry for love, which she calls a stupid custom, and he responds, "I see, you find enough romance in daydreams", at which she is visibly startled, since that is exactly where she has been able to express her desire for romance, the only place for such desires in her life. His assertion, "I know that underneath that prim exterior there are depths of emotion, romantic longings, unfulfilled dreams", is a line that she will later repeat three times when under hypnosis.

performance itself represents another such intermediate space for the expression of emotion. In *Singin' in the Rain*, Don Lockwood (also played by Gene Kelly) prefaces his declaration of love for Kathy Selden (played by Debbie Reynolds) with the lines: "Kathy, I'm trying to say something to you, but I'm such a ham, I guess I'm not able to without the proper setting." He leads her to an empty sound stage and when he begins adding other elements of the movies' atmospheric magic, romantic non-diegetic music starts up. He lights up a backdrop with a purplish-pink sunset and turns on a mist machine. When he turns on rose-colored lighting with the words "colored lights in a garden", the sound of birds appears as well, underscoring his message on the soundtrack. The interaction between diegetic and non-diegetic sounds is complex, with sound effects 'mickey-mousing' Don's actions, and though he has supplied on-screen sources for many of the effects he uses, it is significant that there is no on-screen source for the musical accompaniment. Once he has positioned her on a ladder – "a lady is standing on her balcony, in a rose-trellised bower" – she asks, "Now that you have the proper setting, can you say it?", and he responds, "I'll try". Yet he does not *say* it, he *sings*: "You Were Meant for Me" is the ensuing number. Here, the unreal world of performance – on a stage, with lighting and other special effects for support – is needed for the expression of emotion. Like numerous other musical protagonists who are singers, dancers, or other types of performers, Don is an actor and feels most comfortable expressing his true feelings when acting out a role. Singing and dancing to idealized, off-screen music is a significant part of that imaginary realm, though it is also set apart with other effects such as lighting, conventional pose of Kathy up on a pedestal or balcony, the use of rhymed and poetic rather than prosaic language, and other changes in lighting or filters, such as the colored filters used for several of the numbers in *South Pacific* (1958).

Real – Ideal Distinction

In all these cases, there is a sense in the numbers that music – certainly the supra-diegetic music that is typical of the musical – belongs to an ideal realm, rather than to reality, to a kind of utopia like the one Richard Dyer has connected with entertainment more generally:

> Entertainment offers the image of 'something better' to escape into, or something we want deeply that our day-to-day lives don't provide. Alternatives, hopes, wishes – these are the stuff of utopia, the sense that things could be better, that something other than what is can be imagined and maybe realised.

> Entertainment does not, however, present models of utopian worlds [...]. Rather the utopianism is contained in the feelings it embodies. It presents, head-on as it were, what utopia would feel like rather than how it would be organised. (1981: 177)

The numbers, as the 'highlights' of the musical, so to speak, are a kind of microcosm of the musical as a whole – the utopia the characters escape into temporarily is a reflection of the musical as entertainment for us, the film's audience.

This distinction between ideal and real, work and entertainment, is also reminiscent of the musical's concern in its dual-focus structure[9] with resolving oppositions such as these. In its initial opposition and final coupling of protagonists associated with opposing values, the film musical seeks a resolution. This may mean that "the farmer and the cowman should be friends", as in *Oklahoma!*, or that a good girl and a bad boy can unite their respective gangs, as in *Grease* (1978), but most often this is a resolution to the question of work versus entertainment, a concern that serves to legitimize the Hollywood musical and an entire industry (cf. Altman 1987: 49–51). If entertainment *is* work and vice versa, as in films from *The Jazz Singer* through *Singin' in the Rain* and many others, the dreamers can indeed be productive members of society.

I would like to conclude by examining the 2002 movie *Chicago*, a film adaptation of the 1975 Broadway musical with music by John Kander and Fred Ebb. While most musical numbers, as I have been arguing, have a degree of unreality about them, this film makes that imaginary quality more explicit than most. As a means of motivating the musical numbers, the protagonist Roxie Hart, played by Renée Zellweger, is placed in the role of the focalizer who sees life around her in terms of a vaudeville stage. At the beginning of the film, the first shot establishes Roxie's perspective through an extreme-close up and zooming in on her eye, indicating that we will see everything through her eyes. A kind of Madame Bovary figure,[10] she expects life to be as romantic, not as what she's read, but as a jazz-era stage performance, and sees her life through this lens.

The ensuing number, "All that Jazz", shows an actual – not imagined – performance by the singer Velma Kelly, played by Catherine Zeta-Jones. Roxie is repeatedly shown as a member of the audience, watching in fascination as Velma performs on stage. The scene climaxes in Roxie's transition from mere

---

9 On the dual-focus structure of the Hollywood musical, see Altman 1987, esp. Chapters 2 and 3.

10 Interestingly, musicals are full of Madame Bovarys – see also Manuela from *The Pirate*, who dreams of stories of Macoco the pirate coming to life. The film opens with her reading those stories from a book that bears the same title as the film as a whole.

spectator to a vision of herself in the star's role, as she is suddenly seen in Velma's costume and position on stage, singing the concluding word "jazz" in a phrase Velma had begun with "and all that…". She soon snaps out of her reverie and is seen again in her previous position in the audience when her lover tells her it is time to leave the club.[11] Nearly all the remaining numbers in the film are Roxie's imaginings, a glittery, more attractive version of events as they unfold.[12] Music, not only in *Chicago*, but in many other musicals, represents excitement, sex, fame, romance – in short, the ideal into which we escape when more realistic speech is not enough.

The relationship between words and music in the musical is a complex one, of course, with numerous gradations in the ontological status of different possible worlds created within the film. I don't mean to suggest these are the only possible functions of musical numbers in all film musicals; I have examined only a very few cases, and these films are classic presumably precisely because they are so exceptional. It would be a subject for a future study to construct a typology of the different types of possible worlds created in the musical numbers of a wider range of musicals – on the screen and on the stage – and the way they relate to, are at odds with, or are frequently reconciled with the textual actual world of the film's narrative segments. Another desideratum for future research is the comparison of the musical's use of the modes of speech and song with opera's more fluid connection between these realms through the intermediate form of recitative. The opposition of speech and music in the film musical is also only a single case of the possible interactions between words and music in film, many more examinations of which are necessary to further map out the field as it intersects with the moving image. Yet within the film genre of the musical, I have tried to show that the tension that exists between words and music can be connected to the musical's split between real and ideal realms. The ideal may take the form of dreams, make-believe, of per-

---

11 The scene continues with Roxie's sexual encounter with her lover Fred Casely – who had seduced her by promising to make her a star –, which is cross-cut with the rest of Velma's performance. In this way, sexual excitement and entertainment are equated, at least in Roxie's mind, underscoring the intensity of her desire for fame that will permeate the rest of the film.

12 An exception is "Mr Cellophane", sung by Roxie's husband Amos (played by John C. Reilly), which is sung from Amos's rather than Roxie's perspective. Since it is precisely the fact that no one notices him that is the theme of the song, it would be out of character for Roxie to put herself in his position in this way. The number "Class", sung by Velma and Matron "Mama" Morton (played by Queen Latifah) but cut from the final version of the film, is not witnessed by Roxie and thus not directly from her perspective, though the characterization involved does correspond to her view of these two characters.

formance, or other modes of expression that are freed from characters' rational censorship. It is suited to the expression of feelings characters cannot yet admit to, or that are too strong for (mere) words.[13] While non-musical speech is associated with the real, with the constraints of everyday life, and with the textual actual world, song represents an escape from reality into a kind of utopia – a non-place, the imaginary, one of many possible worlds created by the characters' imagining.

References

Abbate, Carolyn (1991). *Unsung Voices: Opera and Musical Discourse in the Nineteenth Century*. Princeton: Princeton UP.

Altman, Rick (1987). *The American Film Musical*. Bloomington, IN: Indiana UP.

Blue Hawaii (1961). Dir. Norman Taurog. Hal Wallis/Paramount.

Brigadoon (1954). Dir. Vincente Minnelli. MGM.

Buhler, James (2001). "Analytical and Interpretive Approaches to Film Music (II): Analysing Interactions of Music and Film". K.J. Donnelly, ed. *Film Music: Critical Approaches*. Edinburgh: Edinburgh UP. 39–61.

Chicago (2002). Dir. Rob Marshall. Miramax.

Continuum Encyclopedia of Popular Music of the World. Volume II: Performance and Production (2003). John Shepherd et al., eds. London/New York, NY: Continuum.

Deserter (1933). Dir. Vsevolod Pudovkin. Mezhrabpom.

Dyer, Richard (1981). "Entertainment and Utopia". Rick Altman, ed. *Genre: The Musical*. London: Routledge and Kegan Paul. 175–189.

Gilling, Ted (1971–1972). "The Colour of Music: An Interview with Bernard Herrmann". *Sight and Sound* 41/1: 36–39.

Grease (1978). Dir. Randal Kleiser. RSO Records/Paramount.

Halliwell, Michael (2005). *Opera and the Novel: The Case of Henry James*. Ed. Walter Bernhart. Word and Music Studies 6. Amsterdam/New York, NY: Rodopi.

Henry V (1989). Dir. Kenneth Branagh. BBC.

Herrmann, Bernard (1945). "Music in Films: A Rebuttal". *New York Times* (24 June): 27.

King Kong (1933). Dirs. Merian C. Cooper, Ernest B. Schoedsack. RKO.

Larsen, Peter (2005). *Film Music*. London: Reaktion.

Mary Poppins (1964). Dir. Robert Stevenson. Walt Disney.

13 Think also of other outpourings of emotion, not just of love, but of frustration, as in *My Fair Lady*'s "Just You Wait, Henry Higgins" or "Let a Woman in Your Life", or the exuberance of numbers like "I Feel Pretty" in *West Side Story* (1961), ones in *Singin' in the Rain* like "Good Mornin'", "Moses Supposes", or "Singin' in the Rain" itself, and many, many others.

McMillan, Scott (2006). *The Musical as Drama: A Study of the Principles and Conventions behind Musical Shows from Kern to Sondheim*. Princeton, NJ/Oxford: Princeton UP.

My Fair Lady (1964). Dir. George Cukor. Warner Brothers.

Oklahoma! (1955). Dir. Fred Zinneman. 20th Century Fox.

Petermann, Emily (2015). "The Dream Ballet: Intermedial Tensions between Music, Dance, and Language in the Film Musical". *The Ekphrastic Turn: Inter-art Dialogues*. Asunción López-Varela Azcárate, Ananta Charan Sukla, eds. Champaign, IL: Common Ground. 97–108.

Phillips, William H. (2009). *Film: An Introduction*. 4th ed. Boston, MA/New York, NY: Bedford/St. Martin's.

Pudovkin, Vsevolod I. (1960). *Film Technique and Film Acting*. New York, NY: Grove.

Ryan, Marie-Laure (1992). "Possible Worlds in Recent Literary Theory". *Style* 26/4: 528–533.

Singin' in the Rain (1952). Dirs. Stanley Donen, Gene Kelly. MGM.

South Pacific (1958). Dir. Josh Logan. 20th Century Fox.

The Jazz Singer (1927). Dir. Alan Crosland. Warner Brothers.

The Pirate (1948). Dir. Vincente Minnelli. MGM.

The Wizard of Oz (1939). Dir. Victor Fleming. MGM.

Watts, Stephen (1933–1934). "Alfred Hitchcock on Music in Films". *Cinema Quarterly* 2/2: 80–83.

West Side Story (1961). Dirs. Robert Wise, Jerome Robbins. Mirisch.

Musical Form in the Novel: Beyond the Sonata Principle

Jeppe Klitgaard Stricker

Sonata form has traditionally taken – or, rather, been given – the role as one of the primary devices that carries the function of reflecting on the formal structures of novels that in one way or another possess musical qualities. Word and music critics have often asserted that the sonata form model more or less successfully fits the formal scheme or narrative structure of a particular novel, and the reader is then left to wonder what this may signify regarding the work in question – and indeed what it implies regarding our understanding of such works more generally. This essay contends that sonata form is something that cannot be isolated from other musical properties; that it is a musical feature that necessarily belongs to the unique musical design. Consequently, the essay does not make claims for a general solution to the problems that arise from direct analogical comparisons between the art forms. It does, however, offer the view that at least in some music-novels, the notion of music-literary gesture can facilitate a better understanding of the collaborations between music and the novel than the sonata form model provides.

• • •

During at least the last half-century of research in word and music studies, huge claims have been made for sonata form as a device that can facilitate reflection on the formal similarities between music and the novel. The *Grove Dictionary of Music and Musicians* describes sonata form as "the most important principle of musical form, or formal type, from the Classical period well into the 20th century" (Webster online). It is not surprising, therefore, that this particular musical form should also play a pivotal role in word and music studies. Novelists have been inspired by sonata form, and scholars have researched these works in various ways, for various reasons, and with varying success. However, sonata form in the novel is based in a prevalent understanding of musical form as something that can exist outside of music: something that can adequately be described in words. This approach remains remarkably resilient, as literature continues to define itself through music, and critics continue to investigate musical qualities in novels – perhaps hoping to find in literature, as in music, what Lawrence Kramer has called the "almost universal understanding that music appeals to the emotions, moods, the senses, the whole array of

 | DOI 10.1163/9789004314863_015

interior states of mind and body, with unmatched immediacy and power" (2003: 8).

Sonata form as the theoretical abstraction we know can be traced at least to Anton Reicha's *Traité de haute composition musicale* (1826), Adolph Bernhard Marx's *Die Lehre von der musikalischen Komposition* (1837–1847), and Carl Czerny's *School of Practical Composition* (1848–1849). The basic outline goes something like this: a typical sonata form movement consists of a ternary structure (or three main sections) comprising the exposition, a development section, and the recapitulation. An introduction may or may not be included, and a coda may or may not round off the composition. The structure is embedded in a two-part tonal design. The exposition consists of a first theme, also called the first group, in the tonic, and a second theme, or second group, in another key – usually the dominant. The exposition is typically repeated. In the development section the various themes undergo transformation, usually involving a high degree of modulation and other re-workings of the material. Towards the end of the development section, the recapitulation is prepared harmonically for the tonic. The recapitulation restates most of the material from the development section, and second-subject material returns explicitly, if usually undramatically, in the tonic.

This model has demonstrated remarkable tenacity and exerted great influence over analytical practices in word and music studies. I shall give a few examples that are by no means exhaustive. In 1948, Calvin S. Brown discussed the form and its potential in literary analysis in *Music and Literature: A Comparison of the Arts*; in the 1960s and early 1970s, Robert Boyle and Don Noel Smith applied it to each their analyses of *Ulysses* – following a comment Ezra Pound made in 1922 that *Ulysses* was written in sonata form (cf. 1922/1970: 205); in the late 1970s and 1980s, Robert K. Wallace got caught up in sonata form in his comparisons between Beethoven's *Pathétique* sonata and Poe's "The Murders in the Rue Morgue", and in other writings I shall return to shortly; in 1999, William E. Grim described sonata form as one of three levels at which music may influence literature, the other two being the inspirational and the metaphorical levels; and in 2008, it featured in Gerry Smyth's book titled *Music in Contemporary British Fiction: Listening to the Novel* – a book that is theoretically informed by Grim's approach to sonata form as an abstract model (cf. Smyth 2008: 44–47).

Most of these critics have expressed concerns in their comparisons between the sonata form model and literature. Calvin S. Brown, for instance, noted on the relationship between sonata form and literary forms that "certain very general analogies can be worked out easily. But they are so general that they involve only processes which have been independently established in literature already." (1948/1987: 176). Robert Boyle and Don Noel Smith had doubts, too, regarding the analytical efficacy of using this model in their respective music-literary readings, the case in point for both critics being *Ulysses* as sonata form. Boyle seems sceptical, or dismissive, even, of his undertaking which he presents as "the necessity to reduce the complexity of the novel to some kind of manageable order for an interested but overwhelmed class" (1965: 247). Don Noel Smith, on the other hand, begins more confidently: "Since I first saw the resemblance of *Ulysses* to the sonata form independently of Pound, Levin or Boyle, I must conclude that it is rather obvious." (1972: 81) He too, however, ends up disillusioned and concludes: "The analogies music provides are teasing, remaining no doubt more interesting than convincing" (ibid.: 92). In a similar vein, Gerry Smyth finds that "[t]he question of form in the music-novel is extraordinarily complex, because there are a number of different forces operating constantly (although not necessarily equally) upon the text" (2008: 44); and finally, in the proceedings from the first WMA conference, William E. Grim asserts that "sonata form is a musical procedure that is not easily adaptable within a literary context and that its critical use in musico-literary studies should be regarded with a healthy degree of skepticism" (1999: 241f.).

Healthy skepticism indeed. Of course, the model itself can be useful in its musical context. It is certainly true that an outline like this can be observed in many musical compositions, and this outline is probably the best we can do in terms of a general description. A general description, that is, of a particular kind of musical composition that demonstrates a set of similar features, or patterns, across scale, type, historical periods, etc. It is a theory that helps us understand the fundamentals better. It generalizes, just as practice particularizes. Nothing more, nothing less.

The problem is that the model belongs to the fields of musical analysis and composition, in actual music. It is a pedagogical and theoretical construct that cannot meaningfully be isolated from these contexts. Therefore, when we apply it to novels, it is not musical form itself that is being compared to literature. Rather, it is a model that consists of words, not of musical elements. It is an abstraction removed from what is musical. If we take the model to be representative of musical form, therefore, we will be misguided: we will inevitably be looking first for a critical and intellectual condensation of how music should behave, and second for how this reduction is expressed in novels. But when the model is distilled from actual music and applied to literary analysis, the novel being an art form for which it was not intended in the first place, it has by definition already undergone several steps in its reduction to an abstract formal pattern. A pattern that is no longer music.

A brief digression to Ian McEwan's 1998 novella *Amsterdam* may elucidate my point thus far. In this work, originality and musical composition in the context of Beethoven's legacy permeate the plot and contextualise an overarching discussion of the value of art and morality at the turn of the millennium. The point of view alternates between two protagonists, a seasoned composer and a newspaper editor. On a structural level the work consists of five lean parts, each divided into a number of sections. If we wanted to explore the structural analogies between sonata form and this particular novella from the critical practice I have discussed thus far, we would probably begin by looking at which parts of the work we could designate exposition, development, and recapitulation. In that process we would have to dismiss the repetition of the exposition in sonata form music as unrelated to form (a matter of performance practice, for instance) or simply ignore it altogether (the latter is by far the dominating tendency in the criticism I have discussed thus far). We might then move on to talk about analogies between musical themes and the two narrators. Here, we would probably attempt to show that the sections and subsections in the literary work correspond to themes, transitions, etc. in the sonata form model. Ultimately, however, we would most likely reach the conclusion that this analytical approach raises more questions than it answers.

There are also studies that investigate parallels between novels and specific musical compositions. Robert K. Wallace compared Jane Austen's *Pride and Prejudice*, *Emma* and *Persuasion* to W.A. Mozart's Piano Concertos nos. 9, 25, and 27, respectively (see 1983); and in *Emily Brontë and Beethoven: Romantic Equilibrium in Fiction and Music*, he constructed a similar argument (see 1986). Wallace's readings were subjected to extensive criticism, amongst other things because he failed to make convincing claims for his parallels. In *Amsterdam*, too, the validity of drawing specific parallels would pose a significant challenge: the composer in the novella is inspired by Beethoven's 9th, and his plagiarism of "Ode to Joy" ultimately results in his professional, moral and personal end; at the same time, however, a crucial event in the Lake District reflects the composer's musical influence and underscores the pastoral mode that proves vital for the large-scale points McEwan produces on morality and art. Moreover, the novella is structured in five parts like Beethoven's *Pastoral Symphony*. Which of the two Beethoven symphonies, then, should we choose for our comparative reading – the 9th or the 6th? Perhaps more troubling, and even if we could make a convincing argument for either choice, we would still be faced with a comparison between two distinct works of art separated by almost two hundred years. Works by Beethoven and McEwan reflect different artistic values and ideals, and I would be curious to see a comparative reading that can adequately encompass, rather than do violence, to either.

For all its apparent problems, we may wonder why the sonata form model is so widely used. I believe the answer is to be found, not primarily in music, but in its immediate narrative potential. In addition to what A.B. Marx has described as its male and female characters (cf. 1845: 221), the first and second themes, respectively, the sonata form model provides a clear beginning, middle, and an end (more recent musicological research has problematized this, of course, noting that beginnings and middles have cadences, even perfect authentic cadences, too). The form provides predictability and recognition, and if we accept that one of the distinguishing qualities of narrative is time, or at least sequence, the attraction to musical form becomes understandable. But the attraction of sonata form is not the traditional overall shape. The appeal lies in other features of classical and romantic instrumental music; features which are present in sonata form music, and which have been noted by musicologists, but which are not encountered for in the traditional description of the sonata form model.

Let me briefly illustrate what some of these features may be by turning to the first movements from Beethoven's 3rd and 6th symphonies, the *Eroica* (1804–1805) and the *Pastoral* (1808), respectively. The *Pastoral Symphony* contains very few themes that are gradually developed. The themes are light, and they merge into one another so effortlessly that one hardly perceives them as distinct ideas, but rather as different phases of a single melodic harmonic line. The *Eroica*, on the other hand, consists of more direct contrasts. In this work we encounter sharp rhythmic characterizations that underline various individual features, and there are more strongly contrasted themes. Both movements are examples of sonata form: but in the *Pastoral Symphony*, the sonata form elements – exposition, development, recapitulation – are almost static, or repetitive, over long stretches of time. In the *Eroica*, the elements are elaborate, full of contrasts, and constantly in movement. My point is that even in symphonic works by the same composer, in a time when sonata form was arguably at its highest, and in works that are only few years apart, we may indeed observe that sonata form is the general overall scheme. But these works are very different in so many other ways that constitute them as unique musical compositions. This example is elementary, of course. Think only of the differences we would find if we compared various sonata forms across compositional types – piano sonatas, string quartets, and symphonies, for instance – and historical periods with different harmonic aesthetics: Mozart, Brahms, Bartók, Schoenberg. I need hardly go on to demonstrate that in music it is difficult to talk about form in isolation from other properties.

We should also keep in mind that form is not a fundamental category that is somehow above the other properties in a musical work. This is not hard to demonstrate. Should form, for instance, be more important than colour in Debussy's compositions? Is it somehow more essential than rhythmical figurations in Stravinsky? I would say no. But form has been given priority in the type of prose fiction we are discussing here – arguably because the idea of form holds narrative potential, as I mentioned before, but perhaps also because the notion of 'colour', for example, is exceedingly difficult to talk about meaningfully and consistently and therefore does not offer immediate appeal and potential for music-literary analysis. At any rate, it seems to me that when it comes to musical form in novels, we are sometimes willing to disregard what is essentially musical in an attempt to make sense of the relationship between music and literature.

In music, we may interpret sonata form more broadly than its normative and evolutionist usages suggest: we could say, for instance, that sonata form, like other musical forms, is a sense of direction, deeply embedded in a temporal design that also consists of other musical elements such as harmony, rhythm, colour, pitch, etc. It is a design that results from musical ideas and a sense of proportion.

Recent musicology has made advances in our understanding of musical form, and our literary readings of musical form could benefit from these studies. In their comprehensive volume on *Sonata Theory*, for example, James Hepokoski and Warren Darcy touched upon the idea that sonata form may be viewed as a game of chess where each player has a limited number of options at any moment, but where the total number of possible combinations is very high, even within the first few moves (cf. 2006: 432). We need to think more generously when we talk about musical form in novels, too, and the analogy to chess is one example of how we can produce the kind of insight we need to understand the relationship between music and novels better. It is, in effect, an example of the metaphorical reinvigoration Eric Prieto and others have advocated as a fundamental prerequisite for meaningful analysis in word and music studies (cf. 2002: 51). I sympathise with the view that we cannot, and should not attempt to, get over the threshold of metaphoricity in comparative readings. Metaphors are inevitably there, and it is up to us to make them useful in the context of our respective ideological stances and interpretative positions.

I further believe that the analysis of music in novels is generally most convincing if the musical influence is immanently present in the literary work.

What I mean by this is that the notion of music in novels should somehow be significant, carry meaning, and influence the ways we read the novel; if, on the other hand, what we first think of as musical influence can be replaced with something else or removed entirely, we need hardly concern ourselves with it further. If we do find the musical impulse worth pursuing, as it were, we should be wary that our readings do not become so focused on the analogies between musical and literary form that we forget to ask why the author in question wants to direct our attention to the formal qualities, or similarities, between music and the novel in the first place. Eric Prieto gives an example of some of the challenges we face when reading literary works that are structurally inspired by music – here the "Sirens" episode from *Ulysses*:

> The fugue is not the ultimate target of this passage, but a handy metaphor for emphasizing the centrality of the psychological principle of cognitive multitasking. It is pointless, therefore, to argue over how musical or unmusical this passage is, because the musical intertext is the means to an end, not the end itself. To be fully understood it must be thought of in relation to the stream-of-consciousness technique that governs this passage and much of Joyce's novel. For this reason, a complete analysis of the musical intertexts of *Ulysses* must focus on what, precisely, they contribute to the representation of consciousness in the novel. The question of their musical specificity must, ultimately, be subordinated to the underlying concerns that motivate Joyce's use of them. (2002: 58f.)

Prieto's point is a salient one, and our readings could arguably attain a sharper focus if we ask why the literary work insists on using this or that musical structure or device in the novel to begin with. We may ask which points on the relationship between the human psyche and the arts Joyce is seeking to communicate; why music is interesting to Joyce's literary project to begin with; and if his project is primarily a literary one, or if literature is rather the means to another end. My argument here (which I share with Prieto) is that if we dare ask questions like these, the analysis of musical representations would only be one step. One step, that is, on the way to begin answering questions pertaining to what motivates Joyce to use them in the first place.

I hope it is clear by now that I do not think that the sonata form model constitutes the best level at which to study parallels between music and novels. The examples I have given share the idea that the abstract notion of sonata form can somehow be isolated from other musical properties and transferred to the novel: yet they invariably demonstrate that when we do try to apply to literature the theories and tools that were meant for music, both art forms appear elusive. I do not believe that a solution to the problems posed by analysing direct analogies can be found by probing further into how we can make sonata form somehow fit the novel. Instead, we need to embrace the differences between the art forms, and doing so means accepting metaphors as an analytical practice. I would like to suggest an approach that is based on an understanding of sonata form as a dynamic way of organising sound, and a sense of direction imbedded in the individual musical design. An approach, as it were, that more generously allows us to consider the underlying principles of sonata form, but not the form itself.

I propose to think in terms of gesture, as a concept that can help bridge the gap between the two art forms. Let me say that by gestures I am not referring to the linguistic principle that Wittgenstein and others have worked with; nor am I referring to the kind of physical gestures in a musical performance that Karl Katschthaler explores elsewhere in this volume; nor still does my idea of gesture relate directly to the work on musical gesture that Anthony Gritten, Elaine King, and others have undertaken (see 2006; 2011). In music, my idea of gesture is rather simple: when a child begins to learn a musical instrument, he or she may be asked to sing aloud the musical motif or phrase that causes difficulties. The gesture is immanent in the musical score, and its shape becomes clear when the music is played or sung. A musical gesture may consist of virtually anything that is constituent of the musical idea – a motif, a melody, a rhythmic structure, an interval, or even a chord (the 'Tristan' chord, for instance). Its exact shape and expression, as we have already seen in the Beethoven examples, depends on the musical work in question.

In a novel, the purpose of a gesture would be to help manifest ideas, tropes, or other significant thematic material. It would help bridge the gap between words and music. To give an example, let us return to Ian McEwan's *Amsterdam*. In this literary work, Clive Linley, the composer, is heavily inspired by Beethoven and the notion of originality; as the narrative progresses, he becomes increasingly desperate to complete the 'final song' for his Millennium Symphony. In the excerpt below, he leaves London and takes the train to the Lake District, searching for inspiration as generations have done before him. And sure enough, as he is walking in nature, it comes to him:

> [...] he was relishing his solitude, he was happy in his body, his mind was contentedly elsewhere, when he heard the music he had been looking for, or at least he heard a clue to its form.

> It came as a gift; a large grey bird flew up with a loud alarm call as he approached. As it gained height and wheeled away over the valley it gave out a piping sound on three notes which he recognised as the inversion of a line he had already scored for piccolo. How elegant, how simple. Turning the sequence around opened up the idea of a plain and beautiful song in common time which he could almost hear. But not quite. An image came to him of a set of unfolding steps, sliding and descending – from the trap door of a loft, or from the door of a light plane. One note lay over and suggested the next. He heard it, he had it, then it was gone. (1998: 84)

I propose to read this sequence as a music-literary gesture because it does several things with music and literature at once: it has musical significance that cannot meaningfully be replaced with something else, and its associative powers reach beyond the text and point to specific literary and musical historical contexts, as we shall now see.

The notion of birdsong in literature refers to a distinct poetic tradition,[1] and particularly William Wordsworth, Robert Southey and Samuel Taylor Coleridge are known for their relationship to the Lake District. Moreover, the countryside in the form of the Lake District alludes to the musical traditions to which the composer belongs, most notably French Enlightenment and Romantic ideals that entail a 'return to nature'. The sequence also refers to Ralph Vaughan Williams, whose inspiration is instrumental to Clive Linley (cf. ibid.: 21), and particularly Vaughan Williams's early compositions were inspired by city, nature and the pastoral.[2] But of greater significance is the reference to Beethoven who looms large in the narrative. Linley's admiration of Beethoven and his sojourn in the Lake District point, not only to a general tradition of pastoral idyll in painting, poetry and music, but also specifically to the *Pastoral Symphony* and its use of woodwind instruments to resemble birdsong in the cadenza of the coda in the second movement. The "large grey bird" with its "piping sound of three notes" in the literary work underscores the entries – gestures – in the musical score; nightingale, quail, cuckoo. As the plot unfolds, we learn that the well-known melody "Ode to Joy" from the last movement of *Symphony No. 9* becomes of crucial importance, as Linley's

---

1 For instance Robert Frost's "Come In", William B. Yeats's "The Wild Swans at Coole", Samuel T. Coleridge's "The Rime of the Ancient Mariner", Thomas Hardy's "The Darkling Thrush", and John Keats's "Ode to a Nightingale".

2 For example *A London Symphony* (Symphony No. 2); *A Pastoral Symphony* (Symphony No. 3); *Dark Pastoral for Cello and Orchestra*; *The Garden of Proserpine* (set to Algernon Charles Swinburne's 1866 poem of the same name).

plagiarism of this particular piece results in his professional demise. Although he initially regards the birdsong as a gift, it turns out to be elusive and difficult to get hold of, much like the esoteric meaning of music itself. The gesture is strongly associative, and it restates a trope that is already familiar to the reader: Linley's lack of inspiration and artistic originality has been carefully prepared and increasingly problematized up until this point, and therefore nature's *deus ex machina* deliverance from his trials and tribulations will have consequences, no doubt. And indeed, Linley's romantic self-illusion of the compositional process is used to question notions of beauty, originality, and the value of art in a broader perspective. Ultimately, McEwan interweaves musical tropes with points on the loss of morality and art at the turn of the millennium, as the two protagonists gradually fall victim to each their moral and professional decay.

The music-literary gesture cannot stand alone in our reading of the literary work, certainly; but it does offer insights into the ways in which McEwan constructs his argument on the relationship between morality and the arts, and these insights might have escaped us had we chosen to direct our attention to formal analogies between the arts.

The notion of music-literary gesture could potentially be useful to us because it can begin to describe what sonata form cannot. Gesture is not sonata form, of course, but if our aim is to learn what it is the literary work is trying to communicate by means of music, rather than focus specifically on the similarities between the two arts forms, this does not pose a problem in itself. At any rate, we should not be satisfied with repeating the formulaic outline of sonata form when we work with novels. It will inherently keep us from finding out why literature seems so compelled to draw analogies to music: it will take us away from what is musical.

References

Boyle, Robert (1965). "*Ulysses* as Frustrated Sonata Form". *James Joyce Quarterly* 2/4: 247–254.

Brown, Calvin S. (1948/1987). *Music and Literature: A Comparison of the Arts*. 2nd ed. Hanover, NH: University Press of New England.

Burgess, Anthony (1991). *Mozart & the Wolf Gang*. London: Vintage.

——— (1974). *Napoleon Symphony: A Novel in Four Movements*. New York, NY: Alfred A. Knopf.

Czerny, Carl (1848–1849/1979), *School of Practical Composition*. Trans. John Bishop. New York, NY: Da Capo Press.

Grim, William E. (1999). "Musical Form as a Problem in Literary Criticism". Walter Bernhart, Steven Paul Scher, Werner Wolf, eds. *Word and Music Studies: Defining the Field.* Word and Music Studies 1. Amsterdam/Atlanta, GA: Rodopi. 237–248.

Gritten, Anthony, Elaine King, eds. (2006). *Music and Gesture.* Surrey: Ashgate.

——— (2011). *New Perspectives on Music and Gesture.* Surrey: Ashgate.

Hepokoski, James A., Warren Darcy (2006). *Elements of Sonata Theory: Norms, Types, and Deformations in the Late-Eighteenth-Century Sonata.* Cary, NC: OUP.

Joyce, James (1922/1984). *Ulysses.* Eds. Hans Walter Gabler et al. New York, NY/London: Garland Publishing.

Kramer, Lawrence (2003). "Musicology and Meaning". *The Musical Times* 144/1883: 6–12.

Marx, Adolph (1845). *Die Lehre von der musikalischen Komposition,* 2nd ed. Leipzig: Breitkopf & Härtel.

McEwan, Ian (1998). *Amsterdam.* London: Vintage.

Pound, Ezra (1922/1970). "James Joyce et Pécuchet". Forrest Read, ed. *Pound/Joyce: The Letters of Ezra Pound to James Joyce, with Pound's Critical Essays and Articles about Joyce.* New York, NY: New Directions Publishing. 200–216. (Orig. publ.: *Mercure de France.* June 1, 1922: 307–320).

Prieto, Eric (2002). "Method and Methodology in Word and Music Studies". Suzanne M. Lodato, Suzanne Aspden, Walter Bernhart, eds. *Word and Music Studies: Essays in Honor of Steven Paul Scher and on Cultural Identity and the Musical Stage.* Word and Music Studies 4. Amsterdam/New York, NY: Rodopi. 49–67.

Reicha, Anton (1826). *Traité de haute composition musicale.* http://imslp.org/wiki/Trait%C3%A9_de_haute_composition_musicale_(Reicha,_Anton) [09/09/2013].

Smith, Don Noel (1972). "Musical Form and Principles in the Scheme of *Ulysses*". *Twentieth Century Literature* 18/2: 79–92.

Smyth, Gerry (2008). *Music in Contemporary British Fiction: Listening to the Novel.* Houndmills/Basingstoke: Palgrave Macmillan.

Wallace, Robert K. (1977). "'The Murders in the Rue Morgue' and Sonata–Allegro Form". *The Journal of Aesthetics and Art Criticism* 35: 457–463. (Repr.: Nancy Anne Cluck, ed., 1981. *Literature and Music: Essays on Form.* Provo, UT: Brigham Young University Press. 175–183).

——— (1983). *Jane Austen and Mozart: Classical Equilibrium in Fiction and Music.* Athens, GA: University of Georgia Press.

——— (1986). *Emily Brontë and Beethoven: Romantic Equilibrium in Fiction and Music.* Athens, GA: University of Georgia Press.

Webster, James (online). "Sonata Form". *Grove Dictionary of Music and Musicians* [01/09/2013].

Notes on Contributors

Mary Breatnach

is an Honorary Fellow in the School of European Languages and Cultures at the University of Edinburgh where she lectured in French from 1993 to 2010. A graduate in Modern Languages, she studied the viola in London (Royal Academy of Music) and Detmold (Hochschule für Musik) and made her career as an orchestral and chamber music player before completing a PhD in the French department at Edinburgh and deciding to return to academe. Her particular research interest is the relationship between literature and music in nineteenth- and early-twentieth-century France. She has published widely in the field and is the author of *Boulez and Mallarmé: A Study in Poetic Influence*, published by Ashgate in 1996. (M.Breatnach@ed.ac.uk)

Peter Dayan

is Professor of Word and Music Studies at the University of Edinburgh. He is the author of two books on the relationship between music and the other arts, notably in France, in the 19th and 20th centuries: *Music Writing Literature, from Sand via Debussy to Derrida* (Ashgate, 2006); and *Art as Music, Music as Poetry, Poetry as Art, from Whistler to Stravinsky and Beyond* (Ashgate, 2011). His current research concerns the aspects of Zurich Dada which escape words (and have therefore largely escaped academic scrutiny), including Dada dance and Dada costume; he plans to resurrect two Dada soirées in performance for the Dada soirée centenary in 2017. (Peter.Dayan@ed.ac.uk)

Axel Englund

is a Wallenberg Academy Fellow in the Humanities at Stockholm University, Sweden. He is the author of *Still Songs: Music In and Around the Poetry of Paul Celan* (2012) and co-editor of the volume *Languages of Exile: Migration and Multilingualism in Twentieth-Century Literature* (2013). His research centres on twentieth-century poetry and the interplay of music and literature. In 2011, he was an Anna Lindh Fellow at Stanford University, and he has held visiting scholarships at Columbia University and Freie Universität Berlin. (axel.englund@littvet.su.se)

Michael Halliwell

studied music and literature at the University of the Witwatersrand in Johannesburg, and at the London Opera Centre with Otakar Kraus, as well as with Tito Gobbi in Florence. He has sung in Europe, North America, South Africa and Australia and was principal baritone for many years with the Netherlands Opera, the Nürnberg Municipal Opera, and the Hamburg State Opera. He has sung over fifty major operatic roles, has participated in several world premieres and had frequent appearances at major European festivals in opera, oratorio and song recitals. He has published widely in the field of music and literature and is Vice-President and Editorial Board Member of The International Association for Word and Music Studies (WMA), regularly giving lectures and seminars on the operatic adaptation of literature into opera. His book, *Opera and the Novel,* was published by Rodopi Press (Amsterdam/New York, NY) in 2005. He is working on a book: *Myths of National Identity in Contemporary Australian Opera* (Ashgate, 2015). Currently on the staff at the Sydney Conservatorium of Music, he has served as Chair of Vocal Studies and Opera, Pro-Dean and Head of School, and Associate Dean (Research). Recent CDs include a double CD of settings of Kipling ballads and Boer War songs, *When the Empire Calls* (ABC Classics, 2005); *O for a Muse of Fire: Australian Shakespeare Settings* (Vox Australis, 2013); and Amy Woodforde-Finden: *The Oriental Song-Cycles* (Toccata Classics, 2014). (michael.halliwell@sydney.edu.au)

Karl Katschthaler
teaches literature and cultural history and is head of the Department of German Literature at the University of Debrecen (Hungary). His main research interests are multi-, trans- and intermediality in literature, music and theatre and the history of modernity. Recent publications: *Latente Theatralität und Offenheit: Zum Verhältnis von Text, Musik und Szene in Werken von Alban Berg, Franz Schubert und György Kurtág* (Frankfurt am Main: Peter Lang, 2012); *Gustav Mahler – Arnold Schönberg und die Wiener Moderne,* edited by Karl Katschthaler (Frankfurt am Main: Peter Lang, 2013). (karl.katschthaler@arts.unideb.hu)

Lawrence Kramer
is Distinguished Professor of English and Music at Fordham University, the editor of 19th Century Music, and the author of numerous books on music, most recently including *Expression and Truth: On the Music of Knowledge* (2012), *Interpreting Music* (2010), and *Why Classical Music Still Matters* (2007), all from University of California Press. He is also a prizewinning composer whose music has been performed through the United States and Europe. Works recently performed include "Clouds, Wind, Stars" for String Quartet (which won the 2013 Composers Concordance "Generations" Prize), *A Short History* (*of the 20th Century*) for Voice and Percussion (Krakow, 2012; New York 2014), *Pulsation* for Piano Quartet (Ghent, 2013), *Songs and Silences to Poems by*

Wallace Stevens (London, 2013; Belgrade, 2014), String Quartets nos. 2 and 6 (New York, 2013), and *Bearing the Light* for Voice and Cello (New York and Durham, NC, 2014). *Star and Shadow* for trumpet and piano was released on CD/mp3 (iTunes) in 2014. (lkramer@fordham.edu)

Bernhard Kuhn
is Associate Professor of Italian Studies at Bucknell University, where he coordinates the Italian Studies Program and teaches Italian language, culture, and cinema. His current areas of research include Italian cinema, intermediality, and, in particular, the relationship between opera and cinema. He is the author of a book entitled *Die Oper im italienischen Film* (*Opera in Italian Cinema*) and of several articles concerning intermedial aspects of the relationship between stage media and film. (bkuhn@bucknell.edu)

Naomi Matsumoto
trained as a singer at Aichi Prefectural University of Fine Arts and Music in Japan, the Liceo Musicale di G.B. Viotti in Italy, and Trinity College of Music in the UK. After singing in various concerts and opera productions, she commenced her musicological studies and gained MMus and PhD degrees from the University of London in 2000 and 2005 respectively. She has received several awards including the Overseas Research Scholarship, the British Federation of Women Graduate National Award, the Gladys Krieble Delmas Foundation British Award, the Daiwa Anglo-Japanese Foundation Award, and the JSPS Symposium Scheme Award. She is currently an Associate Lecturer at Goldsmiths College, the University of London, and is working on Italian opera of the seventeenth and nineteenth centuries. (n.matsumoto@gold.ac.uk)

Emily Petermann
is an Assistant Professor of American Studies in the Literature Department at the University of Konstanz, Germany. She is a founding member and co-organizer of the Word and Music Association Forum (since 2009) and co-editor of the volume *Time and Space in Words and Music* (Lang 2012). Her monograph, *The Musical Novel: Imitation of Musical Structure, Performance, and Reception in Contemporary Fiction*, will appear with Camden House in May 2014. (Emily.Petermann@uni-konstanz.de)

Beate Schirrmacher
is a Senior Lecturer in Comparative Literature at Linné University, Växjö, and postdoctoral researcher at Stockholm University, both Sweden. Her primary areas of research are intermediality and mediality, German and Scandinavian

Literature. She earned her Ph.D. at Stockholm University in 2012 with a dissertation on the role of music in Günter Grass's fiction: *Musik in der Prosa von Günter Grass* (available online). She is one of the founders of the WMA Forum and is currently co-editing the volume of the WMA Forum's second conference as well as her postdoctoral project on "The Common Ground of Music and Violence". (beate.schirrmacher@tyska.su.se)

Blake Stevens
is Associate Professor of Musicology at the College of Charleston. His research centres on issues in the dramaturgy, aesthetics, and criticism of the *tragédie en musique* and theatre in France. Recent publications include studies of representation in the monologue and the entr'acte in the *Journal of Musicology* and *Eighteenth-Century Music*. A companion piece to this paper, examining the production of dramatic space in Lully and Quinault's *Atys*, appears in *Music & Letters*. (StevensB@cofc.edu)

Jeppe Klitgaard Stricker
is a PhD student at Aalborg University, Denmark. He is particularly interested in the ways in which certain contemporary novels are drawn to the notion of classical music and musical composition. (stricker@cgs.aau.dk)

Laura Wahlfors
is an independent scholar and performing musician. She completed her doctor's degree in music at the Sibelius Academy, University of Arts Helsinki in 2013, and she also holds an MA in comparative literature from the University of Helsinki. Her research focuses on Julia Kristeva's and Roland Barthes's views on music, and on the application of their theories to musical performance studies. She also has an ongoing keen interest in queer theories, vocal sounds, and the piano music of Robert Schumann. (lwahlfors@siba.fi)

Werner Wolf
is Professor and Chair of English and General Literature at the University of Graz/Austria. His main areas of research are literary theory (aesthetic illusion, narratology, and metafiction/metareference in particular), functions of literature, 18th- to 21st-century English fiction, as well as intermediality studies (relations and comparisons between literature and other media, notably music and the visual arts). His publications include, besides numerous essays, reviews and contributions to literary encyclopedias, the monographs *Ästhetische Illusion und Illusionsdurchbrechung in der Erzählkunst* ('Aesthetic Illusion and the Breaking of Illusion in Fiction', 1993) and *The Musicalization of Fiction:*

A Study in the Theory and History of Intermediality (1999). He is also (co-)editor of volumes 1, 3, 5, 11 and 14 of the book series Word and Music Studies (1999–2014) as well as of volumes 1, 2 and 4–6 of the series Studies in Intermediality: *Framing Borders in Literature and Other Media* (2006); *Description in Literature and Other Media* (2007); *Metareference across Media: Theory and Case Studies* (2009); *The Metareferential Turn in Contemporary Arts and Media: Forms, Functions, Attempts at Explanation* (2011); *Immersion and Distance: Aesthetic Illusion in Literature and Other Media* (2013). (werncr.wolf@uni-graz.at)